CRUELTY, VIOLENCE, AND MURDER

CRUELTY, VIOLENCE, AND MURDER

Understanding the Criminal Mind

Arthur Hyatt Williams, M.D. FRCPsych., D.P.M.

Edited and with a foreword by
Paul Williams, Ph.D.

Routledge
Taylor & Francis Group
LONDON AND NEW YORK

First published 1998 by arrangement with Karnac Books Ltd.

2 Park Square, Milton Park, Abingdon, Oxfordshire OX14 4RN
52 Vanderbilt Avenue, New York, NY 10017

Routledge is an imprint of the Taylor & Francis Group, an informa business

First issued in hardback 2019

British Library cataloguing in Publication Data

A C.I.P. record for this book is available from the British Library.

ISBN 978-1-85575-216-0 (pbk)
ISBN 978-0-367-32401-8 (hbk)

To the memory of Dr W Clifford M Scott,
my first psychoanalytic supervisor

— Arthur Hyatt Williams

Contents

Foreword

Arthur Hyatt-Williams was born in September 1914 in a terraced house in an area of Birkenhead, near Liverpool, England. The house and street have since been demolished. He was an only child whose father had trained in engineering but who then became a dairy man and subsequently a dye works engineer, and later a fruiterer and grocer. He never made much money but, although not suited to business, Arthur's father was intelligent and politically minded, with strong socialist leanings. He was adept at construction of all kinds, which reflected his love of engineering, and he communicated this to his son. Arthur's mother suffered from chronic, mild anorexia which led to the family being somewhat underfed. Arthur's childhood was marred by certain deprivations, but the situation was akin to that of many children during the First World War. A mixture of some poverty, close family ties and simple pleasures characterized life for many working and middle-class English families of the time. For Arthur Hyatt-Williams, a source of continuing pleasure during childhood was a love of the countryside. At the turn of the century, Merseyside (like many other areas of Britain that were to become urban complexes) was still virtually rural, with accessible woodlands, beaches, and marshes. These lay only a short journey from Victorian terraces, including many slum dwellings, and they offered a host of natural diversions for eager, young town minds. Arthur spent a great deal of his time discovering the fauna and flora of the Wirral peninsula (the area containing Birkenhead which serves primarily as a residential sector for Liverpool). His interest has remained as alive as it was three quarters of a century ago, only now pursued in rural Oxfordshire where he has a country home.

The Hyatt-Williams family moved from Birkenhead to a different area of the Wirral peninsula when Arthur was still a small boy, and he began school in Great Saughall, near Chester. He was sent to stay with his paternal grandmother when it was discovered that his mother needed to be admitted to hospital in Liverpool, ostensibly with nephritis but which Arthur later came to understand was probably also a neuro-psychological illness. Despite these difficulties the family coped well and Arthur remembers the time with his grandmother as being enjoyable, in part because she was a kindly woman but also because the elder of his father's two sisters took to showing him the countryside surrounding Chester. An undimmed memory of the time is described thus: "We often took long, meandering walks in which my aunt would stop and look at the view of the flowers and trees, and say something like, 'Isn't that beautiful.' She had a capacity to appreciate the beauty and form of nature, which influenced me." Arthur worked well as a pupil at primary school and at 9 was sent to Birkenhead Institute, an excellent school near where he had originally lived. This required the family to move closer to the school, and this time they went to live at the house of Arthur's mother's elder sister, who turned out to be a strict woman, apparently concerned mainly with appearances and social manners. Arthur recalls this as an unhappy time. A year or so later his father acquired lodgings in nearby Rock Ferry, where Arthur lived until he was 18. During adolescence, Arthur became particularly friendly with two brothers, sons of a friend of his mother. One was a poetic individual who was outwardly rather beautiful, while his brother was a down-to-earth and somewhat forbidding character who eventually became an eminent lawyer and judge in Africa. The former played the violin in an orchestra in Liverpool and introduced Arthur to the pleasures of music. He also arranged for him to meet an uncle by the name of Jonty Hanaghan who was then living in Dublin but who originated from Birkenhead and had known Arthur's parents. Jonty Hanaghan was, in fact, the very first person from the North West of England to train to be a psychoanalyst with the British Psycho-Analytical Society in London. He did not complete his training, deciding part-way through that his vocation lay in poetry. He completed his personal analysis, married the daughter of a well-known Quaker family, and subsequently pursued a highly creative life in the arts. On visits to Arthur's house, this small group of boys, together with their admired guest Jonty Hanaghan, would often talk together, sometimes through the night, about almost anything—psychoanalysis, nuclear physics, poetry, art, and biology—with a passion that was to inspire Arthur. It was at this point that Arthur's interest in psychoanalysis was kindled.

One day in November 1927, Arthur made a visit to Liverpool Museum with his mother, who had by now come out of hospital and was well. He became transfixed by a large and impressive collection of butterflies. He recalls an employee of the museum ("a man with a big head and intelligent face") saying to his mother: "Madam, would you mind if I took your son to look at the butterflies we have got behind the scenes here?" She replied that she didn't mind at all, and Arthur was taken into a vast store room filled with exotic species, the beauty and variety of which stunned him. Eventually, when they came out, the man said, "If your son would like to come every Wednesday afternoon, as he is obviously keen, we could give him some unpaid work classifying things." Arthur went to the museum regularly, became absorbed in the work, and eventually decided that he would like to become a zoologist. However, he had no money to pursue such a career, which required several years' study. At the same time, he was about to win a medical scholarship to Liverpool University. After agonizing over what to do, he decided to accept the scholarship and keep zoology as a hobby. At university he met Lorna, a zoologist. They married in 1939, weeks after the outbreak of the Second World War. A son, Jonathan (named after Jonty Hanaghan), was born in 1940 and a second son, Robert, three years later, by which time Arthur was in India serving as a Field Ambulance Company Commander. A third son, Hugh, was born several years later after Arthur returned from war. Adrian, the fourth son, was born in 1951. All four boys followed their father's footsteps into medicine.

Arthur had applied to train in psychiatry with the British Army and had joined the 26th Indian Regiment as hostilities broke out. He was a member of the Company that re-took Rangoon. Throughout Army psychiatry service he kept detailed field notes that were to become the basis of his M.D. thesis. These notes documented many cases of Indian soldiers who had broken down under the stress of war, and Arthur recorded how they had broken down in different ways. After the wartime fighting ceased, Arthur worked briefly as a hospital psychiatrist in Poona, then returned to England and a job as an area psychiatrist in South East London. A memory recounted from many concerning his war service will remind those who know Arthur Hyatt-Williams of the particular quality of care he brought to his work then and later. During heavy fighting with the Japanese in which there were many casualties, he found himself applying field dressings to wounded soldiers wherever he found them. Later on that day, a Japanese prisoner-of-war soldier asked to see him, and said, "I want to live in England." Somewhat taken aback, Arthur asked him why. The soldier replied, "I saw you look after the men who were shot. It did not matter to you which side they were on. You took the same care with all of them. This is the mark of a civilized country. I want to live there."

Arthur joined the Cassel Hospital as a registrar in 1948, following in the footsteps of a quarter of the membership of the British Psycho-Analytical Society. At the same time he began analysis with Elizabeth Rosenberg (later Zetzel). She returned to live in America a year later, obviously ending the analysis. He saw Clifford Scott for a month and then found Eva Rosenfeld, who had established a practice in London after helping Freud and his family leave

Vienna. Arthur qualified as a psychoanalyst in 1952 and began to work part-time at Wormwood Scrubs Prison, where he first treated ordinary criminals and then life-serving prisoners, always using analytic methods. He found his conceptual and personal resources insufficient to deal with these offenders, particularly those with a violent or murderous history, so he contacted Melanie Klein, who agreed to take him into analysis with her. This continued for two years until Mrs. Klein died. Arthur went to Hanna Segal, with whom he had a further eight years of analysis. In the papers that make up this book, it will be apparent to the reader that, in addition to a life-long interest in what he terms the death constellation, Arthur's main intellectual and clinical concern is with the vicissitudes of mourning and its indispensable role in mental health. The many links he makes between the psyche's need for mourning and its loss of place in criminal thinking are an original contribution. He knows perhaps somewhat more about the subject of mourning than most. In 1971 Lorna, his first wife and mother of his children, died in her forties from cancer of the breast. She had completed her training as a psychoanalyst and had a promising career before her. Eventually, Arthur met Shona, a psychiatrist in her forties who also became a psychoanalyst, and they decided to marry. Shona had two children by a previous marriage, Alison and Clare. In an impossibly tragic coincidence, Shona developed breast cancer and died. Arthur's defenses were, as he put it, knocked for six, and this contributed to his decision to step down from the prestigious post of Director of the London Clinic of Psycho-Analysis (the low-fee clinic attached to the Institute of Psycho-Analysis), a decision that provoked criticism from some colleagues, a reaction which Arthur found hurtful and lacking in understanding. Today, Arthur is married to Gianna Williams (formerly Gianna Henry), a distinguished senior clinician from the Tavistock Clinic.

Arthur worked at Wormwood Scrubs for twenty years from the mid 1950s to the 1970s, in addition to maintaining a private analytic practice and undertaking teaching commitments at the Tavistock Clinic, where he eventually became Chairman of the Adolescent Department. His unwished-for decision to leave

"The Scrubs" followed the escape of the infamous spy George Blake, which led to a massive increase in prison security precautions. It was eventually taking visitors ninety minutes or longer to get in and out of the prison each day, and this left too little time for Arthur to see patients. His unique work with criminals was truly pioneering, and often reminded Arthur of his relationships with soldiers during war in that he found many characterological traits in common. He practiced psychoanalytic psychotherapy with delinquent, violent, and often highly dangerous prisoner-patients, whose numbers had increased following the abolition of the death penalty in Britain, and for whom little treatment of any kind was available. Using the theories and techniques of Melanie Klein, Herbert Rosenfeld, Hanna Segal and, above all, Wilfred Bion, he set out to try to understand the severe paranoid-schizoid crises with which these mainly borderline personalities were struggling, although many were found to be psychotic. His interest focused increasingly on projective and introjective mechanisms that can lead to constellations of undigested fantasies and emotions. Left untreated, these constellations can, in certain individuals, come to dominate psychic functioning. In cruel, violent, and murderous individuals he found that such constellations tended to be associated with death in some form, and were either held in abeyance or else erupted in active form under certain circumstances. The existence of these barely manageable constellations prevented any form of reparation or movement beyond that of extreme persecution. Acting out, often of a criminal nature, seemed to be the only method available to the sufferer to unburden the psyche. This temporary solution could give rise to catastrophic consequences, as many of the following papers show. Arthur Hyatt-Williams attempted, with these individuals, to trace the psychological origins and expressive forms of these undigested states in order to try to facilitate the beginnings of a mourning process and hence the possibility of a durable reduction in death-laden, unconscious fantasies.

Because Arthur's work has taken the form of an ongoing research project—a life work, ultimately—the papers selected for this book are all closely related to each other. They represent a series of points at which certain insights have come together around an underlying and evolving theme—the role of death in the unconscious. Stylistically, this means that this theme appears, to a greater or lesser extent, in most of the papers, although in different guises and forms. Nevertheless, it is to be hoped that each paper makes its own original contribution to the subject. Unavoidably, a small amount of repetition has been allowed to stand in order to permit the overall thesis contained in the papers to emerge. One advantage of this is that the reader does not need to read the book from the very beginning through to the end in order to acquire a sense of its subject matter. Any paper may be selected profitably. The names, identities, and circumstances of the clinical cases cited have been altered for reasons of confidentiality, without detracting from the nature of the clinical content.

It has been a privilege to play a small part in contributing to the appearance of this volume. I have known Arthur Hyatt-Williams as a colleague and friend for many years, and I may be speaking not only for myself but also for others if I say that the hallmarks of his work—an abiding faith in potential for reparation latent in his patients, absence of dogma and a devotion to psychoanalytic truth—characterize this collection. Such clinical qualities have earned him a worldwide reputation which is richly deserved.

Paul Williams
London
May 1998

Acknowledgments

I would like to thank the following, without whom the work reflected in this book would not have been realized:

Mrs. Marjorie James of the former Kincardine Trust, who provided financial help and personal encouragement during my early years. I am similarly grateful to the Rowntree Foundation. I owe a debt of gratitude to the late Melanie Klein, who helped me in my attempts to understand the nature of the criminal mind with particular reference to murderousness. The clinical examples given in this book could not, of course, have been provided without the painful frankness of criminal patients who were willing to show the light and shade of their characters. It is to these that I am, above all, grateful.

The production of this book owes a great deal to the enthusiasm of Dr. David Scharff and the very great and extremely thoughtful catalysis of the ideas in the book provided by Dr. Paul Williams, whose devotion to the task has been unstinting in quantity and, above all, quality.

A.H.W.
January 1998

PART I

1

Aggression and Death

Originally, Freud stated that death was unthinkable in the unconscious mind, but was euphemistically felt to have gone away. He was forced to alter this view in light of the curiously lemminglike way in which much of the youth of Europe went to be slaughtered in the impersonal battles of World War I. Dying for their countries seemed to predominate over fighting for their countries, at least in their thoughts and fantasies. When Freud changed his mind about the ideas people have about death, he wrote "Beyond the Pleasure Principle" (1920), in which he set forth his theory of life and death instincts. Later, he seemed to be somewhat doubtful about it all, and at one point said to his followers, "You may accept this theory or not, as you choose" (Hoffer 1952, personal communication).

Melanie Klein took Freud's theory of life and death as one of the cornerstones of her work, both theoretical and clinical. The death instinct and the life instinct, she stated, began from the beginning of extrauterine life (work on prenatal life, particularly in Northern Italy, suggests that these two polarities begin a long time before birth).

Death instinct is manifested actively by destructive and self-destructive behavior, by envy, hatred, and greed, not to mention perversion. Life instinct is associated with construction, love, trust, generosity, and reparation for harm done by the self to others. These two states of being exist in all of us, and in a lifetime there are changes in the balance between the two, an ebbing and flowing of the two opposing tides of life and death. Some people are more grounded and fixed at one end of the scale. In some, "the fierce dispute" between the two is muted, while in others it is fanned into intense conflict by forces from within or outside the self and by interaction between the two. Death instinct escalations are induced by repeated provocation by the subject in a kind of disturbed reality testing. These evoke a reaction from the victim, regarded by the subject as an unjustified attack, further provoking his attacks until a very serious, even murderous, situation is reached. In it, neither the provoker nor the provoked is able to halt the escalation. Similarly, according to Klein, there can be an escalation of positive attitudes associated with good experiences and derived from the life instinct. Klein's basic findings were accepted entirely by Bion. Briefly enumerated, they are:

1. The early *fantasy attacks by the infant* upon the mother's breast and her inside babies are due to experiences of deprivation as well as being generated from within, mainly by envy. Therefore, a fear of reprisal is incubated.
2. *Persecutory and depressive anxiety* derived respectively from the paranoid-schizoid and depressive positions. It was Bion who represented the movement, that is, the transformation between the two positions, with reversible arrows, thus P/S ↔ D.
3. *Splitting.*
4. *Projective identification*, which Bion describes as an omnipotent fantasy in which the infant finds it possible in fantasy to split off temporarily undesired but sometimes valued parts of its personality and put them into another person, primarily mother or her surrogate.
5. The importance of *envy.*
6. *Symbol formation.* In particular, Melanie Klein's concept of an

> inside world, in which fantasies and impulses associated with them can be worked upon, is most important as a springboard for Bion's work. There can be a continual process of reality testing, so that it is possible for a mellowing to take place in the inner world, as a consequence of which there may be no need for external action; if action does take place, it is modified toward less violent and more appropriate behavior than the original fantasy-/impulse-driven impulse. The inner world constitutes a relatively safe harbor of the mind in which states of conflict can be worked through toward some degree of resolution. This working through enables and consists of continual reality testing; also, importantly, there is a degree of internal abreaction that usually saves the individual and the victim from the worst effects of that violence. In some criminals, instead of a maturation in cask, so to speak, a worsening, a fermentation, leads to worse violence.

Between a mindless, pessimistic attitude ("Eat, drink, and be merry for tomorrow we die") and a paranoid, suspicious one ("What is this, I don't know, it must be bad—kill it"), the shared component is the demand for immediate relief by evacuation into action or the "disburdening of the self" of accretions of stimuli. There is no evolution of meaning, no understanding, so there can be no learning from the experience of a threatening situation. On the other hand, if the crucial mental decision is the opposite one, a painful state of mind is tolerated long enough for action to be taken to modify the situation in a favorable way, what Freud calls following the reality principle. The outcome is then better in two ways: first, the action taken is likely to be of more durable benefit; second, the ability to sustain a painful situation without rushing to action heightens the ability to put up with psychic pain on subsequent occasions when it becomes necessary or desirable to do so.

Before considering how these concepts relate to attacks upon life, I would like to emphasize that threats, or persecutions that may result in violence, are generated sometimes inside the self of the individual and sometimes from an overreaction to external provocation, either by accident or intention. The internally generated persecutions may be related to physiological or other needs.

The common denominator, however, is the inability of the individual to tolerate frustration, and often an inability to see a means of gratifying a need without seizing it.

Melanie Klein's views about the paranoid-schizoid and depressive positions, the former associated with part objects, the latter with whole objects, are crucial in the understanding of attacks upon life, the self, and others. Bion's development and use of Klein's views, particularly the theory of projective identification, are valuable in understanding murderer/victim interaction. Bion's chapter "On Arrogance," in *Second Thoughts* (1967a) describes projective identification as a primitive and essential form of communication between infant and mother. A mother capable of reverie unconsciously works on the communication of the baby, preparing the infant's raw communication in a process of psychic digestion, such that the relatively healthy child is able to accept it and use it for further development. This transaction is the fundamental developmental interchange in which the baby's developmental difficulties and growth crises are coped with and modified, allowing the infant to introject the mother's capacity to carry out the transaction. Thus, in normally favorable circumstances, the infant gradually develops an internal, personal, "do-it-yourself" capacity. Serious consequences can arise when this does not occur. The difficulties or snags can be on both sides. For example, mother may not be capable of reverie. She may, instead of predigesting the communications, block them and return raw frustration to the baby. She may, if she is schizoid, strip the communication of all meaning so that what the baby gets back from her is a nameless dread. On the other hand, the baby may be so intolerant of waiting that, with "majestic instancy," she or he demands immediate and total relief from unpleasant states, or total gratification of wishful needs. One is reminded of Winnicott's term, *a good enough mother*. Whatever the breakdown of projective identification, the result is a lack of development of the "do-it-yourself" outfit in the baby. Bion's adult clinical cases revealed a triad of symptoms: "arrogance, stupidity and curiosity" (1967a), all of which are widely separated. The importance of the developmental intolerance of psychic pain cannot be overemphasized because it increases the likelihood of distortion in reality testing and leads inevitably to maladaptation, especially from the viewpoint of attacks upon life. In a worsening situation, which of the life-threatening actions takes place depends on a number of factors that will be considered in detail elsewhere. Freud (1917), in "Mourning and Melancholia," described the intrapsychic impact of the loss of a near person, whether loved, hated, or ambivalently regarded. The survivor is posed with the problem of relinquishing the lost person as a result, and the setup of that person inside him- or herself as an internal object image, distinct from but related to the self. This process takes about nine to twelve months. When it is possible to go through mourning fully, few unresolved residues are left to give trouble later. The essential feature is that the survivor moves toward the depressive position.

If, however, there is an ineffective or arrested mourning process, there is identification with the lost person (Freud 1917), and a pitched intrapsychic battle ensues with the haunting internal image. The mourner able to complete the mourning process ends up enriched in personality, "a sadder and a wiser man" (*Oxford Dictionary of Quotations* 1979, p. 156). This contrasts markedly with the failed mourner, who often becomes psychosomatically ill, hypochondriacal and accident-prone, or, in certain cases, suicidal. Melanie Klein stated that there had to be a thorough working through of the depressive position in the mourning process if there is to be real recovery. What she meant was that if the depressive position can be held on to, that is, sustained, the way is opened up for reparation. In its internal aspect this means restoration of a vital inner world of the subject. In its external aspect, which is evident, there is a turning to good works of various kinds. In manic reparation, the importance of which was stressed by Segal (personal communication 1975), good, external reparative activities can be seen, but not the essential intrapsychic ones. This results in a situation that is glib and unstable intrapsychically. One often sees external reparative activities in criminals; the task of psychotherapy then is to help the individual to sustain the internal work of mourning for damage done to internal and external objects.

Melanie Klein contradicted Freud's view that criminals have a weak or deficient superego, stressing that they have a persecutory *superego* that is often savagely punitive. An aggressive, perhaps destructive child externalizes into dramatic enactments with parents what he or she cannot contain and digest in the way of experiences, provoking parental or other authority figures to treat him or her very severely. These now punishing figures are then internalized and become a further part of the basic personality fabric of the child, worsening a situation that its possessor already cannot contain. In the understanding of this situation, Bion's views of "container and contained" are helpful. Psychoanalysts, beginning with Freud, agree that as a person feels treated by others, so does he tend to treat other people. The rule of talion, that is, the law of retaliation equivalent to an offense, is pervasive. This applies to the inner as well as the outer world. It represents the original paranoid-schizoid position situation before any developmental and maturational advance to the depressive position. An increasing capacity to treat others as one would wish to be treated can occur, but only insofar as the depressive position is achieved. Worse for a person than living by the talion principle is domination by paranoid delusions. In action, this is seen in the way in which, because of their mounting suspicion and fear of an attack, some violent criminals forestall it by attacking first.

Bion, in *Elements of Psychoanalysis* (1963) and *Attention and Interpretation* (1970), states how and why he uses an alimentary model of the mind. It represents the first essential process for life and growth. He then considers the question of food for the mind. This food he regards as the truth. He goes on to show that the protein, fat, and carbohydrate breast may, in states dominated by adverse attitudes, become split off and separated from the breast which is associated with containment, alleviation of fears and anxieties, and the giving of the truth and appreciation of beauty. Separation of physical needs from psychic emotional needs—the satisfaction of the former and the starvation of the latter—is the incubator of brutalized children and therefore, later, of criminals. Bion differentiated between the task to be carried out and the intrapsychic apparatus to enable it to be carried out. This is stated in his papers on thought disorders and, in particular, in "On Arrogance" (Bion 1967a).

Early in my study of murderers, prior to the work of Klein, I was puzzled by how something inside the mind of a potential killer sometimes remained in limbo for years and then broke loose into murderous violence. Klein later emphasized to me the nature of the splitting involved and how a person can remain for years dominated by one of his or her selves. Eventually he or she can short-circuit, so to speak, and suddenly operate from what seems like a different self. Werthem (1927) described in *The Show of Violence* how, in his view, murderousness was activated into the deed of murder. Before the deed, conscious efforts—sometimes unconscious ones, too—were designed and devoted to keeping the murderous encapsulations from action. Then something took place internally that broke loose the murderousness from its cordoned-off status so that the whole of the energies of the individual became devoted to enacting the murderous deed, after which a precarious restoration of balance usually took place. To this catastrophic event Werthem applied the term *catathymic crisis*.

It is over the understanding of the relationships between inner and outer worlds, the interaction of character with traumatic experiences known or thought to have detonated the catastrophic crisis, that I obtained important help from Kleinian and post-Kleinian sources. As a result, I began to envisage a sort of intrapsychic gang, the activities of which militated toward destruction and death. It was a narcissistic organization, closely associated with power obtained and used irresponsibly. This internal organization became evident externally in individuals when they participated in small and large groups and in organizations. Meltzer and Rosenfeld, followed later by many others, described the intrapsychic narcissistic gang associated also with a negative therapeutic response. The patients they described were usually not indictably criminal, and in this respect were not the same as my criminal patients. After several years, as psychoanalytically oriented psychotherapy went on, various changes were noted in some of the patients. Depression was expected and occurred, sometimes alarmingly, because of the continuous defensive tendency to act out. Hysterical identification with former victims, hypochondria, and psychosomatic illnesses were frequently encountered. The theoretical framework of Klein, together with the extension by Bion and other close post-Kleinians, provided me with a map and a compass, enabling me to find out more about what was going on in the unknown territory of the criminal mind. In addition, Bion's and, later, Meltzer's views of catastrophic change as a break*through*, not necessarily a break*down*, helped to give me confidence to press on with the therapy rather than quell the turbulence and avoid a real working through of the underlying encapsulated or psychotic part of their personalities.

Essential to the analysis of psychotic and borderline patients, as Bion stated, is the use of countertransference. Linked with this is the need for the psychoanalyst or therapist to preserve what Bion describes as the indispensable aloofness necessary for the study and elucidation of the unknown. The therapist acting as a container allows deeper meaning to accrue, thus giving back a fuller understanding to the patient without too much of the therapist's psyche being added to it as a contaminant. The many snags and obstacles in this include idealization of the therapist and using him or her as a container for excitement, thus ensuring that the therapist is entertained.

2

The Death Constellation (I)

Introduction to the Problem

For many years I have been endeavoring to disentangle the complicated ingredients that contribute to the relatively uncommon crime of homicide. Although I have collected startling and at times shocking data in great quantities, there appeared to be no precise, underlying formula. Years ago I suggested the possibility of an intrapsychic patterning to which, naively, I gave the name *blueprint for murder*. Although this phrase was too sensational perhaps, it may be useful here. What I used to term a "blueprint" is quite common in people who do not commit discernible attacks on life processes. It also seems to be present in more people who commit crime than is readily recognized. What goes on in the inner worlds of conscious, and especially, unconscious, fantasy in these people requires investigation. Is homicide only one of the possible end points? Attempted suicide is common in the premurderous histories of persons incarcerated for homicide. Also, a large number of murderers attempt to or actually commit suicide after committing homicide. During the course of serious and persistent attempts to give psychotherapy to convicted murderers in one of Great Britain's prisons, I observed that when the responsibility for the crime begins to be recognized and owned, the murderer usually develops hypochondriacal complaints accompanied by an increased incidence of psychosomatic illness ranging from colds to rectal bleeding or even, in one case, a radiologically confirmed peptic ulcer. Another man developed leukemia and died, though cause and effect cannot be proved.

In studying previous records of people convicted of homicide, one notes a high incidence of accidents in which someone else has died, though the responsibility for the actual death is usually not easy to designate. Here we have a situation in which there are attacks upon life. How widespread they are can be inferred from the behavior of human beings, especially men, in settings in which attacks on life receive encouragement and approval by an acknowledged authority, as in war or in guerrilla activities such as those in Northern Ireland and elsewhere. When one looks at the low incidence of homicide in England, only 0.6 per 100,000 of population per annum, and even in Colombia, the world's highest for homicide, the figures are 34.4 per 100,000 (Wolfgang and Ferracuti 1967), one wonders if what one is seeing in homicide itself is merely the visible tip of an iceberg. Perhaps the invisible seven-eighths of this complex psychological condition could be brought into focus by looking at other kinds of attacks upon life processes.

It may well be that some attacks are expressed harmlessly or are even sublimated. I am thinking of the wide appeal of crime reports in the press, and also of the mass readership of crime fiction, especially murder mystery paperbacks. Is there a continuum from thoughts and fantasies about murder to actual attacks on life? Or is there a break in the scale or spectrum at some point so that on one side there is no risk of an attack being carried out and on the other, great risk? The individual may be pushed one way or another by external circumstances, or may gravitate to one end or the other because of what is going on in his inner world of fantasy, thought, feeling, and impulse.

It may be useful to assume that everyone begins life by being at risk. The difficulty in symbolizing and the tendency to slip from depressive anxiety to paranoid-schizoid anxiety causes the not fully developed capacity to symbolize to revert to concrete thinking (symbolic equation, described by Segal [1981]). At this point there is a tendency to act out concretely. The polarization between life and death instincts normally achieves a better balance; also, as psychic conflict between life and death instincts can be managed less dangerously, the individual is later able to resolve or mitigate attacks on the processes of life. This is important, as individual strength and the ability to carry out such fantasies increase enormously as growth proceeds. Some young children and people who are limited in their capacity or opportunity to carry out dangerously aggressive actions seem to have vividly aggressive and destructive fantasy worlds. One is compelled to wonder whether attacks on life processes in others are brought about by the need to externalize something to do with death, perhaps first internalized forcibly owing to some traumatic external experience. Or it may have arisen from within the individual, or perhaps by a combination of both. Young, weak, and vulnerable individuals, and perhaps powerful, instinct-driven, exceedingly muscular, strong people whose controls do not match their physical prowess, may give us clues about the vicissitudes of this constellation concerning death.

Before trying to relate these ideas to any contemporary psychoanalytic theory, it would be timely to define what is meant by a grave attack upon life processes. Any activity that irresponsibly risks death as far as the individual or other people are concerned constitutes such an attack. The deflection of attacks from human beings onto other creatures is commonplace; for example, the well-known caricature of the English country gentleman who says, on a Sunday afternoon: "It's a lovely day, let us go out and kill something." The tragic spectacle of the bullfight, which always attracts the crowds, is another such externalization.

One murderer, referring to *Moby Dick*, a film he had seen in prison, said to me on my subsequent visit: "I know how Captain Ahab felt about that whale because I felt that way about the child I attacked and killed." I could not understand what he meant until he repeated the statement. I then remembered that as a small child he had been viciously treated by another child who in many ways resembled his later victim. It seemed clear that intrapsychic reality had become confused, dangerously reactivating the traumatic experience. The entire constellation had to be enacted upon a new person who reminded him of the old. The paranoid resentment and experience of aggrievement distorted his reality-testing ability, facilitating his murderous revenge upon a child who had accidentally crossed his memory shadow.

Another adolescent boy complained of a pervading impulse to kill slightly younger boys by knifing them from behind up the anus, or by stabbing them in the lower bulge of the abdomen, making them bleed inside. These murderous impulses with two variant forms, the anal attack and the abdominal attack, dated from childhood when they consisted of a fantasy system. It was not until he himself reached puberty that the fantasy pattern became energized and the impulse to kill began to trouble him. In the case of this man, the drive to act out his murderous fantasies was associated with a perverse sadistic sexual organization directed with anticipatory relish exclusively toward members of his own sex. Only those who fulfilled certain specific requirements attracted him. In his childhood there had been another baby, a brother whose birth had been difficult and who, in the course of a traumatic delivery, had suffered physical damage, a feature of which had been internal bleeding. The grievance over "mother's other baby," originating with her long hospital stay because of the delivery complications, had been elaborated over time into a complicated fantasy pattern. What kept this pattern going and prevented its being mitigated by all the other favorable experiences of childhood, and thus finally healed, seemed to hinge on his original capacity to seize upon a grievance and nurse it. It was further potentiated by the excitement and gratification associated with the retaliatory measures and the subsequent sexualization of the whole system. This would appear to be due to a severe defect in his psychic digestive ability.

Without going into details, let us contrast this case with numerous others in which traumatic experiences in childhood were successfully worked through and where adversity seemed only to deepen compassionate concern for, and identification with, other human beings in a state of distress. Yet there are cases in which a neurotic inhibition of achievement is the outcome. Others, though materially successful, seem to enshrine disasters of the past not in the form of grievances, but in painful symptoms of a neurotic or psychosomatic kind.

What are the factors involved in the criminal or delinquent way of dealing with the adversities of life? It will be apparent that I have widened the field by including criminality and delinquency. The difference between criminals who actually attack and those who attack life processes will be considered later, and, if possible, their nature will be delineated. Despite histories of hitherto apparently blameless lives, all murderers seem to have a criminal personality organization. I do not intend to suggest that a criminal could not also have neurotic and/or psychotic components. Nor, for that matter, need a neurotic be entirely without a delinquent component. Perhaps there can be a transformation from one to the other, and vice versa. If so, why do potential murderers not slip into neurotic illness and preserve their victim from the threat to life? This question requires scrutiny and study. One example occurs to me.

> During a period of difficult fighting during wartime, when a division was surrounded, a young soldier developed a state of typical acute battle anxiety, shaking and becoming almost speechless. No psychiatric help was available as the psychiatrist had been killed. He was sent to sleep beside the chaplain for the night, but the latter became exhausted in trying to deal with him. Combat the next morning was even worse and all available personnel, including the casualties who could walk, had to man the perimeter defenses. In the evening a calm young man reported to the chaplain and thanked him for his kindness the previous night. The chaplain was mystified at the transformation and asked what had happened. The young soldier reported that a number of the enemy had at-

tempted to break through the perimeter at his location and he had killed two of them. After doing so, his tremors and fears disappeared.

In retrospect, I believe the young soldier was more horrified by the thought of killing than of being killed. Evacuation was not feasible as the troops were surrounded by the enemy. His immobilization due to battle anxiety increased the risk to his self-survival as well as his risk to other people. When the attack by the enemy developed before his very eyes, he was able to feel afraid of the murderousness of the enemy, and much less afraid of his own murderous impulses. In a surge of self-preservative murderousness, he fought, helped by his comrades, and eventually the enemy attack was repelled. He had contributed in his way to a successful defensive operation. The switch in himself seemed to be fairly stable.

What can we learn from this example? Somewhere in the situation there was a fear of his own death and a fear of his own murderousness. The conflict between the two fears could not be resolved by the injunctions of the officers and NCOs, nor by the social climate of the division in which he served. In other words, this young soldier resisted brutalization even when it was necessary in the external reality of the moment. As his situation became more desperate, he finally could see that because it was happening in front of his own eyes, action was necessary. When he saw the enemy to be the murderous attackers, a switch took place and his internal conflict was resolved, at least for a time, by the external crisis. The enemy were designated as aggressors. They had to be attacked or at least repulsed. Here was a case in which a young man was so reluctant to switch into a killingly self-defensive frame of mind that he was regarded as a social deviant relative to the norm that prevailed in the military campaign.

Unfortunately, there was neither the knowledge nor the opportunity to investigate whether his reluctance to kill the enemy was due to a reaction formation against an unresolved murderous constellation hidden within himself, or whether it was structured differently. One did not know whether, when it came to killing, he enjoyed it and felt elated, or whether he felt that it was distasteful but managed to accomplish it.

Murderousness may result from a fear of being murdered and the act can be regarded as one of self-preservation. If the internal or intrapsychic reality is one in which a fear of being murdered is experienced and the feeling is not founded on any external reality, the murderous act may feel like self-defense. To the victim, and later to the authorities, it may be regarded as a totally unprovoked attack or one in which the response to minimum provocation was out of all proportion. In other words, some murders are committed because a constellation of the inner world of the murderer is projected into a victim who becomes enmeshed in a situation that preexisted within the psyche of the murderer. The victim is given a part to play, and sometimes the role is to be the murdered person. The entire process is a sort of "dance of death."

I have given a hint that the victim of murder is not an indifferent person. Some victims have their roles thrust upon them, but there are some who seek to be killed. In the developing drama in which escalation of murderousness mounts in the murderer, there are cases in which the victim, by his every countermove, makes the fatal outcome more inevitable. In other cases the person selected for the role of victim does not fit it, and his every move counteracts and ultimately prevents murderous escalation. Two examples spring to mind. The second murder in *Night Must Fall*, a play by Emlyn Williams (1935), is one in which an old woman helps to excite the character Danny by entering into his game. Eventually she panics and refuses to go on with the game, but because of the escalation of excitement in which she has already participated, she makes her own death certain. The second example is of a man who saw a young woman and decided in his mind to approach her with the aim of raping or murdering her. His designated victim, a judo expert, threw her assailant. He got up and tried again, with the same result. Finally the aggressor slunk away, saying under his breath, "It's not fair, she won't play."

What was to be "played" was a deadly game, but its significance was treated by the would-be murderer in childish, naive terms. What he wanted to do was to act out a disturbing constellation in his personal inner world in the mistaken and delusional belief that he would feel better permanently. When in a nonmurderous frame of mind, this man was perfectly fair and generous in his dealings with males and females. A split-off encapsulated intrapsychic constellation in which there was unmitigated murderousness had been triggered in him. It was a delusional system that had not responded to life's favorable experiences but had remained for years unmodified. It needs to be stressed, however, that this man would not be thought of as suffering from psychosis when he was not in a delusionally murderous state of mind.

Murder and murderousness are complicated. I have had a great deal of help from H. V. Dicks's (1972) study of SS killers in his book *Licensed Mass Murder*. Dicks's designation of the "high F" syndrome ("highly Fascist personality"—identifying with a brutalizing father and idealizing violence and a subculture) helps to pick out individuals who are indifferent and often hostile or criminally irresponsible toward life processes. Characteristics of this syndrome are as follows:

> The common characteristic of the "high F" syndrome is the indifference towards human or, in fact, any life, especially when compared with their staunch sometimes fanatical support of ego-inflating experiences. Shame seems to predominate over guilt. Pride is brittle. There is arrogance and scorn for most other people. In some, even the idealisation of the leader is grudging. In others, there is a wide polarisation between idealised and denigrated objects. Narcissism predominates and, in the idealised person, stands for the idealised self-image. Relationships like this, of course, are necessarily tyrannical. [p. 71]

3

The Indigestible Idea of Death

Some years ago I was asked to give dynamic psychotherapy to a man who had been convicted of murdering another man. The patient had been sentenced to death and reprieved, with the sentence commuted to life imprisonment. Later I was asked to treat several more men serving life sentences for murder. What struck me most was the presence in the mind of the convicted murderer of a constellation of fantasies, dreams, thoughts, impulses, and ruminations to do with killing, annihilating, and obliterating. During the next few years, I tried to see if, by means of psychotherapy given by a psychoanalyst while the patient was in prison, the intrapsychic configuration I flamboyantly called the *blueprint for murder* (see Chapter 1) could be worked through. The aim was to work through to such a degree that the intrapsychic situation became relatively safe and the "blueprint" no longer remained the threatening encapsulation it had been.

Having achieved some limited success with the patients treated in prison, I turned my attention to people not in prison, people who had not committed murder but were thought to be in danger of doing so, or who themselves felt afraid that they might do so. Some of these patients had been picked out by colleagues—psychiatrists and psychologists—because they were thought to have a "blueprint for murder." The psychologists recognized the situation when they studied the responses made to projection tests: the patients complained of murderous fantasies, dreams, or impulses. There was no difficulty in getting them to therapy (psychoanalysis in two or three cases). When the blueprint was found in people who had no conscious awareness of murderousness, the problem was whether to let the trouble remain in intrapsychic limbo or to draw attention to it. If the complaints for which the patient had been referred had a life-threatening element that was recognizable in them, it was thought advisable to link the test findings with the symptoms.

One of those to whom it was possible to give psychoanalysis was a 16-year-old adolescent boy who complained that he was impelled to kill boys somewhat younger, 14 or so, who were just emerging into adolescence. The complaint was made by the boy to his parents that he did not know how much longer he could *contain* the impulses without acting them out. The pattern in this patient consisted of murderous, sadistic, and homosexual fantasies that were worked out in his mind concretely and vividly in great detail. The fantasy constellation was always present in consciousness and linked with his masturbatory activities. Later on in analysis, it was found that the fantasy constellation was the prerequisite for orgasm in masturbation. Later still, it was found that masturbation with a murderous fantasy constellation prevented the enactment of murder, yet, perpetuated the state of murderousness (i.e., potential murder) needed to attain orgasm. When murderousness is closely linked with sexuality, it makes sex a matter of death and killing rather than about creating a new life.

I gradually became aware that a fairly constant factor in the development or retention of the blueprint was experienced by individuals later found to have it as fear for their lives. These people were terrified of death, and in most instances the experience had been one in which the future patient, in a state of terror, had been forced into a passive position, pinioned and unable to do anything.

The young man mentioned above remembered an incident that seemed to act as a bridge between a childhood in which he had an uncontaining mother and a brutal father and an adolescence in which he was haunted by murderous fantasies and impulses.

The incident consisted of his being kidnapped by rough boys in a town he and his family had just moved to. His captors had acquired a broken iron railing with a top like a medieval lance, and it was with this crude weapon that they threatened to impale him unless he agreed to swear that he would undertake to be their slave. What he did become was a slave to a life-threatening intrapsychic situation: a massive life-threatening introject, an inner representation of the leader of his former assailants. He later proceeded to reverse the situation so that he was to be active and his potential victims passive. He would be frightening instead of being frightened. He would be the aggressor rather than the victim. Something like this probably happens whenever there is an identification with the aggressor.

Many other, similar instances could be described. These communications were thought to indicate that the blueprint for murder was a function of sadism of very early origin, stemming from a tilting in the balance of life and death instincts toward death. This may be true, but in surveying the range of life-risking activities, it is clear that the term *blueprint for murder* is restrictive and I came to call this kind of intrapsychic constellation the *death constellation*. It can thus cover the transformations that occur during the course of battling with, or yielding to, the problem of death inside the self. In particular, the term covers those prone to attack the self, even to the point of suicide. Also included are those who defy the fear of death by life-risking sports, or by deeds of valor. It was found that in addition to the well-known high incidence of suicide attempts in murderers after the crime, many people who subsequently committed murder had made one or more serious suicide attempts before the murderous deed. In addition, psychosomatic illnesses, some of which were life threatening, were found in a high proportion of convicted murderers serving prison sentences as well as in persons with murderous impulses that they had not acted upon.

At this point in my study I happened to be asked to see the adolescent children of two families in which a parent had been murdered. In one family the brother and sister—adolescent when I saw them—had found their mother lying dead in a pool of blood on the floor of their home; the girl was 4½ at the time, the boy just under 2 years old. The children of the other family were two boys whose father had been murdered when the brothers were 4 and 2 years old.

In the first family it was the 16-year-old girl who had murderous fantasies and impulses. She was more afraid of becoming a victim than of perpetuating a violent crime. Not only was there an identification with her dead mother, but her reaction was more in line with female emotional development. Also, as the trauma had occurred when she was nearly 5 years old, she had adequately verbalized her stark fear and grief.

The two brothers, as each turned 15, were bothered by fears of becoming victims of murder—a clear identification with their murdered father. They also had impulses to kill an older man—an identification with the killer of father. I was able to give some psychotherapy to the younger of the two brothers. He brought dreams, all of which consisted of a struggle between a father–man versus a son–youth: sometimes the fight followed the story of Oedipus and his father, Laertes, and sometimes it followed the pattern of Sohrab and his father, Rustum.

In all cases, the weapon (of which there was only one) changed hands from one to the other in the course of the struggle. The point seemed to be that murderousness lay in the weapon of power rather than in the individuals involved in the struggle.

A similar theme occurred in the case of a 15-year-old youth referred because he was filled with murderous intentions toward policemen. He wanted to—and simultaneously did not want to—kill one or more police officers. The family's recent history was tragic. His older brother, six years his senior, had been hanged for his involvement in a gang killing during which a person had been robbed of a few coins. The brother had tried to stop the killing, but was found guilty and executed according to the law at that time. Within a couple of weeks of the brother's execution, the father died of cancer. Mother and sisters were completely overwhelmed and the adolescent was without a containing parent during his grief. Fortunately, a gifted probation officer acted as a containing person for both the boy and the bereft family. I was able to offer weekly supervision to the probation officer. After about five years, an impressive recovery had taken place and it was difficult to find anything grossly dangerous in the youth's intrapsychic situation. The probation officer had facilitated the restoration of what remained of the family network and, even more impressively, the growth and development of the adolescent himself.

In the group of patients described above, the common denominator was a psychically indigestible experience to do with death suffered by young and vulnerable individuals. The term *death constellation* seemed to me to be appropriate. The therapeutic problem was to bring the life–death polarity back into balance after it had been tilted toward death by one or more traumatic experiences to do with death. The relish of death was found more difficult to treat than the fear of death. After a traumatic experience involving the sight or threat of death, the intrapsychic situation usually oscillates between a kind of excited preoccupation with the experience—and fears of becoming both the victim and the agent of death—and a wish to become that agent.

In states of psychic health, the state of mind is reflected in Shakespeare's words spoken by Julius Caesar: "The valiant never taste of death but once," or else from birth to death, a person may be like the well-known stanza of Gray's *Elegy* (*Oxford Dictionary of Quotations* 1979):

> Far from the madding crowd's ignoble strife,
> Their sober wishes never learned to stray;
> Along the cool sequestered way of life
> They kept the noiseless tenor of their way. [p. 235]

Many factors may interfere with the "cool sequestered way of life." Among these are:

1. Predominance of hatred over love
2. Strong endowment of primal envy
3. An inability to contain an overriding need for a containing person (e.g., good enough mother)
4. An inability to grow to take on the containing function (i.e., to internalize and sustain the image of the containing person inside the self)
5. Lack of good early figures or an inability to use such figures
6. Early life-threatening experiences (e.g., one of my patients was a battered baby who grew up to be a murderer)
7. Prolonged painful illness
8. Early and repeated witnessing of cruelty and death (see, for example, the French film of the 1940s, "Les jeux interdits")
9. The linking of the death constellation to sexuality in a sexual perversion, so that sexuality means destruction (death), not creation (life)
10. Narcissistic personality structure and organization
11. Arrogance
12. Obedience to a gang leader outside the self or, in a narcissistic character, obedience to the sadistic murderer's intrapsychic gang leader, or to use Alvarez's book title, *The Savage God* (1971).

A largely unanswered question concerns the prevalence of murderous fantasies or killings appearing in remembered dream sequences in comparison to the infrequency of the deed of murder. Some detoxication of the intrapsychic situation must occur in most people. Two issues arise: 1. Can the death constellation be rendered completely innocuous? 2. Is there always the possibility of relapse into murderousness?

There is probably no absolute answer to these questions. In surveying my own psychiatric experience I would conclude, perhaps somewhat obviously, that there are many people who could never be brought to the point of committing a murder. Less clear is the situation in war when there is social sanction for impersonal killings. The people I consider highly unlikely ever to be brought to the point of committing a personal murder are characterized by their having made a fairly good negotiation of the depressive position in the first year of life and on subsequent occasions that demanded a renegotiation of it. They were in a state in which feelings of guilt and responsibility generally predominated in their intrapsychic and interpersonal relationships. This does not by any means suggest that they were wishy-washy or sentimental do-gooders. As a result of their relative psychic poise and balance, they were not afraid of themselves or others, except in a reality-based way. On the other hand, people who have impulses to harm and/or kill other people are suspicious and lack trust in themselves or others. As a person actually, or in fantasy, treats others, so by projection he feels that he is, or will be, treated by others. If the inner world is frightening, one gets the situation as Shakespeare put it:

> And in the Night imagining some fear
> How easy is a bush supposed a bear! [*A Midsummer Night's Dream*, V, i, 7]

It was striking to me that all the murderous patients whom I studied, whether they had committed the deed or not, were bogged down in a state of mind in which persecutory anxiety predominated over depressive anxiety. Persecutory anxiety is a primitive response to threat, internal or external, actual or supposed. It is a state of mind in which aggrievement is rampant and responsibility muted. Action to silence, quell, obliterate, or annihilate supposed persecution is felt to be totally justifiable. The victim or other people are felt to bear responsibility for the persecution.

Even in those who had not committed murder in the external world, but only in the inner world of fantasy, it became clear that what I was seeing was tantamount to a late stage of development. Many depredations had taken place in fact or fantasy. There had been in some patients a working toward the acceptance of responsibility, that is, toward the depressive position. What had sent the process into reverse was the pain of insight as the subject saw he had damaged, in fact or fantasy, a person or the intrapsychic representation (image) of a person who was innocent of the accusation. Paranoid fear and resentment were responsible for the accusation.

The Indigestible Idea of Death

The psychic pain itself became persecutory and so there was a slipping back into a state of mind dominated by persecutory anxiety. Those who threatened and smoldered for a long time—months or years between the first murderous token action and the full enactment of the deed of murder—shared a somewhat different picture. Somewhere, it appeared to be true that the low morale and damaged self-esteem resulting from the failure to make a real negotiation of the depressive position compounded the problems of a relapse into a state dominated by persecutory anxiety. It was these very people, however, who in psychoanalysis or psychotherapy were able to use help and, later, to make a better negotiation of the depressive position, resulting in mitigation of the intensity and threat of the death constellation. When such mitigation has taken place, there was found to be a greater tendency to keep and hold the attacks within the self, rather than to act out murderous fantasies and impulses upon other people. In other words, there comes a phase of therapy during which the suicidal threat constitutes the major problem. Later, token action becomes the order of the day. Without a renegotiation of the depressive position each time, there is an efflorescence of death constellation activity and *the risk remains.* It is important to recognize that when the death constellation is active within the individual, a surge of self-preservation impulses may result in what looks like a total relapse, but which is found to lead to *token* life-risking attacks on others and not the full deed. In several of the cases I saw, these activities took the form of dangerous driving of a motor vehicle.

Some mention needs to be made of the way in which a victim is chosen by his or her assailant. Sometimes a victim is a person hated, wanted, or simply in the way. This is the direct method of choice. Sometimes the victim is chosen narcissistically, that is to say, in the image of the self of the aggressor. Sometimes the victim is chosen in the image of the hated parent, wife, sibling, or child who is also loved, so that a dangerous situation is compounded by the fact that the scapegoat victim chosen for attack is not loved, but receives only hatred and destructiveness.

There is no safe alternative to a satisfactory negotiation and renegotiation of the depressive position. When there is but a poor negotiation of the depressive position or no negotiation at all, attacks upon life, though not inevitable, are much more likely and there are a number of possible outcomes, just as there are important factors involved in determining the outcome.

1. At best, there is a transformation of the death constellation brought about by work at the depressive position, so that the person with such a modified psychic balance is less dangerous to himself or others. In some, it can be said that there is minimal risk.
2. There may be a precarious intrapsychic equilibrium, possibly lasting over many years, until the general decrease in the pressure toward action of the impulses renders the situation less dangerous as far as acting out in a life-risking way is concerned. It must be emphasized, however, that risk of action is exacerbated at times of crises. Such times are menopause, the male climacterium, retirement, bereavement, loss of employment, being left by a spouse, and so on.
3. In some cases, defenses are elaborated. By this I mean unconscious psychological defenses that in several of the patients I saw consisted of obsessional organizations. The murderous deed was then committed in phantasy many times. You may recall the line: "Nice cup of arsenic, my dear!" as the husband brought the tea to his wife in Dylan Thomas's *Under Milk Wood.* In one or two patients the constellation was hedged with so many prerequisites that the chances of all the conditions being met at a particular time became extremely unlikely.

An example of this is a young man who was impelled to attack and kill young adolescent boys. He required his victims to fit in with a prefabricated phantasy in detail: they needed to be good-looking, with a slightly plump figure, well dressed, neat and clean with a hairless, slightly smug face and a slight bulge in the lower abdomen (as if they had something good inside), and above all, a shiny seat to their trousers. It is evident what a small likelihood there was for all these requirements to be met at the same time. Another potential murderer, a young adult, required his potential victim to be a girl aged 9 to 11 years with no signs of puberty, but with an innocent prettiness and, above all, a helmet-type hat on her head. There are many other similar examples.

Important in the change from a state of mind in which attempts to control and contain murderous impulses are operative to one in which the main energies of the potential murderer are switched to the task of committing the murder itself is the collapse of the capacity to symbolize. What Segal has described as the "symbolic equation" becomes operative. This consists of an increasing concretization so that thoughts are equated with and become actions. The switching of effort and determination that occurs when the potential murderer is about to become an actual murderer was described by Werthem as far back as 1927 in his book *The Show of Violence*. The transformation, Werthem's *catathymic crisis*, consists of a takeover bid by the death constellation of all the rest of the psyche of the murderous person. After the enactment of the deed, some kind of intrapsychic equilibrium, albeit a highly precarious one, was gradually restored. In one case quoted by Bion, a young man projected the intrapsychic images of anti-sex parents into his actual parents and killed them in the delusional belief that he would thereby be freed to have sexual relationships with the girl with whom he had supposedly fallen in love. The projection triggered the catathymic crisis. A few days later, when some kind of intrapsychic equilibrium had been restored, or, in other words, sanity had returned, he, accompanied by the girl, went to a police station and asked to be arrested.

The transformation from a murderous thought to a murderous deed is related to the following:

1. A collapse of the capacity to symbolize
2. A rapid shift from depressive anxiety (depressive position) to the paranoid-schizoid position
3. The frequency and intensity of murderous phantasies and dreams
4. The inability to sustain adequate mourning for the victim(s) of the murders committed in phantasy
5. The pervasiveness of arrogance in the self of the potential murderer with the consequent reduction of the potential victim(s) to:

(a) Subhuman status
(b) A concatenation of parts (part-objects)

6. The strength and pervasiveness of manic currents that sweep aside any growth of concern, or guilt—in fact, any states that, if tolerated, would be likely to enhance movement toward the depressive position
7. Factors to do with the social environment:
   (a) Credibility of the deed of murder
   (b) A murderous or a murder-tolerating superego figure, for example, parent, teacher, religious leader, or political leader
   (c) A potentially lethal weapon that implies a readiness to use it in certain circumstances
   (d) The witnessing of killings of humans, or sometimes animals, so indigestible psychically, causing the vulnerable individual to identify with the killer or with the killed, or to oscillate between the two

The situation is complex, consisting as it does of intrapsychic and interpersonal factors. It would be easy to let our investigation rest at the point of recognition of the multiple etiology. In this case we would assume that murder erupts when too much happens in too short a time. In such circumstances the potential murderer, that is, the person with the death constellation, cannot psychically digest the recent input of experience and its effect on what was already present in him intrapsychically. Instead of de-escalation into a safer state of mind, there is escalation so that symbol turns into symbolic equation and the deed is committed. I have encountered a significant number of instances in which there was a de-escalation, an increasing capacity to symbolize, and hence no murder. In favorable cases there is no killing at all, but there are cases in which there is a reintrojection of the whole constellation and a killing of the self. I knew a man whose job it was to send out income tax demands to people. These figures were prepared by an arrogant, ruthless tax inspector who would brook no modification of his demands. The patient felt guilty about being the agent of this man. He decided that he would kill the inspector, so he followed him for nine miles in a fog with a sword cane at the ready. All the time, he was in a "to be, or not to be" state of mind. Finally he let his victim escape into the fog, returned home, and made himself the victim.

Some people do not digest or metabolize intrapsychically the death constellation, but remain for years "suffering" from murderous fantasies and dreams. The death constellation seems to have become chronic, so to speak. Sometimes one is told dreams of killings by patients whose external activities appear to be devoid of murderousness until one looks more closely into the way in which relationships, projects, creativity—their own or that of others—are the victims. One such person used to say of creative projects put to him, "I will kill it! I will kill it stone-dead." Another kind of destructiveness can be found in a study of accidents that endanger life—that of the subject, or the lives of others. Sometimes the workings of the unmetabolized death constellation can be found in the psychosomatic illnesses of a life-endangering kind. The link between these various indications of the activities of the death constellation can be found sometimes in convicted murderers in psychotherapy and frequently in patients undergoing psychoanalysis.

One patient who was particularly "stuck" in his personal analysis used to bring dreams of killings. He was usually the onlooker, afraid to intervene. He then brought the following dream: "A threatening, rather mad woman was about to kill me. At the last minute, a hooded man came up behind her, seized the knife with which she was about to kill me, and cut off her head. I was relieved and horrified. There was a hue and cry; I knew that I had to protect the man as he had saved my life, but at the same time I knew that, knowing it was he who killed the woman, I had him in my power. The whole story would have been difficult to tell to the police, who might jump to embarrassing conclusions." In associations he felt that the hooded man was myself. His main stumbling problem was his inability to mourn, focused around the death of his devoted and overindulgent mother many years previously. His relationships with women always followed the same pattern of idealization, collapse, denigration, and then utter rejection of them by him. They were left to mourn. He had projected his murderous part, derived from the death constellation, into me. I had a superego role as well. Like his mother, I protected him from the consequences of his actions: he had made the woman murderous, and then he had me in his power as he felt he had had his mother. He was then in a position to blackmail me so that I, not he, could bear the burden of his internal (and symbolic external) murders and things would remain unchanged. This dream and its working through did initiate a significant change.

The usual findings in those who have persistent unmetabolized death constellations are:

1. The ascription to someone else of the responsibility for the murderous wishes of the subject
2. The conviction held by the subject of the need to kill in order to stay alive
3. The association of sexual perversion with fantasies and/or impulses to kill
4. The experience of the death of the object as a persecutory rejection of the subject
5. The annihilation of the object (psychically), resulting in the lack of an internal containing object so that the subject cannot progress

In analysis, the analyst can (secondarily) become the required containing person if he or she is allowed to function, but if the analysand evacuates the problems associated with the death constellation into the analyst, he sometimes becomes terrified of the analyst and breaks off treatment. This fear seems to be based upon the paranoid fear that the analyst will be taken possession of by the murderousness that has been projected into him.

> Weave a circle round him thrice,
> And close your eyes with holy dread,
> For he on honey-dew hath fed,
> And drunk the milk of paradise. ["Kublai Khan," *Oxford Dictionary of Quotations* 1979, p. 157]

4

The Death Constellation (II)

In 1956 capital punishment was suspended in England, except for certain kinds of murder. I was approached by the prison medical authorities and asked to take on for psychotherapy first one, then, soon after, several more prisoners who had been convicted of murder and were serving life sentences. The object was to see whether, and how, the psychic state of prisoners serving life sentences could be helped. If, as was envisaged, many (if not most) of them were deemed safe as far as further killings were concerned, they could then be assessed regarding the wisdom of parole. I was appointed as a part-time psychotherapist because I was—and am—a psychoanalyst, not despite it.

The first two lifers I saw had been selected because they were intelligent, verbally gifted, and, apart from the crime for which each had been convicted, not diffusely psychopathic. Later, the selection of patients covered a wider spectrum of disturbance.

It turned out that mainly these prisoners were fairly ordinary persons, but they possessed within themselves a part that was quite capable of killing someone, enemy and/or persecutor. In the earlier referrals I saw, there was a good deal of remorse: I do not mean self-pity. There seemed to be little evasion of the truth, though later, as therapy proceeded, it was often found.

Freud's theory of life and death instincts in 1920, particularly as taken up literally by Melanie Klein (1946), was helpful to me in this work. I was beginning also to think of the possibility of a split-off encapsulation that was murderous—a kind of time bomb, or unexploded bomb that could be detonated into death-dealing actions under certain circumstances. I was then lent a copy of Werthem's (1927) book, *The Show of Violence.* In it, I found that Werthem had envisaged and postulated a state that seemed to cover the buildup prior to the actual deed of murder, and then its short-term aftermath. In people who had murderousness in themselves, murder in situ, so to speak, their available energy was normally directed toward keeping this murderous enclave from being acted out. When this containment began to break down, the healthy, antimurderous part of the psyche was invaded by the murderous part he called the *catathymic crisis.* Following this crisis, virtually all of the individual's energy became directed toward the enactment of murder, after which a precarious equilibrium was gradually reestablished. The entire process was lived out according to the character of the individual. Some evaded, some lied, some gave themselves up to the police, and some killed themselves. At this point I felt that an unexploded bomb signified a process too acute and too immediate to describe what happened during the catathymic crisis; I called it a blueprint for murder, as mentioned in earlier chapters. The factors that activated this configuration were varied, but usually involved a connection to a situation to which the particular killer was especially sensitive, a sort of Achilles' heel. I used the term *allergic,* and then thought of *anaphylaxis,* in which an earlier sensitization to foreign proteins can later be fatal to the individual. It is the reverse of immunization. Indeed, many of the prisoners serving life sentences had experienced events ranging from severe exposure—to bombing and seeing dead, dying, and grossly mutilated people—to much cruelty. Also, they tended to do actively what they had once been forced to suffer passively. In one instance the baby boy battered by his father grew into a father-killing man. His victim was not his own father.

I had already derived benefit from Kleinian theory and knew some of it in practice, but one event was so striking that it expanded my view of murderousness and its blueprint. I was allowed to walk around the grounds with a prisoner patient suffering from a fatal illness. On this occasion I developed a strong fear that he was going to kill me. I argued silently to myself that this did not make sense. Having told myself that it must be something in reverse, I thought of Klein's description of projective identification and reconstrued what the prisoner patient had put into me by this unconscious method: it was his fear of his own death. What I was then able to do was to ask him about it: "It feels that you are conveying to me your fear of death." He relaxed and told me that he had learned that he was going to die, and thought it would be fairly soon. During this communication our physical situation had in no way changed, but my having picked up the patient's fear of death had helped him cope with the harsh reality of his illness. He died not long afterwards, but with help from me and the nursing staff, which he was able to use, he died peacefully.

The view of murderousness as an evacuation of an indigestible fear of death began to crystallize in my mind. The battered baby who became the killer of a man who threatened to annihilate him physically (not his father, but a substitute) acted in panic and fear of his own death, but his reaction was potentiated by anger and revenge displaced upon somebody standing in the place of his cruel father.

The prisoner patients who responded to psychodynamically oriented psychotherapy developed a number of psychosomatic illnesses. In one, it was bleeding "per anum," but an examination found no hemorrhoids or other organic cause. Peptic ulcers and recurrent attacks of laryngitis were among the conditions presented. One prisoner patient who had strangled his victim developed a bad throat each year around the anniversary of the killing. This clearly was an identification with the victim, and seemingly a step toward mourning. This was later shown to be so. It illustrated how concretely states of mind were experienced by those who had at one time resorted to actions that had killed another person. Perhaps it was an inability to work through a murderous state of mind in fantasy life, without resort to action, that lay at the core of the original psychic indigestibility as well as subsequent psychosomatic versions. I noted that though psychosomatic symptoms tended to be associated with a favorable prognosis, hypochondriacal symptoms were the reverse. In the former there was evidence of identification with the victim, based on depressive anxiety. In the latter the unconscious statement seemed to be: "I am ill and am persecuted by pain in the belly, pain behind the eyes, swallowing over a lump, et cetera," which expressed: "I am persecuted by what I have done and not said." The process was experienced in very physical terms.

External factors are not the only ones of importance in the movement from the death constellation to murderous actions. Envy, as Klein stressed, attacks the good experience, the help given, good objects, and good principles. This applies especially to therapy.

One prisoner patient, not a lifer, with whom I thought I had a good therapeutic relationship, required more treatment when the end of his sentence came. I made arrangements for him to be admitted to a hostel from which I could see him under National Health Service facilities, and hoped to continue to treat him. He agreed, and thanked me, but when asking for his rail warrant had it made out to a place exactly the same distance from London but in the opposite direction! There was another patient who found himself saying under his breath: "I would rather cut my throat right through to the bloody bone than let that fellow Williams help me." In fairness, both of these individuals were compulsive alcoholics: addiction to destructive parts of the self imposes particular stresses upon the psychological processes of such people.

Only a small minority of persons who suffered from a projective identification-blocking mother or mother surrogate commit murder. Many more, at least in Britain and in Western Europe, commit suicide when there seems to be no person externally, but more particularly internally, to whom they are able to turn for help. This is the area in which the Samaritans and other organizations can provide help by making the situation less dangerous at times of crisis. If the introjection—the holding inside the self of a death constellation—is impossible, and if there is a risk of suicidal action, projective identification (consisting of putting into another person the death constellation at times of special risk) may relieve the immediate danger. When this happens, the suicidal impulse has been countered by a surge of the self-preservation drive. The next step is complicated. What one would expect would be relief at getting rid of the death constellation. But, as Bion (1967a) stated, projective identification is an omnipotent fantasy, a state of mind conveyed to another person. We need to recall that the person with the death constellation (at risk of committing murder) thinks in concrete terms, like the psychotic, but with a difference. The person into whom the death constellation has been put by projective identification is felt to contain that part of the owner of the death constellation. There is also a supposition that the death constellation can be bounced back into the owner as and when the latter feels threatened. At this point, there is acute danger of a murderous attack upon the person into whom it is imagined that the death constellation has been put. Sometimes the projector reintrojects his intention, sparing his victim. An example springs to mind—the case of a young man with an immediate desire to rape, but who was also aware that somewhere in his mind was a wish to kill and a plan to do so. He lay in wait for an attractive girl who came by on a bicycle, put a stick through the spokes of the front wheel, and overpowered her. She fell into the long grass at the side of the road, virtually into his arms. He got hold of her and was about to rape her, but the beautiful girl sobbed and her would-be rapist felt a surge of pity for her. He loosened his grip and dried her eyes, saying that she was free to go. She said that he would be caught. He replied, "That will be my fault, not yours." He was caught and convicted for attempted rape. This strangely determined young man pursued the line of action upon which he had decided, but was able to change course and pursue an opposite, noncriminal course with the same determination. This kind of behavior is by no means rare: the murderous projective identification is a forcing into the victim of the death constellation, itself dangerous and ultimately parasitic.

Bion's (1967a) paper "On Arrogance" discusses a triad of characteristics—arrogance, curiosity, and stupidity, all widely separated—that can be observed in the analysis of certain patients. Bion concluded that what is seen is evidence of a primitive disaster. This he viewed ultimately as a failure either to have had, or to have been able to benefit from, a projective identification-accepting object (mother or surrogate). This had led to the absence of an internal version of a projective identification-accepting object, resulting in an inability to digest and metabolize experiences. Indulgence without love or understanding can be corrupting to the morale of the individual by fostering materialistic, greedy expectation and arrogance.

Let us suppose that curiosity is evidence of an endless search for a projective identification-accepting object that is pursued long after the quest seems to be fruitless. The sign of breakdown in functioning is the outcrop of stupidity to which Bion referred. Arrogance, in spite of failure, carries overtones of manic defiance. More psychotically, however, it can signify a resort to hallucinosis, in view of reality repeatedly having turned out to be fruitless and disappointing, in object relationships.

As one treats one's objects intrapsychically or externally, so one feels that one is or will be treated by objects, internally or externally. A talion justice reigns in the mind of the owner of a death constellation and, of course, in everyone else. In many cases the murderous sequence of projective identification of the death constellation exists in the mind as a totality. As was stated by one prisoner patient: "It has already happened in my mind, and I feel bad about it. I then have to go out, find somebody to do it to, do it, and then at least for a while, I feel a lot better." Here we have a differentiation between conscience pain and the pain of containing violent impulses. He feels conscience pain when he has committed the crime in fantasy, experienced in a highly concrete way. To repeat, "It is as if I have already done it, and I feel bad. I go out and do it and for a time, I feel better." This illustrates the burden of living with a death constellation, and with no adequate internalization and development of a projective identification-accepting object. A current external situation, perhaps in the family or the wider social milieu, may contribute to a disastrous outcome. The deficiency of an internalized projective identification-accepting object is relative, and what may allow the individual to get by in times of relative calm may be totally inadequate when too much happens too soon.

Returning for a moment to the nature of the death constellation: in the precatathymic crisis state of "murderousness in situ," which is not yet triggered into a catastrophic action sequence, one may think of this as being analogous to its physical homologue, namely, a carcinoma in situ. In its interpersonal dimension, it represents the containment of an enemy force that is adequate unless and until the advancing army runs into trouble, whereupon the enemy promptly breaks out of the containment. The death constellation tends to break out of containment when a person who hitherto had been able to contain his intrapsychic troubles can no longer do so as the result of events such as the illness and/or death of a loved one; loss of a lover; involvement in disasters like football, rail, or air accidents; or, at a more chronic level, loss of a job and subsequent unemployment. The finding of a good object, cause, or belief can help to compensate for the inner impoverishment, and in time may be an object willing and capable of accepting projective identification. A lifer released on parole found that he was totally accepted by a certain well-known religious group, with no onus on him to be anything but himself. He became able to mourn for the woman he had killed, an innocent person representing his more punitive mother and used as a substitute victim. The capacity to continue to mourn enables the life of the individual on lifetime parole to continue reasonably satisfactorily.

Many persons with a death constellation who have killed do *not* become able to mourn, however much they may wish that they had not killed. I interviewed in depth a lifetime parolee who had killed and served a long prison sentence. He had had some psychotherapy, and I found that the ability to mourn did exist, and it developed. This man had experienced a worse than noncontaining mother regarding the projective identifications of her young child: she was very nearly a schizophrenogenic mother. Nevertheless, the child had been able to use containing persons in the caring services meaningfully, and had made significant steps in the internalizing of a projective identification-digesting part of himself. It is likely that a detoxication of the death constellation depends for its effectiveness on the capacity to mourn. What makes mourning an interminable process in those who have willfully killed another human being is the impossibility of restoring that person to life. Reparation to the internal representation of someone whose life has been taken by the self reaches an impasse, so that the mourning goes on and on. King Henry III mourned Thomas à Becket in this way. I have also mentioned certain lifers on parole who stated that unless they continued to mourn each day, they started "to go to pieces."

The question arises whether the death constellation, once established but without the individual's being compelled to carry out an actual killing, can be totally resolved. It may be that, although some psychic digestion and metabolization of the death constellation follows from its detoxication, it can be reactivated by an excess of adverse circumstances. Factors that will influence the situation are:

1. the relative strength of life-hazard factors as against life-preserving factors
2. unconscious envy
3. love predominating over hatred

The prisoner patient who committed the crime in fantasy, and then had to go out and commit it in external reality, had an experience that in a healthy person would have been different. Something would have happened to the remorse about the crime committed in fantasy while it was still in a pre-enactment state. The prisoner patient who enacted his fantasy wrote a chart of his variations in mood, which went as follows: happy and feeling genial and generous, dissatisfied and touchy, depressed, persecuted, angry, murderous. I think the healthy stages would have gone from happy—depressed—persecuted—more depressed—not persecuted to recovery and then a period of peace and relative harmony.

> One man, serving a life sentence for killing his wife, experienced just such an oscillation trying to cope with a death constellation. He and his wife had not developed a mutually helping relationship. He was depressed and suicidal and had taken some poison from work, intending to take it himself. His wife chided him for being selfish when he was about to drink a glass of fruit juice, which she did not know contained the poison. After a number of "You take it," "No, I'll take it," "No, you take it," statements, it eventually ended by his yielding to her demand for the drink. It must be remembered that he knew, and she did not, that the juice was poisoned. As soon as she had drunk it, he telephoned for an ambulance and tried to make her vomit, but she died. He was guilty and remorseful and very depressed. A sudden urge to live had gripped him, while his wife was felt to contain the death wish—his own death wish.

This was not a suicide pact, because she did not know about the poison. Suicide pacts are a special issue, as rarely do both pact-makers die. In the past, the surviving person used to be charged with manslaughter.

> An example was the case of a 20-year-old woman who was the survivor of a suicide pact. Her partner was a young woman of the same age who shared the despair that led to the act. They had both been pregnant for the second time. The parents and other authorities recommended therapeutic termination of the pregnancies. Despite pressure from their respective mothers to yield to the terminations, the girls did not agree: nevertheless the terminations were carried out. The girls felt guilty, depressed, and demoralized, and decided to steal sleeping pills from a young man who had given one of them the key to his apartment. The plan was carried out. They settled themselves

on the river side of an embankment, took the tablets with some vodka, and went to sleep. One girl rolled into the river and drowned. The one who survived fell against an embankment wall and was picked up by the police and taken to the hospital, where she recovered after several days of intensive care. Her problems were increased by the guilt and sadness over the death of her friend, with whom she closely identified. She had nightmares in which her friend called her name from the river to come and join her, and to look after the two aborted pregnancies, now babies under the water. After therapy at the Tavistock Clinic, which lasted for about two years, she improved greatly. It was revealed that it had been her father who had insisted on the abortion. He came across as a very anti-life person. It did not surprise me that he had been suffering for a long time from a life-threatening illness. Eventually she stopped attending the psychotherapy sessions, as she lived some distance from London. A few months later she telephoned for an appointment and asked if she could bring her fiancé, as she would like me to see him before she decided on marriage. He was younger than she and rather naive, but with an obvious allegiance to life. She married him after having become pregnant by him, defying her father who had put up a feeble case for another abortion. I reached the view, however, that she had hidden her own antipathy toward having a baby behind her father's overt antipathy. There was no further news until four years later, when she came to ask for advice in handling her three young children, stating that her husband, though nice, was very much a fourth child.

The idea of death sometimes seems to be so deeply rooted in the character of the individual and to be psychically indigestible without professional help. In the foregoing case, what became clearer after the young woman had recovered was that she had been abused by her very disturbed father, not sexually but by the projective identification into her of his own eroticized fear of death. This had a component of dread and one of excitement, and an element of defiant brinkmanship. It reminded me of a child's naughty life-risking game called Last Across. The baby, for the young woman, was very vulnerable to this projective identification from her father. Her mother, on the other hand, had found the means of refusing the projective identification from her husband, which laid open the daughter as the main receptacle. Despite her relative inability to digest what was put into her, she made good use of psychotherapeutic help when it was obtained as a result of a catastrophe and a near-death experience.

5

Other Manifestations of the Death Constellation

In one family, Caribbean in origin, that I treated there was a tough stall holder at a street market father in his late fifties, a mother a few years his junior, three sons, and a daughter. The mother could just about read and write, but was not of subnormal intelligence. The eldest son, in his mid-thirties, was a successful solicitor, entirely interested in young women. The second son, two years younger, was a carpenter, skilled at his work, but with a tendency to become depressed and inactive. The third son was a slick, clever businessman, a wheeler-dealer. Both younger sons lived with women many years older than themselves, clearly representing mother. The youngest sibling was a girl, attractive and wayward, who had caused her parents much anxiety by her unamenable, undisciplined behavior over which they had little influence. The family had been affluent, but times had changed and their standard of living had fallen dramatically.

The impression I got, through treating the oldest brother in as near to psychoanalytical therapy as possible, was that father was bright but operated at the frontier of criminality. He was kind, rough, quick to avenge grievances, proud, resourceful, and with a smoldering, explosive temper. Mother had bouts of depression, including some severe ones for which she had been given several courses of electroconvulsive therapy. She had made suicidal attempts from time to time, one or two having necessitated treatment in an intensive care unit. The second son had also made two suicidal attempts, or at least gestures, toward suicide.

At one juncture I was asked to recommend a colleague so that the mother could be assessed for psychotherapy. The father denigrated both the project and the recommended colleague, and so the situation dragged on.

Suddenly an SOS arrived from the daughter in their home country, indicating that she was in mortal danger from her lover. Both had been, or were, on a variety of drugs. The next message came from a hospital. Mother and eldest son arrived to find the young woman near death in the intensive care unit. She had many injuries, the worst being gross contusion of the brain, and died. The oldest brother was grief-stricken and felt guilty at being slow to go to the Caribbean after his sister's first SOS. Father was moderately retaliatory, wanting to murder the murderer but not doing anything about it. Mother went blank. Middle son became depressed, and youngest son said he was sorry but with little affect.

I began to suspect that murderousness was located in this family, probably in the father. I knew that father was not only aggressive but also very afraid of being attacked, robbed, wounded, or killed. I also knew that he kept a loaded gun at home, allegedly for protection, but this precipitated the next catastrophic event. Mother took her own life.

Massive turmoil ensued in the residual family. The careful planning of the mother's suicide made me think that she was not the shallow-minded woman I had been led to believe she was. Some months later I discussed the tragedy with the colleague whom I had suggested for help for the mother. He felt that a terribly murderous atmosphere emanated from the husband, and that the husband had been determined that his wife should not come to psychotherapy. The attitude of the eldest son was a sort of depressive nihilism; it seemed to him as though there was a curse on the family, that they were held in the grip of a lethal fate. What could they do about it? Most of all, what could he, the eldest son, do about it?

Some years ago I was involved in family therapy with a different family comprising two parents and two children in which violence seemed to be the main problem. During the therapy, which lasted for two years, the mantle of violence settled upon each member of the family in turn, finally achieving resolution during the "second round" of its allocation.

I think that something like this was happening in the family described above. What was being passed around was death in the form of murderousness, suicide, and, in the youngest boy, accident-proneness. The oldest son murders in his mind and has occasionally risked death in fights. Where did the idea of death and its indigestibility arise? The entire family tended to get bogged down at the paranoid-schizoid end of the anxiety spectrum. As Bion said, P/S denotes part objects and a state of disintegration, or leads to a state of unintegration upon relapse from approaches to the depressive position. The state reached is worse than the first. Beta elements and bizarre objects consisting of beta elements with ego and superego traces clinging to them exist as residues of relapse from the depressive position. They are suitable only for projective identification or for acting out. Certainly, each member of the family showed these characteristics. The eldest brother, as a child, kicked in a door while in an uncontrollable rage. The lack of containment this implies was a shared characteristic of all members of the family. Acting out was extensive. As far as I can tell, mother looked after the physical needs of the four children well. She was not satisfactory, however, in her ability to work with the projective identifications of the children and relay back to one or another of them an improved situation that could be accepted by the child, the projective identifier, and then worked upon by him or her. Of course they were displaced persons.

Little wonder that ideas about death should have proved to be so psychically indigestible. The result, as far as one can see, was that each family member was left with a disturbingly powerful constellation connected with death within the psyche. I would postulate that mother took in a good deal of this, but could not detoxicate it. It seemed to be this inability that resulted in a prolonged failure in development that affected the family in different ways.

Son A could be destructively aggressive if opposed. His kicking down the front door when somebody inadvertently locked him out was an example. He later ruthlessly punched a motorist who outmaneuvered him in a parking lot.

Son B dealt with aggression in the face of frustration by a paranoid-depressive withdrawal from conflict. He was suicidal and accident-prone, had time off from work, and avoided provocation.

Son C was a wheeler-dealer, a fast car driver, and had dreams of strangling the girl he lived with.

Father was quite intelligent but lived by threat and counter-threat—a profoundly antidevelopmental way of life in this country.

Consider the factors that operated in the death constellation that led it to remain strikingly undigested and unmetabolized in this family. As far as I could ascertain, only the eldest son did a significant amount of work on the problem. He could and did feel guilty, and sometimes made serious attempts to make reparation for the damage he felt he had done to other people. The father rationalized his own shortcomings. The mother retreated into narcissistic inaccessibility. The middle brother retreated into illness and opted out, stating that he could not face the situation. The youngest brother consciously brushed aside blame.

The detoxication of murderousness depends on the ability and willingness of the burdened individual to mourn, and by that I mean more than a token mourning for the deeds enacted in fantasy. It includes mourning for murderous dreams. If this mourning process can be sustained for a sufficient length of time, the murderous enclave within the individual tends to be detoxified, so that there is recovery. The likelihood of a life-taking or life-risking deed will be substantially reduced, if not entirely eliminated.

P.S. One summer's night the oldest brother telephoned me to say that the middle brother was attempting to kill himself, claiming that he would get to be with mother first! A psychiatrist injected him with Valium, and the patient slept, waking up in a relatively unsuicidal state.

PART II

6

The Nature of Aggression

Aggression consists of the use of force to express feelings and to achieve aims. It is used to intimidate, to impress, to manipulate, and sometimes to subjugate other people and the environment and the various things contained in it. In former times the vanquished, whether other human beings or animals, were not necessarily killed but were enslaved so that they became subordinate factors and aids to achieve the further aims of the victor. Aggression is used for purposes of self-preservation and in the service of species preservation. It is used at times to save, rescue, and defend. These functions contrast markedly with the opposite functions mentioned above, namely, to dominate, to annihilate, or simply to seize and use. Aggression thus has a positive developmental function as well as a predatory function exercised for egotistic purposes, usually to the detriment of other people.

Pathological Aggression

These two aspects of aggression might be termed as normal parameters, but in addition to these there is a kind of aggression that from the first is essentially pathological. In this type of aggression, which may be characteristic for the particular individuals who use it as the habitual currency of their interpersonal relationships, there is violence and destructiveness beyond the need of the task in hand. Some of these people smolder sullenly for long periods of time only to burst out into flagrant aggressiveness in an episodic way for adequate or sometimes totally inadequate reasons. The important point is that the severity of the explosion into aggrievement greatly exceeds the provocation that triggered it off. This suggests that something rather like a time bomb inside an aggressive kind of individual is so situated or anchored within the psyche that certain kinds of provocation can detonate it. Sometimes the detonating agent seems minimal and totally inadequate.

What is this condition? It is insufficient to say that some people simply have a chip on their shoulders that makes them trigger-happy without inquiring into how this state of affairs came about in the first place. It is particularly with those people whose aggressiveness is excessive, odd, or in one way or another inappropriate that we wish to concern ourselves. I refer especially to those in whom aggressive action appears to be built into their way of life so that aggression is an invariable extension of diplomacy and for them a usual substitute for verbal negotiation. As far as words are concerned, there seems to be no give and take in these people. In their method of physical confrontation, what usually occurs is a bipolar situation in which they either boss other people about if they can subjugate them or kowtow to stronger individuals (or groups). The underlying principle is based upon the maxim that might is right.

The other features of the syndrome are that there is usually neither tolerance of difference nor espousal of a democratic interaction with the aim of achieving a negotiated solution acceptable to both sides. Control or be controlled by somebody else is the order of the day. These people are authoritarian, but not necessarily perverse. As far as child abuse is concerned, what is often encountered is an excess of punitive zeal in quelling turbulence so that, in the case of an unruly or disturbed child who finds it impossible to conform to rules, the individual resorts to cruelty amounting eventually to gross abuse. This occurs when the child resists the conditioning of the authority. One of the most difficult features of the situation is how the parental or other authority retains an attitude of moral righteousness and a belief that dreadful punishments are being inflicted for the child's good. Sometimes, mounting aggressiveness is found to be exciting to both the authority and to the defiant, provocative child. This excitement can be quite sexualized, the one side practicing brinkmanship and the other pursuing a cat-and-mouse game that gets more dangerous even to the point of being life-risking as the excitement mounts.

Provocation of Aggression

The various provocations that trigger such an escalation of violence may be due to disobedience, defiance of moral codes of behavior or persistent acquisitiveness such as stealing. Sometimes the child is greedy and the demands upon the parent(s) or their substitute(s) go beyond the need of the subject and beyond the capacity or willingness of the objects. Sometimes the demands for food, toys, money, privileges, or love are from one specific individual, the mother, and sometimes greed is diffused into all relationships, including particularly those with siblings. Demands may be made aggressively and, when unsuccessful, the aggression may mount into quite frightening violence. To cope with this, the parents or other authorities may find themselves responding by violent retributive actions in an attempt to get the greedy child back within certain boundaries so that he or she is not felt to be a threat.

Sometimes the need of parents or schoolteachers expresses itself greedily and a perfectly ordinary child receives punishment for not fulfilling the ambitions of parents or other authorities. A child who was being trained by her father to be a swimming champion collapsed and died through being forced to do strenuous swimming at a time when she was physically ill. The ambitious greed of the father made his daughter into an infantile prodigy at swimming and obscured his capacity to think of the child's needs and rights and the limitations of her capacity. Greed may be expressed in the implementation of sibling rivalry, in which case aggressiveness and cruelty tend to mount. Greed directed against parents felt to be depriving by the child can result in violence either way so that the child threatens the depriving parent, who in turn feels threatened by the child. Violence breaks out, and in an escalation of this kind the killing of the weaker is not unknown.

Envy is more dangerous than greed. Although the greedy person makes quite outrageous demands on his or her object— parents, their substitutes, or their latter-day derivatives—at least they are based on a kind of love, and the need for more and more does indicate a presupposition that something good exists. This contrasts with envy, which, as Chaucer said in the fourteenth century, is the deadliest of all the deadly sins because it attacks all the virtues and destroys all goodness. The envious person attacks the good object because that object is good and has something to give. The envious individual bites the hand that feeds it and makes nothing of the best endeavors of the most giving and generous people in the social environment.

Being punished for badness, default, or dissimulation is what the average child expects and is usually quite willing to tolerate, as long as the punishment is regarded as full atonement to be followed by forgiveness and rapprochement. If, after the punishment, there is continual harping in the form of nagging, reproach, or reminding the young person of his or her wrongdoing, a secondary rebellion may flare up and eventually result in a further delinquent act. Sometimes authorities, including parents, are envious in such a way that they exploit the contrition of the young person and penalize constructive remorse that, if fostered, could have a good outcome in relation to future personal growth and development, and in its psychosocial repercussions. The worsening cycle of malevolence, in which an envious adult often pillories an envious child or vice versa, may end in a surge of destructive aggression.

This may be initiated by the child or by the parent, but in either case escalation of the violence can and often does lead to a beating, a battering, a maiming, or even a killing, usually of the smaller and weaker person. Most often there is a constant interchange of violent projections. *Projective identification*, the term suggested by Melanie Klein (1946), is used a great deal. This splitting off and projection of parts of the self and the forcing of them upon another person who may then be attacked for seeming to be responsible for those parts is a pathological use of the unconscious psychic mechanism and method of communication we might call *normal projective identification*. Sometimes the recipient of the projective identification feels taken possession of and may shout out phrases such as, "Stop it, you'll drive me mad!" Such outbursts are not meaningless expressions of intolerance. Sometimes aggression is unconsciously designed to put madness into somebody else, that is, to drive him or her mad in the hope and expectation that the subject may remain sane.

Disburdening the self of feelings regarded as being unbearable is what every baby does to his or her mother or the person acting in the role of mother during the earliest period of the life of the infant. To lesser degrees, the father—and after him more peripheral family members and people outside the home—comes in for this kind of treatment. The mother or her substitute may make what is communicated to her by projective identification somewhat better, and then relay it back to the infant in a form that the latter is able to accept and utilize. This course of interchange is obviously the desirable and healthy one. It leads to emotional growth and development. There are other possibilities, however. For example, the mother or her substitute may block the communication—or even make it worse—and feed back to the infant a worsened version of it. Blocked communications are very provocative as far as a flare-up of aggression is concerned. Just as parents can block the communications of children, children can frustrate parents. This may be intentional, unconscious, or coincidental, in which case it is likely to consist of a spillover of their own disturbance in the capacity to communicate. For example, sometimes a pain is so frightening and persecutory to the child that he or she cannot talk about it clearly but conveys to the parent a misleading story. Some even go so far as to locate the pain in some part of the body far away from the part that actually hurts. This seems to be a spillover and spread of the wish to deny the existence of the pain at all. I have known parents to be drawn into this kind of displacement and denial for some time, resulting in dangerous delay in calling for appropriate help.

Aggression and the Victim

We all have an aggressive component. The question is, how is it linked with other parts of the self and how does it function or cause a person to function in relation to other people, that is, in a small group or larger social setting? Within the self the aggressive component may be stronger or weaker. It may be directed toward the preservation of good internal object images and by externalization of their outward representations in the form of good people or worthy causes. On the other hand, the aggressive component may be used to defend or to perpetrate externally bad, undesirable parts of the self, including engagement in cruel, aggressive, greedy, or destructive external projects. More complicated still is the situation in which bad methods are used in attempts to further good aims. These people are difficult to deal with because they feel so self-righteous, and it is hard to show them what they are doing in the course of their activities. When conducted in a solitary way by an aggressive loner using destructive methods, often of a kind that can risk the lives of other people, the individual who perpetrates acts of destructiveness tends to become increasingly personally unstable. This is shown in several ways. Sometimes there is an escalation of violence, or an increasing paranoia that would be manifested as self-reproach if the feelings were allowed to operate on the self and not projected onto other people. However, because they are repeatedly projected into the outer world, members of which are then attacked, the actual hostility of society or the police is increasingly aroused so that the individual tends to bring upon himself a concretely expressed persecution. To match this, there is even more persecution from internalized figures in the fantasy life of the aggressor and a constant reinforcement of external and internal forces and vice versa. This process could be termed *the brutalization of the solitary aggressor.*

When the various depredations are carried out by a group (or gang), the situation develops somewhat differently. The presence of like-minded people with a common aim tends to give to the group a coherence of its own in isolation from the rest of society. This coherence consists of an ascription of all good things to the in-group—the group members—while the bad characteristics are projected or ascribed to outer society. Thus the aggressive group can carry on for a lot longer than the loner. Nevertheless, when disruptions occur within the group, the fact that general brutalization has taken place is shown in the cruel and violent measures used to maintain group solidarity and pull back potential deviants into the group on the basis of "conform to the group's standards or be rejected absolutely" (not infrequently by execution).

In child abuse a parent or parental surrogate may behave like the loner described above or a family or institution may operate like a gang or criminal group. In this case the leader is likely to be the sickest member of the group, family, or institution. Families can behave like gangs in certain circumstances and then a scapegoat victim is usually selected, often quite unconsciously. This individual, often the baby or the most overtly weak member of the family, becomes the target for the projections of the family group.

> In one such instance a violent family with shared delusional ideas about their aristocratic status and origins made their older daughter the receptacle of most of the family mental instability. At first she developed a state in which she behaved as though she were mentally subnormal. There were marked learning difficulties, so that she was unable to read or write until she went away for some months to an adolescent inpatient unit, where she suddenly found that she could learn to read. The family consisted of an intensely variable, warm and loving but violent father; a mother who was cold, distant, critical, and dignified; and an older brother, younger brother, and

> younger sister. It became clear that the individual psychotherapy eventually given to this young woman had little or no possibility of succeeding. With hindsight it was evident that the family, largely unconsciously, set about dismantling everything favorable that was happening in the therapy of this girl so that she was constantly and repeatedly reinstated as the family scapegoat. Quite often the mother would ask to see the therapist and complain about the lack of improvement in her daughter. She would inquire when the treatment was going to work, as if complete health and recovery would occur when the therapist found the magic word with the "open sesame" effect.
>
> Eventually, when some small amount of ground had been gained from the furious family inundation, the therapist was confronted with a catastrophic relapse in the patient, who seemed to be back at or even beyond square one. On inquiry, it was learned that the father had picked up his daughter's very special pet cat, which promptly scratched him, whereupon the father, in front of the daughter, seized the cat by its hind legs and bashed out its brains against the wall of her room. Each subsequent improvement was nullified by an overdetermined, contrived catastrophic event ranging from a serious head injury sustained by the sister in a strange fall from a hitherto docile horse to a damaging car crash involving the older brother, who had passed his advanced driving test.

Without going into further details, the lesson to be learned from this therapeutically unsuccessful and frustrating experience is that the whole family must be seen and treated together when it is found that one family member is carrying the crippling and disturbing burden of all the family projections. When it is the baby—perhaps the baby who was unwanted in the first place—who is subjected to the process of scapegoating, there is considerable risk to mental health and even to physical survival in a disturbed family setting. In child abuse the cruel parent and his or her relationship with the young victim is often only the visible part of the iceberg. The invisible part is situated in the unconscious mind of one member of the family or is shared between members of the family. It may be focalized in one parent, and that parent enacts concretely the fantasies shared by the other family members.

In some cases a disturbed child with an unconscious sense of guilt stemming from secret fantasies or actions evokes cruel punishment from a parent or sibling in order to assuage and mitigate the uncomfortable feelings of guilt. Often there is an interaction between the fantasies and impulses of the aggressor and the needs of the victim. The interaction may remain low key, muted as it were, for long periods of time, so that violence and cruelty may erupt episodically. Alternatively, there may be a tendency to overcontrol, with eventual eruptions of violence that may or may not escalate.

The question arises, "What makes some cases of violence appear to be self-limiting and, on the other hand, what makes for escalation in some cases?" In the former category the aggression seems to be expressed, but once it had broken, it is like a wave breaking harmlessly upon a sandy beach and thereafter receding. In the latter category the characteristics are of a tidal wave, mounting in successive stages until finally it overwhelms everything in a terrifyingly destructive catastrophe.

When some cruelty has been perpetrated and the aggressor sees the damage he or she has done—damage to a child, for instance—healthy feelings of guilt and remorse are usually able to make themselves felt and so limit the wave of cruelty, which then recedes as the anger and rage die down. Most cases are like this, but in a minority of cases, a dangerous minority, something different happens. There is a tendency for the sight or even the thought of harm done to the victim to result in further attacks being made upon the self-same victim. The intrapsychic processes in the aggressor seem to be as follows: the sight of damage done to the victim shocks and dismays the aggressor and remorse begins to make itself felt in a painful manner, but the pain of the experience is felt to be unbearable and causes the psychic state of the aggressor to slide down from the more advanced and civilized feelings of depression and sadness over harm done to the victim into one of mounting persecution. It is then that the eyes of the victim are felt to be boring into the aggressor with persecution and reproach. To end this situation, and in a state of mind that is essentially paranoid, the aggressor attacks the victim further. This process can and often does go on until the victim is masked and obscured by defacement or even more completely obliterated. In the 1966 play by Peter Shaffer, *Equus*, this situation is shown clearly in relation to the horses blinded by the emotionally disturbed young man who loved them and practiced a perverse sexuality with them. When he fell for and had sexual relations with a young woman in the stables and the horses stamped their feet, he felt that he had been unfaithful to them and that they were looking at him with tremendous disapproval and reproach. He could not bear it and therefore attacked and blinded them.

We have not as yet dealt with primarily sadistic aggression, in which the aim is for the subject to derive pleasure from the infliction of pain upon the object, the satisfaction being enhanced by the obvious signs of pain and distress that can be seen in the victim. In some families one or other parent may behave in a sadistic manner toward one or more of their children. Some schoolmasters derive pleasure from the infliction of pain upon young boys. In sadism it is important to recognize the sexualization of the pleasure in the cruel transaction. It is largely the sexual excitement that causes sadistic behavior to be repetitive. The role of the victim of ill treatment or more serious injury is complicated and, of course, many victims are masochistic. The masochist derives pleasure, ultimately of a sexual kind, from the infliction of pain upon him or her. There is a male/female sex linkage with the pair of opposites just described: there are more male sadists and more female masochists. The study of aggressor/victim relationships, called *victimology*, is still in its early stages and needs much more investigation. Let it suffice to state that the pairing of aggressor and victim is rarely a matter of chance. They tend to select one another mutually for definite though usually unconscious reasons and purposes.

Reparation and reparative aims and activities are undertaken to put right, as far as possible, the injuries and depredations committed by the aggressor against his victim or victims. Reparation can proceed only if the pain of guilt and remorse about harm done can be borne and sustained significantly for sufficiently long periods of time. If the self-reproaches and remorse are switched unconsciously and automatically into persecutory feelings, the result tends to consist of further attacks on the victim rather than further reparation. It is easy to see how serious the consequences of aggressive damage done can be when we are dealing with that kind of person. It is to be emphasized that some of the further damage may be due to the mental image or representation of the victim within the mind of the aggressor. The acting out with further damage to the actual victim may be immediate or delayed, sometimes delayed by many years.

Working Through the Depressive Position

How do people become so different in their attitudes and actions, so that at one end of the scale intrapsychically something is built in that limits aggression, whatever the provocation, and at the other end a much less favorable situation prevails? In the people at this other end of the scale, aggression tends to escalate. Although there are no clear-cut boundaries in nature over this issue, there does seem to be something like a watershed. The question is, can this be related to any situation or phase in infantile or childhood development that, if dealt with satisfactorily, leads to a capacity to limit aggression and, if left un-negotiated in an unsatisfactory state, leaves such people with no capacity? These are the people who tend to be goaded by the sight and realization of damage inflicted upon a victim. At the risk of repetition, it is necessary to explain the development of the depressive position and of the partial substitution of the more primitive, persecutory form of anxiety by the more integrated and "civilized" depressive anxiety in the human being.

In the first months of life the infant has relatively undeveloped perceptual powers and only limited capacities to conceptualize;

mother or the person who looks after him or her is perceived not as a whole person, but as parts. These parts are apparently relatively unrelated to each other. At this stage a feature of normal development is the sorting out of experiences and objects into gratifying experiences stemming from good, even idealized, sources and into painful, depriving, and frustrating experiences, supposedly derived from bad, denigrated part objects. Without going into detail, the frustration and deprivation due to the absence of a good part object can be experienced as being caused by the presence of a bad part object.

Just before the middle of the first year of life, neurophysiological and psychological development is far enough along for the infant to recognize mother or her surrogate as a person, that is, as a whole object. The realization of a whole-object mother results in the untenability of the previous polarization into good and bad part objects. The infant's own hostile feelings toward and fantasies about the bad, depriving part object (e.g., the breast) are felt to have harmed, even destroyed, the good, gratifying, loved breast. As a result of relating these two opposite attitudes, namely, love and hatred toward the same whole person (mother), the infant now experiences a different feeling. This new feeling amounts to depression, sadness, and concern for the mother lest his hostile feelings predominate over his loving ones. To this stage Melanie Klein gave the name *depressive position*. Some holding on to the painful anxieties at this phase by the young infant, that is, some negotiation of the depressive position, is important for future growth and maturation. Without such negotiation the infant remains dominated by the more primitive kind of anxiety called *persecutory anxiety*, which is based on a feeling of being got at and threatened, and is productive of an abiding sense of grievance. With some success in dealing with the depressive position, depressive anxiety, which has to do with anxiety over harm done by the self predominantly to one's good object, is able to be felt and sustained. This kind of anxiety leads on to feelings of responsibility and hence to attempts at reparation for harm done, to sublimation, and to every form of creativity.

The working through of the depressive position in the middle of the first year of life is never complete. Renegotiation of the anxieties and relationships to do with the depressive position is necessary again and again, particularly at times of personal crisis and developmental change such as adolescence, menopause, and the midlife crisis in the thirties described by Jaques (1965). Successful renegotiation of the depressive position is followed by a further efflorescence of integration of the self and therefore of favorable psychosocial repercussions.

Although the depressive position and its negotiation does indeed constitute a watershed in emotional development, it must be stressed that the situation is not an all-or-nothing one but one of degree. If this were not so, it would stultify the numerous and complicated efforts on the part of many people who work in the caring and remedial services. Not only can there be some improvement, even in the most disturbed people, when there is some secondary negotiation of the depressive position, but also disturbed individuals, including those who are most violent, can be helped to contain their violent feelings and impulses without immediately seeking to enact them in full in action upon another person or persons.

Several kinds of mitigation may take place. One is the expression of violence against things instead of people. The man who smashes the telephone or breaks a glass rather than beating up his young child with whom he is annoyed has made a considerable step forward. Further steps lead to an increasing ability to contain violent impulses without acting them out at all. These impulses are often expressed in conscious fantasies or in dreams; although it is recognized that some fantasies may be the precursors of action, I am referring to the extremely important use of fantasy as a substitute for action. Harmless substitutes for violent and aggressive actions may be sustained in the absence of a containing environment or they may be able to stop at a fantasy level only in such an environment. Violence tends to occur when too much happens too quickly or when hostile feelings accumulate in those people and in situations where psychic digestion is impaired or when a sudden rush of violent experiences exceeds the capacity of the individual to digest them. Often it is at this point that urgent intervention of a professional kind is required and can have most influence. The way in which there can be a drift from fantasy to action is usually by means of the following series of steps:

1. A loosening of the grip on depressive anxiety gradually replaces persecutory anxiety, as shown in D ↔ P/S (D = depressive anxiety and P/S = paranoid schizoid or persecutory anxiety).
2. Then follows the designation of the potential victim as a persecutor. He or she, whether child or adult, becomes singled out as the enemy.
3. Gradually, the potentially violent individual suffers from an increasing distortion of his perception of the persecutor. For example, in one case, a disturbed adolescent girl experienced her stepfather as a large, bearlike animal who gradually became regarded as a bear with all the implied threat of sitting at breakfast with a grizzly bear.
4. There is then a breakdown into part-object perceptions, so that the persecutor, in the case of the stepfather as seen by the adolescent girl, changes: all she could see finally was a knife and fork threatening to stab her and carve her up.
5. The capacity for and use of symbolization gradually breaks down so that what would stand for something else becomes experienced as that thing-in-itself. For example, the phallus of the rapist is regarded as being a sword or a dagger. In retaliation or in the interests of self-preservation, an actual knife may be picked up and used against the threatening persecutor. Another example of a breakdown in symbolization is when burning feelings become concretized into an impulse to set something on fire which is then indulged and a fire started with incalculable results.
6. What has been said demonstrates how action, which is dynamized by persecutory anxiety, is likely to be of a violent, destructive kind.
7. After the violent episode has run out of power and drive, a precariously held equilibrium is gradually restored.

The restoration of equilibrium may be hastened by appropriate action on the part of the social agencies. Far better, of course, is the recognition in advance of the mounting danger of violence.

When the violent escalation has not gone too far, social agencies—and, in particular, knowledgeable, caring, and understanding individuals working for the social agencies—can be significantly successful in helping to restore equilibrium without the violent acting out taking place at all.

7

Violence and Psychic Indigestion

No disregard for the role of other factors in the etiology of violence is implied by my decision to write on how psychic indigestion can and does account for many acts of violence. There are constitutional, cultural, and social factors in the origins of violence, and these have been stressed by many authors over many years. The role of what may broadly be called *traumatic experience* has not been entirely neglected in attempts to understand how violent states of mind are initiated and maintained: however, I do not think that its importance has been sufficiently stressed.

Psychically indigestible experiences are varied. Sometimes something is witnessed, like a motor accident in which one or more persons are killed or maimed, or perhaps a train or air crash. The event may have been part of a war or even a surprise attack by unseen guerrillas. It could be an armed holdup or a psychically unacceptable act of cruelty. Not all such experiences lay down a blueprint for future psychological trouble. Sometimes the individual witness of such events is able to work through the emotions aroused by the experience in the presence of a containing person. Sometimes a working through is undertaken unaided, together with some resolution or detoxication, as I prefer to call it. More often help is needed. This is often given by a parent, a close relative, a teacher, or a family friend. The characteristic of a containing person is that he or she proves to be able and willing to bear some of the burden of what has happened on behalf of the traumatized person to whom it has happened. But more important still is the capacity to accept the burden, work on it, and pass back to the person at risk a situation improved by clarification and by differentiation between the actual wrong suffered and any imagined or supposed harm. This process it is hoped is prophylactic against the buildup and persistence of an intrapsychic enclave that would pose a danger later, perhaps even years later.

If there remains such an enclave or intrapsychic constellation, a breaking out from what appears to be a kind of emotional limbo tends to take place at a time of stress. This may be during a psychobiological crisis like bereavement, divorce, or loss of employment (including retirement). Personal illness, particularly if there is pain, with or without a threat to life, is a powerful experience during which psychic limbo may be disrupted. The situation is like anaphylaxis: the original situation acts as a sensitizing "dose" and, if unmetabolized psychically, is put away, but not safely. It remains a danger when there is a *shocking* event that is capable of reactivating the earlier situation and results in overreaction to the second situation.

What is going on in the intervening period, often over many years? Sometimes the individual knows something going on in layers of his or her mind to which there is poor access and about which there is little understanding, perhaps none. In some individuals evidence from dreams and other outcrops of unconscious activity enables us to infer that there is a frequent going-over of the traumatic situation, probably in an attempt to detoxicate it. Other strategies can be aimed at converting threat and pain into peace or even pleasure. Sometimes this is carried out by turning a passive, painful experience in the mind into an active, pleasure-giving one, possibly by transferring to someone else the pain and the passivity. If this "works," the individual repeats and repeats this pattern of fantasy. When fantasy no longer gives relief or pleasure, there is a tendency to act out the fantasy constellation upon someone else. This other person—a willing partner, an accomplice, or a victim—in each case is made to bear the state of mind evacuated by its owner.

What prevents improvement in psychotherapy or psychoanalysis in such patients? The obstacles vary widely, from fear of the mobilization of uncontrollable forces, despite the reliability and discernment of the therapist, to the inability or reluctance to relinquish an addiction to destructive parts of the self. An addiction is discernible in masturbation practices and their associated conscious and unconscious fantasies. From a practical viewpoint there are important implications. One patient got himself locked up in a mental hospital in what turned out to be a defensive retreat into a psychotic breakdown. His masturbation fantasy was necrophilic and his object was the dismembered body of a young girl. This girl represented a combination of his much envied sister and a young girl of great prettiness with whom he had fallen in love as a child, at a distance.

The difference between individuals who have a worse prognosis lies in their capacity to feel sad and regretful rather than to develop an increasingly paranoid attitude when psychic pain related to what they wanted to inflict upon someone else becomes severe during therapy. Unable to work through this situation, one prisoner patient could not hold in consciousness the fact that he had killed a young person. Repeatedly the memory was re-repressed, even though that meant a jeopardizing of his prospects of release. Another young man had killed an older woman; rather than sustain remorse and guilt, he broke off therapy. In both these examples the victim had been a scapegoat who at the time of the crime represented (symbolized) an ambivalently regarded, needed person; in the first example, wife, and in the second, mother. These men who killed females had been seriously wronged by their respective near relatives, but in no way wronged by their victims. Sometimes this kind of violence is worked out not upon the person who did the injury, nor upon an external scapegoat, but on themselves in a self-injury, a suicide attempt, or a self-killing. In some cases the self-injury is more unconscious; for example, a severe hypochondriasis or psychosomatic illness.

The basic rule is that what cannot be psychically digested, that is, worked through to recovery by detoxification, persists in the form of an *identification*. This is as Freud (1917) stated in relationship to healthy mourning leading to recovery and pathological mourning leading to an identification with the lost, but not relinquished, object. It applies to intrapsychic fantasy situations as well as to those enacted in concrete external reality.

The preparedness to accept violence (even as far as accepting the possibility of the death of the self or of someone else) can work both ways. I suppose the "good" soldier or officer has this kind of preparedness. Such a person can differentiate between good persons who have to be protected, sacrificing, if necessary, one's life for them. The darker side of this "heroic" character is in the gusto with which injury and death are inflicted or suffered by the self.

Another category of violent person is the paranoid individual. He can be recognized by, among other things, his dourness. He is unforgiving and vengeful. Sometimes he is spotted by his capacity to divide and minimize any good experience that comes his way; at the same time, any affront or grievance is multiplied and maximized. A typical example is an affront, slight, usually involving actual injustice, evoking the usual amount of ill grace. In succeeding days, instead of a slow detoxication taking place, the anger and persecution increase. With this escalation of aggrievement, threats are made. Then one day, after a period of false calm, an aggressive, possibly murderous crime is committed. It is regarded as revenge by the perpetrator. As opposed to this, sometimes something favorable takes place in the course of what looks like a serious violent escalation. A de-escalation follows so that in the event, either a token crime or no crime at all is committed. An example of an unfavorable outcome is that of a young man whose enemy, in an outburst of swashbuckling competitiveness, boasted of his sexual experiences with his rival's girlfriend when in fact there had been no such liaison. The paranoid, violent boy brooded until, in a mad fulmination of violence, he sought out the competitive young man, beat him up, and, while he was unconscious, threw him into a stretch of deep water where he drowned. Love was nowhere involved in this sequence, which was based on paranoia, arrogance, and narcissistic rage. An example of the switch into de-escalating violence is that of an older man equally deluded and paranoid who fixed on a derogatory statement alleged to have been made about him by the family doctor to his (the patient's) wife. A series of token attacks were made and at times it looked as though a very violent escalation might be taking place. However, the violently affronted man sought therapeutic help and the situation became less and less ominous. It ended in an ironic joke being played on the doctor that demonstrated the identification between the paranoid husband and his object of persecution. Significantly, the doctor was the only other man who had a right when requested to do so to examine the body, including genitals, of the patient's wife. There were echoes of Freud's Schreber case in this sequence (Freud 1911a).

For a threateningly violent situation to go into decline and resolve in the manner I have described, there must have been a good deal of work done psychically. This includes remorse and mourning over the crime of violence committed in the mind in fantasy. It is the work of mourning and regret that gradually detoxicates the constellation. If this is halted or goes into reverse, there is a return of violent, ultimately paranoid attitudes. In quite a number of the individuals seen after there had been a violent crime, careful history taking showed that the violent, threatening situation had ebbed and flowed for years before the intrapsychic state of affairs had been matched by external circumstance so that a crime occurred. At this juncture the criminal action appears to be so automatic that it follows a prefabricated sequence. It also depends upon how the intrapsychic constellation is situated within the mind of its owner and whether it is easily triggered or not. The external circumstances in which it is likely to be detonated are also crucial. If all the "necessary" conditions coincide and a crime of violence is committed, new problems arise. If injury but not a killing occurs, the task of working through regret and remorse is possible: sometimes it can be worked through satisfactorily. Frequently, however, there is a failure to work through it and the victim comes to be regarded as a persecutor. From that moment on either the original victim is liable to be attacked further, or some other victim is chosen.

It will have become evident that Klein's views on depressive and persecutory anxiety (complementing Freud's [1917] views on mourning and melancholia) are central to my thoughts about violent activities and their resolution or ominous escalation and even repetition. Persecutory anxiety stems from the beginning of life and is ubiquitous in the animal kingdom. It is based on fear of malevolent attack and, if severe enough, amounts to a fear of being mutilated, maimed, or killed. In the reaction that follows, in nature one sees fight, flight, or freezing in an attempt to turn the tables on the persecutor. The objective is to get away from it or to become so merged with the background that the predator does not observe the potential victim. In humans the fight–flight mechanism operates but the freezing comes to be represented by conformity or by presenting a story that consists of a texture of lies, as in Munchausen Syndrome by Proxy.

Depressive anxiety on the other hand is about anxious regret over harm done by the self in phantasy or in external reality to one's good objects—including principles, causes, and so on. In civilized groups (and possibly in others) it includes regret over harm done to enemies, starting with regret over excessive retaliation, regret over reaction to threat, and a general regret over the collapse of one's essential humanity. This anxiety is almost, but not quite, confined to human beings. When an individual can tolerate depressive anxiety, the way is open for favorable developments, important among which are the reparative drives. At the persecutory end of the spectrum no such progress is made. The best that can be expected is freezing, that is, conformity or acceptable behavior due to a fear of retaliation, punishment, or physical pain.

In early infancy, when conflicts between persecutory and depressive anxiety first reach prominence, and always thereafter, persecutory anxiety is associated with part objects and depressive anxiety with whole objects. What is the practical use of these conceptual models in thinking about violence stemming from psychically indigestible experiences? *It is easier to attack a person as a part object than as a whole human being.* Trigger part objects often initiate violence.

The Yorkshire Ripper's last victim had "Best Rump" written on her jeans across one of her buttocks. One of the individuals whom I worked with for a long time perpetrated a seemingly senseless fatal attack on a middle-aged woman as the result of seeing a shaft of sunlight shining through her auburn hair. After a lot of therapy this was shown to be the feature that ignited memories of his loved and hated reproachful mother.

One reason why there can be progress and successful working through while the individual is able to tolerate the self-blame of the depressive position is that attention (therefore work) is focused on the negative, destructive aspects of the self. At the paranoid end of the anxiety spectrum attention is focused on threats to the self posed by unreasonable, savage, often relentless persecutors. These are more often than not perceived in part-object terms. It is always easier to attempt to alter the external environment rather than to focus attention on the involvement of oneself. Yet what about those who are severely self-reproachful, who injure themselves and sometimes end up committing suicide? Without going into detail here, this seems to be due to attacks on internal persecutors as part objects lodged within the self. Here again, the individual is operating with part objects, not with images of whole people.

What happens in those cases in which the psychically indigestible experience cannot be detoxicated inside the self and help is either not sought or is not available? Inside the self there exists an identification with the aggressor, that is, with the person who inflicted the original (or subsequent) violent experience. This identification may be a total one or there may be a split-off encapsulation of it, so that an alternative self is manifested at times of threat. These are times of stress both external and internal. Painful illness, by repeating the pain of the original violent experience, can reactivate the split-off part, forcing it away from psychic limbo and risking an acting out of the entire preexisting sequence. In some cases there may have been no hint of what will happen, while in others small eruptions give an indication of a dangerous intrapsychic constellation. One clinical example is that of a young man who went out with a switchblade in his pocket into a dangerous district of London. He saw a policeman being confronted by threatening youths, and went in with the conscious intention of helping him. The rapid change that then occurred within him was in line with his previous experiences: he stabbed and killed the policeman and consciously did not know why he had done so. A latency child, aged 9, put the matter clearly when he found a dead man under a bush behind a summerhouse while playing with his younger brother (aged 2½). He was in an internal conflict with his idea of father at the time, which was normal except that his father had fairly recently returned from war service overseas. He said, "It is not that the sight of the dead man frightened me, but it has lit up fears which were already bothering me." When questioned further, all he said was, "It showed that death is real and not like just thinking about it." In the case of the toddler brother, the memory was much more of a screen memory. After the event the little boy developed a phobia of any shelter (like a summerhouse); when questioned a few months later, he said, "We found something nasty there." When asked what, he said, "It was a snake—a poisonous snake." The phobia cleared up with only parental treatment.

If the traumatic experience involving violence, pain, or injury matches the contemporary phantasy situation, it is likely to be compounded in a way that makes personal (normal) working through difficult or impossible. It is important that parents and teachers recognize that something is going wrong. In milder cases parents can help the young person to work through the situation. There are extra difficulties if the caring adult or adults themselves have been involved in the traumatic experience, for example, a major accident. Then, for the time of stress, no caring, containing adult person who knows the child may be available. Two brothers, 6 and

4, whose father had been murdered, encountered immediate problems relating to their lives. These were dealt with at a children's psychiatric outpatient unit. In adolescence both boys ran into further internal difficulties and both had fairly long psychotherapeutic intervention at an adolescent department. Their phantasies at the time consisted of a compound of the earlier trauma and their adolescent problems with father figures. In these boys, matters were made worse by the absence of father and the known reason for it.

The length and intensity of therapy varies with individual need, of course, but in my view only psychoanalysis or psychoanalytically oriented psychotherapy affords satisfactory results in the long run.

In line with Freud's findings (1917), experiences that cannot be worked through persist intrapsychically by means of identification. The identification may be partial or total. If the individual at risk can be helped by understanding persons who tolerate but do not appease, he or she may recover and most improve. The process of recovery necessarily takes place within the psyche of the individual at risk. If he or she remains bogged down and immovable in a state of persecutory anxiety, a sound improvement is precluded. A chance of apparently trouble-free conformity on a psychosocial (not intrapsychic) basis is then the best possibility.

When thorough detoxication has taken place by means of mourning work at the depressive position, I would regard relapse as highly unlikely.

8

Escalating Violence

Anyone who stands at the edge of a sandy cove will have noticed how the power and fury of a stormy sea expends itself as the broken wave runs up the sloping sand and then gently runs back down the beach, leaving a smooth expanse of sea-washed shore. This is what happens in ordinary circumstances with the ebb and flow of the tidal cycle. Under some conditions, however, forces such as cyclones, storms acting upon the sea, earthquakes, or other volcanic actions stir the depths. They infuse a more inexorable menace into the situation, so that instead of losing power and slowly flowing back into the matrix of origin, each successive wave, more powerful than its predecessor, escalates the violence, sometimes to the destructive crescendo of a tidal wave.

Violence is an essential part of each one of us and, like the sea, it can run a benign course or it can escalate to a dangerous and destructive crescendo. An example of nondestructive violence is a man I saw who fainted and fell into fairly deep water. I was on the point of jumping in to save him when my colleague, a man so slow and gentle in ordinary life that we liked to call him "the sleeping clergyman," was in the water before me. His organized sequence of violence ended with successful artificial respiration and the relatively quick recovery of the man. When things were calm, I mentioned that his rapid, life-saving, violent action seemed to contradict his everyday behavior. My colleague replied, "It had to be done. I don't expend energy unnecessarily."

In contrast, a violent 22-year-old man released from prison after a short sentence for violent behavior went out on his bicycle, which he loaded up with firewood from a forest near London. As the wood he was taking was rotten, he was doing no one any harm. A policeman stopped him and questioned his authority to take the wood. The young man flared up in anger out of proportion to the suspicion, and attacked the policeman with his wood chopper, injuring him seriously. For this he received an appropriately long sentence. He wrote to the wounded police officer and said: "I do hope you realize that there was nothing personal in my regrettable attack upon you. This letter is not in any way intended as a plea for a more lenient sentence, but is just a personal apology to you." The young man later encountered further circumstances that he experienced as highly provocative and he reacted to them similarly, in a violent way. He was a bland man so long as he was not provoked, but once action had started, the escalation of violence proceeded automatically, and if unchecked, either by onlookers or by some retaliation on the part of the victim, a killing was likely to take place. This young man agreed with my anxiety about the murderousness of the situation. Consciously he regretted every bit of violent aggression. Unconsciously there seemed to be an inner source, like the phenomena that cause a tidal wave. Can we make progress toward an understanding of these two types of violence, and the many states between the two extremes?

In personal or group confrontation, the goading of an opponent by his adversary is common. It was alleged that the violence at the tragically fatal football match in Brussels between Liverpool and Juventus some years ago was triggered by posters stating that the British were animals. This goading may sometimes demoralize the opponents, but more often than not it leads to an enormous intensification of violence. Somewhere in the hurling of slogans as missiles, rather than more concrete objects, there is probably a hope that the enemy will, like the walls of Jericho at the sound of the horn, fall. At a primitive level it can be conjectured that the hurling of abuse is meant to undermine the self-esteem and the will to fight of the opponents, to demoralize them and hopefully cause them to collapse without further violence. In many instances, however, the aim of the goading is to intensify the violence. This objective may be compounded by the destructive wish to provoke an intense fight and to emerge victorious, or, where moral issues are involved, to goad the enemy into doing something wrong or stupid so that he or they are wrong-footed either morally, practically, or both. But there seems to be another process at work when the supposed demands of necessity are overestimated and exceed actual necessity in such a way that they become transformed into a retaliatory atrocity expressed in action.

Some explanation of terms is required. They are: *part-objects, persecutory anxiety, depressive anxiety,* and *depressive position.* In the first months of life the infant has relatively undeveloped perceptual powers and a limited capacity to conceptualize. Mother is perceived not as a whole person, but as parts—eyes, breasts, hands—initially experienced as relatively unrelated to each other. At this stage, a feature of normal development is the sorting out of experiences and objects (experienced as part-objects) into pleasurable experiences, stemming from "good," even idealized sources (good part-objects). At the opposite end are painful, depriving, frustrating experiences derived from "bad" and denigrated part-objects. Frustration and deprivation due to the absence of a "good" part-object can be experienced as being caused by the presence of a "bad" part-object.

About the middle of the first year of life, the infant becomes able to recognize mother or her surrogate as a person, that is, as a whole object. The realization that the whole-object mother exists results in the untenability of polarization into good and bad part-objects. The infant's fantasies about the bad, depriving part-object are felt to have harmed, even destroyed the good, gratifying part-object. As a result of love and hatred towards the same whole person, the infant experiences a different feeling. This amounts to depression, sadness, and concern, lest hostile feelings predominate over loving ones. Some holding on to the painful anxieties of this phase by the young infant, namely a negotiation of the depressive position, is important for growth and maturation. Depressive anxiety leads to feelings of responsibility and, hence, to attempts at reparation for harm done, to sublimation, and to every form of creativity. The working through of the depressive position in the middle of the first year of life is never complete. Renegotiation of the anxieties and relationships to do with the depressive position is necessary again and again, particularly at times of personal crisis and developmental change such as adolescence, the menopause, and the midlife crisis. Each successful renegotiation of the depressive position is followed by a further efflorescence of creativity.

It takes a considerable degree of maturation and integration to mourn a crime committed in the mind; yet it is a good deal less difficult to do that than to mourn a crime that has actually been committed, especially if it has killed or injured someone. In the intrapsychic world of fantasy, the desirable state to reach is one in which there is accurate foresight of action that might be taken so that its consequences may be foreseen. Something is interposed between impulse and action. If there is sufficient psychic digestion during this process, a successful psychic metabolism can proceed.

An accumulation of traumatic events tends to be more provocative than traumata that appear singly. In such circumstances there can be more of a tendency to explode into violence. Sometimes the outburst is directed against the self, but more often it is directed against either the person or persons supposed to be the cause of the trouble, or toward a scapegoat. For example, a young man, quick tempered but without a record of criminal offenses, felt that he loved and wanted to marry a young woman. He had introduced several other girls to his mother, but she had disapproved of them in some peculiarly hostile way, managing to get them to turn away from him. In this instance he felt that the girl was so pleasant that his mother would approve, but she was off-putting in the usual way. Despite the protestations of the young man, the mother rejected the young woman, who in turn rejected him. The situation worsened in his mind over the next few days, after a minimal overt reaction. Ten days later he passed by his mother's best woman friend, who was on her way to work. He knocked her off her bicycle into a ditch and she drowned. As he had no grievance against her, he wondered why he had done it. It is clear that he retaliated with escalated savagery in a single but fatal act of talion.

Another example is that of a man whose wife became sexually involved with a married man in the small, isolated community where they lived. He felt rejected, angry, and vengeful. The same thing had happened once before, years previously. It was as if he had had a sensitizing dose years ago, and the second occasion became the shocking dose, as in anaphylaxis. As his wife was evasive when questioned, he sent messages to the man to discuss the matter, but received no reply. Eventually he met the man in a railway waiting room and brutally attacked him. Fortunately, others prevented him from doing worse damage and even killing him. The likelihood, however, was that the attack would have gone on to murder.

If the extreme state of mind reaches psychotic proportions in its deviation from what could be regarded as ordinary reality, the containing forces (police) may find it very difficult to contain by any means other than violent force, though I know of several successful curbings of escalating violence by police officers who found within themselves expertise and insight at the time of need.

At least part of the explanation lies in two situations in the inner world:

1. The degree to which the individual (or group) is bogged down in a state of persecutory anxiety
2. The degree to which psychic pain can be borne without a rush to evacuate it, to alter the external situation, or to break loose from internal persecution in the belief that action will deal effectively with it. The view taken of a persecutor or persecutors may be realistic, it may be a view as seen through the eyes of the child

> part of the self, or it may be experienced as a nameless dread to which a name is given and a source described.

I know of a young man, 26, who had been sentenced to prison several times for attacks on young girls aged 10 or 11. He had put his hands tightly around the throat of one girl and then, having intimidated her, touched her genitals and finally put his penis against her vulva and had an emission without penetration. In a therapeutic session with me, he said that when he had carried out the assault and had had the emission onto the girl he began to feel guilty, and then felt very sorry for the girl. All feelings of hatred, fear, and the wish for revenge disappeared. I asked him to explain hatred, fear, and, especially, revenge, as far as he could. Eventually his history as a toddler was revealed. His father had died unexpectedly and his mother took on the task of earning for the family. He, as the youngest child, had to be disposed of, at least temporarily, and was put into a children's home. There he remembered nothing but trouble. Two children, a brother about his own age and a sister about 10 or 11, got together and worked out how to deprive him of a tricycle his mother had given him as a consolation present for having to go away to the home. I have no doubt that he projected into the new and strange environment his hatred and fear, and invited ill treatment from the people there. When he complained about the stealing of his tricycle, the girl forced him into various sexual activities for which he was quite unprepared and unsuitable. She drew out his penis by the foreskin and then put it between her strong little thighs and nipped it with her adducter muscles. He was barely 3 years old and she must have seemed enormous to him. While this is not an example of escalating violence on a large scale, it had the potential of being so. It went into de-escalation by the way in which the man was able to do actively what he had formerly been forced to suffer passively; when that cycle was completed, he began to identify with the victim and then to be reparative toward her.

What of escalating violence? The sight of damage caused to a victim sometimes stimulates in the aggressor not compassion, but triumph. I have, however, encountered many cases in which compassion and regret were aroused. Sometimes the current of compassion and remorse can be sustained, in which instance one wonders why the aggressor needs to be violent at all. In some cases it would appear that a split in the personality has been short-circuited so that a split-off, compassionate self takes over from the violent, vengeful self. In either of these circumstances violence is likely to be episodic rather than escalating. Quite commonly, however, remorse and regret cannot be sustained at the depressive end of the anxiety spectrum, and when psychic pain cannot be tolerated a slipping back to the paranoid-schizoid end occurs, a switch that can occur very swiftly. The responsibility for psychic pain is then ascribed to the victim. The responsibility for causing the injury is denied by the aggressor and the pain by this time is persecutory in nature. The aggressor proceeds to injure the victim by attacking him or her again, probably far more violently. In severe cases this cycle is repeated a number of times, with the violence escalating at each successive cycle—this is the parallel with a tidal wave. In these severe cases the victim is not only murdered but repeatedly defaced. When the aggressor has felt accused and reproached by the eyes of the victim, I have known instances where the eyes of the victim have been destroyed. This was due to the mistaken idea that by obliterating the accusing eyes, the aggressor would be spared the reproaches of the victim. In these transactions projection and projective identification have been prominent, so that the destruction of the eyes supposedly frees the aggressor from having to or being able to see what he has done. The delusional nature of the transaction is brought home to the perpetrator of the destruction by the return of the eyes, sometimes the whole face of the victim, in his nightmares and in other dreams.

Fortunately, the acting out in full of a crime like the ones we have considered is relatively rare. Far commoner are related fantasy constellations, sometimes conscious, sometimes partly unconscious, and sometimes wholly unconscious. Intrapsychic work to mitigate the severity of fantasy constellations can and does go on, so that some de-escalation may have taken place before the crime. In that event what is perpetrated in action is a watered-down version of what was present as the original fantasy constellation in the individual. Sometimes de-escalation goes so far as to result in there being no action at all, or a harmless token of what was envisaged originally.

Violent individuals do, however, have particular difficulty in containing and working through painful feelings. For example, following an accident, an attack upon them, or a severe illness or death of someone near to them, they are particularly vulnerable. I have carefully avoided the term *love* in relation to these painful feelings because for such persons love is more of a possessive, tyrannical feeling than a caring tolerance. *Revenge* is more likely the word they would use. In the case of illness it is often the doctors or nurses who are blamed and who become indistinguishable from the illness itself. It is in the mind that violence escalates in most cases, except those mentioned where the sight of harm done provokes rather than hinders violence. A man who had distinguished himself in a military elite force was involved with a young woman whom he intended to marry. She was wooed, if not seduced, by a man whom our suitor despised. He gave several ultimatums to this man and finally said, "If you do not stop I will kill you." This he enacted in a coldly detached way and then asked the person who had witnessed the "execution" to call the police, after he had first handed over the murder weapon. The transaction had taken place mainly in the mind of this man, who also was prepared to kill and/or be killed. One man who had been decorated for bravery in World War II dreamed, "When I killed those labeled the enemy under orders, I was praised. When I killed *my* enemy, I was imprisoned for life."

Sometimes an individual seeks external provocation or threat, which is used as an excuse for violent action. An intrapsychic violent constellation can then be expressed and moral justification claimed by the perpetrator. One man who was violent but empathized with the underdog became addicted to lighting fires, which seemed to leave him without the compulsive need to resort to personal violence. There was a split between his attitude toward authority figures and the underprivileged, including anyone who was threatened. During a prison sentence for incendiarism, he saved a prison officer from attack and was himself hurt severely. He then felt something change inside him. In the psychotherapy he had had from me earlier, to which he had responsed plausibly, no real improvement had occurred. Upon release from prison he had no impulse to light fires and no impulse to be violent. I think that the bringing together in his mind of authorities who were not always hard and arrogant and underdogs (in the form of criminals) who are not always decent, and who had proved themselves to be violent toward somebody who had not provoked them, enabled him to identify with a benign kind of authority. Later on he got a job at a hospital. This expressed a wish to help people and to direct them, an identification with me—in those days I worked in a hospital.

There are other types of escalating violence: baby battering, for example, gang violence, violence associated with drug or alcohol intoxication, and need and violence erupting in the case of a pyrexial physical illness. In addition, there is violence that is put into another person by means of projective identification and is returned to the prospective identifier with increased force. The escalation is potentiated by its having been put into someone else and returned to its originator. A variation of this process is when a person, often an authority figure like a teacher, youth leader, or lecturer, verbalizes a violent idea or series of violent ideas, never intending them to be expressed in concrete reality. In some vulnerable individuals a preexisting violent constellation can be activated from its psychic limbo and acted out in full, often in a way that adheres to the communication of the authority figure. I am reminded of the results of King Henry II's statement, "Who will rid me of this seditious priest?"—ending with the murder of Thomas à Becket. Some years ago, in the film *Rope*, two students killed a third for no reason but that the phantasies of their lecturer were taken in by them and acted out concretely—the film was based on an actual murder of this kind.

Baby battering tends to begin in a minor way and to escalate over a period. Battering sometimes arises because of the father's jealousy of the baby and the love and attention the latter is getting from the mother. This may result in actual neglect of the father, but there is usually a *supposed* neglect. The crying baby can awaken the crying-baby parts of the father, who may have managed to contain them—just—since babyhood. Mothers can be provoked into baby battering by the crying baby through the stirring of similar baby needs, so that she becomes competitive with the baby rather than caring. Lack of acceptance by the baby of a mother's efforts sometimes stirs up violent retaliatory action in the mother. She may be unable to cope for want of a satisfactory supportive network, and becomes frantic and violent, in which case the battering is a plea for help and a danger signal. Serious long-term effects can and do result for the baby as well as more obvious short-term injuries, which in some cases lead to death. I treated a man who had killed a father figure for reasons that seemed remarkably flimsy until I learned that I was dealing with a person who had been a baby battered by his father until he became too big to batter. This man, carrying the traumatic experiences of cruel battering by his father, killed not his father but a substitute who in some way impinged upon an intrapsychic encapsulation. The scapegoat victim thereby lost his life.

Criminal gang violence has two main forms: violence as a means of carrying out gang policy, and violence escalating in a clash with victims or with the police. Of these two forms, the first is more alarming as it is conscious and chosen. Usually the leaders are ruthlessly power-greedy, or acquisitive of material wealth that is acquired in a predatory way. They may use hit men who have a tendency toward violence, rather like the murderous man just described. When violence has become an extension of diplomacy (to misquote Bismarck), the consciences of the individuals involved tend to become less and less effective, so that a state of brutalization is reached and then no holds are barred.

I should like to make some mention of violence in relation to alcohol and/or drug taking. Although an enormously increasing amount of crime is engendered through the acquisition of drugs and, to a lesser extent, alcohol, this is different from the violence that erupts and often tends to escalate during states of drug or alcohol intoxication on the one hand or the frantic states of deprivation in persons who are addicted and dependent on the other. During intoxication, violence tends to be triggered by actual or supposed persecution and to be conducted without the controls or limits that fairly healthy people have. There is usually a paranoid element, but this tends to spread out in a diffuse, often indiscriminate way. *Reason* never works if it entails opposition, particularly direct opposition to the intoxicated person. Attempts to deflect attention to less dangerously escalating violence are often successful.

The drug-deprived individual, in attempts to get the drug he or she must have, is associated with a more ruthless and unscrupulous, well-directed violent drive, and is likely to stop at nothing to get supplies. This is an increasing problem with which I can deal only sketchily. Not all drug-intoxicated individuals are incapable of coherent action or of knowing what they are doing. For example, drugs may be taken in order to be able to commit a crime or series of crimes. After all, hashish derived from the word *assassin* and was taken, along with alcohol, before going out on a criminal sortie. I have seen such sorties overseas during quiet periods in the course of World War II.

The common denominator in violent action is the dominance of persecutory feelings and anxieties over depressive ones. The former, clustered around the paranoid-schizoid position, are based on the experience of a threat—perhaps to life itself—aggrievement, and resentment. Violence contains a wish often felt as a need for action of a retaliatory, vengeful kind. The latter are associated with self-blame rather than its avoidance or evasion. What have I not done? What have I done incorrectly, ungenerously, or badly? These are the questions asked of the self, if I am somewhere near the depressive position. In the case of the persecutory situation, the question is, "How do I stop these persecutors getting at me?" The depressive position question is, "How can I put things right and make amends for my shortcomings?" It is easy under stress to slip back from depressive to persecutory pain, partly because of the tendency to slip back to more primitive stages of development. This we know as regression. At the depressive position whole persons are involved; at the paranoid-schizoid position the same people are experienced as parts of people, or part objects. It is far easier to be ruthless and destructive to parts of people than to whole people.

Often regression in a violent person is a state that lasts only for a short time. If during times of crisis the violent, persecuted individual can be *contained* by a stable relative, a doctor or a probation officer, a policeman or a nurse, the crisis can often be negotiated without escalation of violence. When hostages are being held in a hijacking or other situation, the police are usually skilled, patient, and containing. They are aware that it is important to state facts to the person or persons whose violence is liable to escalate, and never in any circumstances to add threats or recriminations. One hijacker who was on the run with a hostage eventually said to the police officer who had talked to him over many hours, "I will give myself up to you because you understand me." *There should be no question of appeasement in such containment.* One encounters similar, less dramatic situations with adolescent patients who are disturbed but not basically criminal, and of course with children in one's own family or among their friends. The same procedure usually proves helpful.

We have been dealing with crises. To deal with personality disorders in which there is a tendency to escalate into violence, treatment needs to be deeper and more prolonged. Such work is carried out in many places, including at the Tavistock Clinic. In fact, both kinds of help are given at the Tavistock, and a crisis intervention patient may well be taken into therapy after the acute crisis has been dealt with. Therapy and crisis intervention have a common denominator in that the aim is to facilitate a movement from the paranoid-schizoid position to the depressive position. In a crisis the urgent task is to prevent the violence from escalating. In the latter case the aim is to facilitate a steady reaching and sustenance of a state of depressive anxiety based on responsibility rather than a state of persecution, aggrievement, and readiness for violence.

9

Cruelty and Cruel Behavior

It has been stated that criminals are deficient in conscience, have no consciences, or have no ability to distinguish between right and wrong. Melanie Klein drew attention to the fallacy of these views. She stated that the delinquent had not a deficient conscience, but rather possessed a different kind of conscience, in which there were savage, cruel, or primitive internal authority figures. It is generally known that an individual has the ability to tolerate only a certain amount of blame. If this quantum is exceeded, a feeling of responsibility (related to depressive anxiety) is replaced by a feeling of being "got at." In this case the individual is in the sway of another kind of anxiety, persecutory anxiety. What quantum of reproach can be tolerated varies from person to person and from time to time in the same person. Some people can tolerate blame as long as it is just, that is, so long as the external authority and the internal or conscience authority are in basic agreement. Some people react in exactly the opposite way. If the external authority and the internal one are not in line with each other, the capacity to tolerate may be exceeded and a switch from depressive to persecutory anxiety takes place. The difference between the two as far as emotional development and growth are concerned is profound. When anxiety is depressive, there is a capacity to learn from experience. In some cases of persecutory anxiety there is conformity because of fear, but never because of love. The strange and complicated Mayan civilization disintegrated in an untimely way because of its being founded and built up on rituals and devices whose aim was to propitiate savage deities.

Another mental mechanism of paramount importance in the understanding of cruelty is splitting. In effect, there may be two or more aspects of an individual so separated and different that it is like dealing with two or more different persons. Splitting is not the same as repression. There can be repression and splitting in the same person. An aspect of the self can be split off and unrepressed or split off and repressed. When there is a return to consciousness of repressed thoughts or impulses, there is always anxiety. When there is a short-circuiting across a split there may be no evidence of anxiety. The movement from one split part of the psyche to another may or may not be associated with a period of confusion.

When a feeling of guilt impinges upon a personality structure that cannot bear the psychic pain involved, there are several possibilities. The situation may be repressed or split off, or manic mechanisms may take over, or there may be a combination of all three processes. In general, the neurotic individual deals with what he cannot bear by repression. If the quantity of repression accumulates, there may be other consequences that cannot be dealt with here. The splitting processes may be multiple, shallow or deep, or varied. If deep splitting occurs, what results is two or more selves, or virtually so. One of these may have the characteristics of a Dr. Jekyll; the other, that of a Mr. Hyde. Manic mechanisms consist of projective identification, splitting, idealization, denial, or omnipotent control of objects, that is, people in the life of the individual or represented as images in the psyche, or both. The splitting in the manic defense differs from that in more paranoid-schizoid conditions in that it is more highly structured and organized.

As a result of splitting, there is a variety of different object relationships. If splitting is into idealized and demonized figures, by projection of the demonic figure onto another person, an outside person may take on these qualities and be attacked on that account. By keeping the demonic image inside, there may follow demonic activity or, if the internal image is attacked, suicide. If splitting is into a criminal self and a noncriminal self, there is an alternation in behavior. Sometimes a split-off part is held in check for a long time, only to break loose violently on some occasion. The breakout usually takes place when the controlling or containing energy is depleted, for example, by physical illness, accident, bereavement, or other misfortune. Some examples may help to make the matter clear.

A young man deserting from the army and hitherto not violent became very hungry. He saw a middle-aged woman, decided to rob her, struck her violently with a piece of wood, and took her money. In his childhood he had seen his father hit his mother violently and had been extremely shocked by this incident. He had forgotten it but remembered it subsequently in the course of psychotherapy. Another youth, while his father was dying of cancer and looking terrible, went out with a gang of youths, knocked down and robbed a man who died as a result of his injuries. In the army I remember a man who shot his warrant officer. At the time of the crime the aggressor was nursing a severe malarial infection.

When depressive anxiety cannot be borne and shifts to persecutory anxiety, there may be a further shift into a state of not caring at all. This callousness is part of a manic reaction in which cruelty is common. If it is directed inward, it may be observed as a manifestation of masochism. If directed outward onto another person, animal, or inanimate object, it appears to be sadism or destructiveness, or both. The state of mind pervaded by or characterized by not caring is not casual or indifferent. There is no tolerance in it. There is cruelty and destructiveness and the not caring applies to the concern that would be associated with a sense of responsibility and a resulting moderation of behavior. The compassionate elements of the psyche in such cases have been split off, denied, bypassed, and in some way put out of action. The more the frenzy and the less the moderation of action by the setting of the compassionate elements against the destructive ones, the more cruelty there is in the criminal activity that takes place.

Reality sense varies greatly from individual to individual and also, to some extent, from time to time in the same person. Destructive violent cruelty may be part of the life of the individual—for example, when these urges are associated with sexuality—or they may be split off and accessible only under certain specific conditions—for example, provocation of one kind or another. One individual committed cruel deeds only after he did not attack the person who had offended him, but instead attacked a weaker individual who really stood for himself. He identified with the aggressor and perpetrated upon a victim what he felt himself to have suffered, but he multiplied the punishment in severity many times over. This particular person did not lose his reality sense except in the circumstances outlined above. The difference between the fantasy of what he wished to do to a victim and the action he perpetrated is that he thought of killing a youth by stabbing him in the abdomen and gouging out his guts. What he actually did was to punch a youth in the abdomen and hurt his testicles, letting go when the young man yelled out with pain. Many acts of cruelty are tokens in real life of a frightful fantasy system of extreme cruelty.

Occasionally, as in one murder case of note, the full horror is acted out upon a victim. In this case there seemed to be marked manic elements associated with the devaluation and scorning of other people: "They are only a lot of cabbages." There was a perverse preoccupation with sadistic subversive literature, for example, de Sade; a seductive proselytization of accomplices through a manic showing off to them of how utterly ruthless the perpetrator was; the luring of victims, the playing upon their weaknesses if these were known, and an increasingly savage and cruel torture of them. Sexual cruelty seems to be compounded of similar factors. Let us look at what these factors are, some of which stem from manic defenses.

What are manic defenses? They are defenses against psychic pain of any kind. Typically they act against feelings of tenderness, unrequited need such as the need for love, feelings of compassion and concern both for the kind and tender parts of the self and for the well-being of others. They also act against feelings of inadequacy, smallness, lack of intelligence or skill, inability to compete with others, lack of beauty or of social graces. They operate by the denial of adverse factors, often idealization of favorable factors, splitting of the object into good and bad at a level more integrated than in the splitting that characterizes the paranoid-schizoid position and the pathology directly in line with it. There is also a manipulation of objects (the term object is, of course, used to describe a person—a figure or someone in the life of the individual standing for an important figure, e.g., father, mother, brother, or sister). This manipulation, if extreme, becomes an attempt to control in an omnipotent way. The object who will not be manipulated or controlled is attacked in one way or another, often by scorn. The compliant object is given less and less freedom and it too becomes the target for scorn. In the case just referred to, the victim who complied was treated like a "vegetable" and the one who showed some resistance was attacked in a frenzied manner and destroyed most cruelly.

When sexual perversion is present, the cruelty is involved in the sexual fantasy, so that cruelty becomes an indispensable part of the program. This is very dangerous as the situation is not a once-and-for-all crime, but one likely to be repeated again and again. The key to the understanding of sexual cruelty lies in the elucidation of the unconscious fantasy constellation leading up to orgasm. Almost always there is a masturbation fantasy system or pattern that contains and expresses the perversion of which cruelty is a part. It can be stated categorically that when there is sexuality approximating to the normal, the hostile negative elements are eventually overcome by the loving, reparative, and tender components. Token aggressiveness with a show of cruelty may well figure in the foreplay but in the end, tenderness and loving elements triumph. When the cruel elements cannot be mitigated, splitting takes place so that the individual behaves as if he were two separate and distinct people, one loving and kind, the other full of hatred and brutality. Sometimes the cruel and the kind behavior are toward one person. Sometimes cruelty is reserved for one person and kindness for another. This pattern is seen fairly commonly when a man ill-treats his wife and reserves a tender relationship for his mistress. Also quite common is the man who is tender and kind to his wife but not very potent sexually. With a prostitute, however, he can be cruel and very potent. The tender and aggressive components of sexuality remain unfused. This can be a dangerous state of affairs in that aggressiveness and cruelty, stemming as they do ultimately from the "death instinct," are unmitigated by the love and compassion that stem, of course, from the "life instinct." Thus it may be that one day a crime of violence, even murder, may be perpetrated against the recipient of the cruelty.

Clinical Example

> A man who practiced sadism managed to get women to submit to the cruelty, or went to prostitutes who specialized in this kind of activity. The sadism consisted of a buildup of threats, flogging, and "nettling" the bare buttocks of the woman, who had to be tied up. He would humiliate the woman in certain ways, and then would suddenly release her and proceed to have sexual relations with her in which there was no sadism and her satisfaction was a point of honor. The turning point from cruelty to kindness followed a homosexual pattern, in which he had been the passive recipient of the same cruelty followed by kindness during his youth. It is to be noted that he had switched from being the victim to being the aggressor, from passive to active, and from homosexual to heterosexual. The whole dramatized performance was repeated over and over in a compulsive way so as to produce the maximum amount of threat and even pain, and then to make things right again.

Letting situations get as far out of control as possible and then bringing them under control again is part of the defense against the mental pain of feeling that situations are out of control. The trouble is that the practice of brinkmanship is fraught with danger, and one day the victim suffers too much and dies or takes fright, or the turbulent aggressive impulses of the sadist leap out of control and turn into a frenzy of cruelty. This must have happened in the case of Heath, a notorious British murderer, a number of years ago when his first murder of a young prostitute was followed by a much crueler and more frenzied murder of another young woman.

Cruelty may not be present in a loose state, so to speak, but may become detached from other forces that would normally offset it; this process of unloosing does occur when the individual is in a state of emotional distress due to rejection, affront, bereavement, and so forth. Then a good deal of cruelty may be unleashed, sometimes directly on the person who is thought or known to be responsible for the injury, sometimes on a victim who has done the aggressor no wrong and is, in fact, a scapegoat. The motive is one of revenge but the decisive factor seems to be the inability to bear an internal situation that has become extremely painful. Action is designed to reduce this internal state of distress. The less the reality sense of the delinquent, the more immediate the relief sought and the future disregarded. A case that comes to mind is that of a man who killed his sweetheart. She loved him, but as he was married she was trying to get him out of her mind. He became paranoid about the rejection and killed her. Although not insane in a clinical sense, he was sufficiently out of touch with external reality that he was unable to discern what the girl was doing. He also disregarded his unfair bargain with her. He was able to be extremely cruel to her verbally and, finally, physically, too, by shooting her.

Cruelty to animals must be as common as that to human beings. The same factors are present. Manic mechanisms enable the rationalization to be made. "Oh, it is only an animal." How many a fox hunter has said, "But the fox likes it as much as we do." If an animal is the victim of a person who tries and fails to exercise omnipotent control over it, there may be considerable torturing of the animal by way of reprisal. Animals can be made to stand for people. A man normally gentle and kind killed a cat by strangling it because it made a noise at midnight carousals with other cats. Sometimes provocation is used to excuse violent and excessively brutal reprisals. A schoolboy kicked by a pig kicked the pig so severely that it died. Another boy was disturbed at night by baby pigs squealing. He smashed their heads together.

Sometimes the cruelty seems to be unprovoked and quite meaningless. It is nearly always possible to trace the action to the unconscious constellation if time is spent on the task. The methods I use are: systematic dream analysis and methedrine abreactions.

If the person who has committed the act of cruelty knows why he has done so, or thinks he knows, he is asked to relate the whole incident or series of incidents down to the last detail. Sometimes the explanation is directly available, as in the following example. A violent man witnessed the attempted homosexual seduction of a pleasant lad by a deceitful and dishonest proselytizing homosexual old enough to be the boy's father. The witness could not contain his fury and eventually, apparently quite suddenly, jumped up and smashed a tureen into the face of the seducer.

Sometimes the meaning has to be sought in the symbolic nature of the activity. The Hanratty case is one in which a man and a woman were held up; eventually the man was killed by a younger man who then tried to rape the woman. The oedipal nature of this crime of violence is fairly clear. The Gravesend murder in which a young couple were marched at gunpoint into the marshes and there killed separately would seem to have similar oedipal elements, but what happened to the girl? The assailant amputated her breasts and took them away with him. Here was jealousy of the couple that, once acted on, triggered an envious frenzy in which there was a strong homosexual coloring in that the assailant sought to possess the breasts of the girl.

Another man hallucinated on the face of a young girl who was trying to cheat him in a food bartering deal the face of his wife who had succeeded in cheating him in their marriage. He stabbed the girl with a knife he was holding, ostensibly peeling an apple.

He was normally a kind man and this act was so unacceptable to him that he rid himself of all conscious memory of it.

Chronic cruelty is different. When a person repeatedly behaves in a cruel way almost as a matter of policy, either to another person or to an animal, it is usually because he ascribes to the object undesirable hated qualities of the perpetrator himself. He solves an internal situation, in which a cruel conscience or conscience figure persecutes him for a certain characteristic or group of characteristics, by projecting the whole undesirable constellation into a victim, then punishes it in the victim. Thus personal psychic pain is avoided. The victim may be subjected to physical or mental cruelty or both. I know of a senior officer in World War II who had a pet monkey in a forward area. Horrified when he saw the monkey masturbating, he tried to restrain the pet from repeating the act. When he failed, he took out his revolver and shot the monkey dead, then burst into tears. The monkey stood for himself. The killing of the monkey, which to onlookers seemed both cruel and out of character, was a projected suicidal act reversed by the projection, but the manic killing did not endure and for weeks afterward the perpetrator of this deed against the naive and devoted monkey was very depressed.

Another sadist found a female masochist with whom to act out his disability. No physical cruelty was ever committed. It was all in the talk and the mime. In this deed what was suggested was a fantastically cruel murder with a butcher's knife that was even brought down to touch various parts of the girl's body, but not a scratch was made. The girl could not get sexual gratification without this monstrous ritual in the foreplay. The man could not be satisfied without his part. The control was perfect, but such situations are dangerous as there can be a breakthrough of primitive destructive urges; the control may collapse and suddenly the destructive deed is done.

The need to spoil, and the callousness of the active perpetrator of the spoiling—including indifference to the suffering of the victim—is compounded of a number of factors. There is envy, sometimes of the happiness or good looks or gifts of the victim, plus feelings of inferiority giving rise to malice and spite. A Borstal boy was put in a room as a punishment and some of the other boys came to see him. He was taunted by them, although they had come to bring him some tobacco. He flew into a rage and jabbed at their eyes with a peg of wood he found at hand. One boy's eye was severely injured.

Another kind of cruelty is really a reversal of a childhood trauma, as in the case of the sadistic man who reversed the situation in which he had been made to suffer painful, essentially homosexual, assaults. In these cases there has been a situation or series of such situations in which the individual has been forced to suffer and could do nothing about it. The suffering itself seemed to have been internalized and then split off or isolated within the psyche so that much later on in life, when some chance circumstances detonate it, the whole tragedy is repeated but reversed.

It seems that an attempt should be made to classify cruelty. Two main subdivisions are cruelty aimed at attacking the bad in another person, and cruelty constituting an attack on the good. After a few projective and introjective transactions, the situation becomes confused and the motivation becomes more and more mixed.

A further subdivision, which is a quantitative one, is the degree of cruelty. Is cruelty designed to control and dominate, which includes coercion and extortion, or is it aimed at the destruction of another person? In other words, is death the ultimate aim? This would apply to authorities as well as criminals, and the immediate example that springs to mind is the cruel, murderous Nazi authority. Clearly there is a spectrum with milder cruelty at one end and major cruelty, reaching to death or even total obliteration, at the other.

Cruelty can constitute a testing of the object. It may be designed to see if the person or animal will turn nasty, or, at its severest extreme, whether or not the object is dead or will die. The aim is to go as far as possible without a fatal ending. It is an extrusion into external reality that occurs when certain individuals feel they have injured or destroyed the images of their loved ones within themselves. This situation may become so unbearable that external persons are attacked. These are either the loved ones, if the attack is direct, or anyone standing for those persons, if the attack is indirect.

When death is the aim of cruelty, it may be that for a long time token acts of cruelty suffice, but there is the danger that the token deed in time proves insufficient to satisfy the internal drive toward death. If this drive is expressed by projection, the result is murder; if by introjection, the result is likely to be suicide. The categories of cruelty due to the possession by (and inability to digest and metabolize) cruel objects introjected as a result of having experienced cruelty, and being in possession of an unmetabolized constellation of death, are very similar. In the one case it is possible that the cruelty perpetrated upon others will be limited in degree; in the latter it leads inevitably to death itself.

In a way, we have been dealing with cruelty that is projected, or rather evacuated, into another person or perhaps an animal. This evacuation results in transitory relief for the perpetrator. Some cruelty, however, is based on an acquisition of something from another person or animal. If it is of a detached possession, the only cruelty that may be expressed is the deprivation of the owner. Into this group would fit the starving of people and animals. Sometimes, however, the acquisitive urge expressed cruelly is a devouring one, and the aim is to orally incorporate the person or animal. Within certain limits such an urge is regarded as fairly normal in regard to animals. Direct cannibalistic token attacks, however, are quite common. One man, quite unconsciously, bit the nipple of a woman severely. In one well-known case a man actually bit off the nipple. In some cases tender elements of sexuality do not predominate over, and finally eclipse, aggressive ones. How much of this is due to an unconscious need to ill-treat the object (person) on whom the aggressor has become dependent is an open question. How much is a repeated revenge displaced from an earlier experience or multiple experience, or how much is a lack of maturation into tenderness, is also difficult to delineate. What is certain, however, is that the cruel relationship is a primitive one, whether expressed toward friends, enemies, or scapegoats. One has only to look back in history to see innumerable examples of cruelty, cruelty of authorities, or criminals, of ordinary people in ordinary and in extraordinary circumstances, to conclude that cruelty is a component of the personality of man. What circumstances, internal and external, resolve this cruel component and what cause it to remain as a dystonic, undesirable, or even disastrous island of savagery within the mind of an individual? We do not yet know all the answers to these questions, but we do know some of them, thanks to the work of Freud, Melanie Klein, and W. R. Bion (see earlier chapters).

What are the possibilities of prevention and treatment of persons who are liabilities as far as outbreaks of cruelty are concerned? Specially designed psychological personality tests are likely to make the diagnosis reasonably certain. Treatment, on an individual or group basis, whether given by psychoanalysts, psychiatrists, lay psychotherapists, or probation officers, has to give due weight to the task of restoring psychic digestion and metabolism so there can be learning from life's experiences. Persecutory anxiety will have to diminish in quantity and intensity if the depressive position can be reached and to some extent worked through. A more normal kind of relationship with external people and with their internal images in the psyche of the individual gradually becomes possible. Relapses are frequent, and must be negotiated. Therapy takes a long time, but if the whole chain of human suffering that emanates from one sadistic crime is taken into account, the slow and costly task of treating individuals can be seen in the correct perspective. It is one small contribution to the process of mental hygiene that, when aggregated with other contributions, militates toward a better state for the next generation.

At present we are still in an exploratory state, but the results with individuals are promising.

10

Brutalization and Recivilization, or Wildness and Civilizing for the First Time

Differentiation is necessary between an original learning process and a reclaiming of ground lost during the process we call brutalization. The latter is a reaction to circumstances that are persecutory, perhaps through their seductive temptingness, as with drugs, alcohol, perverse or in other ways unwise sexuality or acquisitiveness, or aggressive behavior that has stirred a powerful counteraction by the agents of the law. In general, the relearning or reclamation of the brutalized person stirs up more resistance in the individual or group being reclaimed than the taming process in the young untamed person. The late Esther Bick once said that little boys were either naughty or nasty. You could do a lot with naughty boys, but far less with nasty ones!

I came across a good deal of brutalization in the course, and later in the aftermath, of World War II. One man mentioned earlier, a very good soldier and later a noncommissioned officer (NCO), killed someone in civilian life some years after the war had ended. In prison he said: "When I killed people I was told to kill when I didn't hate them at all, I was praised and given a medal. When I killed someone who had really wronged me, I was given a life sentence."

None of us is ever completely free from the processes of brutalization, though they occur mostly in far less dramatic ways: for example, being overly severe with one's own children, or enacting reprisals for deceptions in life and work, or driving a powerful vehicle ruthlessly. Unless looked for, these manifestations could be passed by, but they are in fact the milder expressions of brutalization. A schoolteacher can discern the signs in his or her class; parents can discern them in their own children. One of the least attractive features of brutalization is that it tends to be copied by its victims, as indeed the process in war is copied by identification with the brutality of war, and sometimes of the enemy. The brutality can be watered down and attenuated, so that it is not as bad as that under which its perpetrator suffered. In people who are naturally paranoid, or when the cruel, persecutory person cannot be gotten out of one's mind, there tends to be an identification with the aggressor, as Freud described.

I once decided to ask a number of Borstal boys, each separately, what he would do if in the course of a friendly fight his opponent fell down. To my surprise, each one gave the same reply: "Kick him, of course." Here in close-up is the process of brutalization. One aspect of this is promising, namely, that none of the boys expected to receive better treatment than he was prepared to give to others. In even more severely alienated people, one finds that they give no kindness but expect to receive it by right.

Several linked but different features occur in brutalization:

1. Pleasure in the pain of the victim or victims.
2. The formula "I am not going to suffer" is pervasive. "You are going to do the suffering" is implied and acted upon.
3. "I cannot *contain* what I feel in the way of fear, anger, or persecution, and so must evacuate it into somebody else." This evacuation to relieve the self was described by Freud (1911b) in "Formulations on the Two Principles of Mental Functioning," and later studied by Bion.
4. Some people do suffer but cannot digest or metabolize the internal situation and it appears that instead of being resolved, old hurts get worse in their minds until what is acted out is far worse than the original suffering.

Three clinical examples mentioned in previous chapters may be useful. They include the little boy who, after his father's sudden death, was sent to a children's home where his toys were stolen and the somewhat older daughter of the couple who ran the home repeatedly abused him sexually. After a self-destructive attempt so serious that he was hospitalized for a year, the child pleaded successfully with his mother not to send him back to the home. On reaching puberty he began to threaten prepubertal girls, ending up by sexually assaulting one of them. The assault was limited and relatively mild, an almost precise reversal of what he had suffered at the hands of the prepubertal girl, and his behavior during the assault ended with a much kinder pattern of relating to his victim. This could be traced back to how he had wished the assault upon him had turned out. He was "saying," in his action, "This is how it should have gone."

The second example is that of the young man in one of the armed forces who was homosexually assaulted by a ruthless NCO many years his senior. The victim deserted the unit and spent some weeks on the run. Short of food and with no money, he took to mugging and robbing people, treating his victims with the same kind of violence he had received during the assault by the NCO. The only difference was that the patient's assaults were predatory rather than sexual.

The third example was the most sinister and serious. A man had been cuckolded by a brash, younger man who had allegedly raped the subject's fiancée. Whether it was rape or seduction was impossible for me to ascertain. Once she saw her fiancé's violent reaction, the woman tried to minimize the situation, but the intrapsychic state of the angry man did not improve as the weeks passed by. On the contrary, he became more and more paranoid and, in his mind, beat up, punched, and annihilated his adversary. Weeks later he actually beat the man into unconsciousness. There was no contrition, only loud, assertive self-justifications and what sounded like righteous indignation that was paranoidly psychotic. This is the apotheosis of brutalization.

I turn from these examples to examples, also mentioned earlier, of the opposite process, namely, the restoration of healthy standards of humanity in dealing with others who wrong or appear to have wronged one. One man had a highly traumatic escape from a burning and sinking oil tanker in the North Atlantic in World War II. A genital injury incurred at the time required his hospitalization. When discharged from the hospital, he found himself to have become a compulsive incendiarist with a strongly sexual, perverse aspect. He served three prison sentences. I treated him psychodynamically during the second sentence, during which time some part of the compulsion must have been loosened but not remedied. He had begun a long course of debrutalization and reestablishment of standards of behavior that seemed to have been driven into eclipse by the trauma and its sequelae. Not all his standards had disappeared, however; he retained a keen sense of justice and fair play. During his third sentence, he witnessed a savage, possibly murderous, attack by three prisoners on a prison officer whom he described as a "decent chap." The compulsive incendiarist, without regard to the risk, saved the officer from severe injury even though he himself was injured. When he was released, to his surprise, he found he no longer had any impulse to set things or places on fire. I saw him once after that and was impressed by the favorable change: his whole appearance had altered and he looked a much gentler, less alienated person.

Sometimes the reparative activities are not nearly so dramatic. One man with a history of violent crime started to write significant poetry and won a prize for some of it. Poetry writing is not uncommon in prisoners who are becoming restored to healthy behavior from brutalization, at least as far as human civilized standards are concerned. This man did not produce an idealized writing, thereby risking missing the mourning for the harm he had done in his previous state. The sequel to his writing of the poems was an impressive rehumanization but at the cost of ongoing regret and mourning for the harm he had perpetrated in his various crimes in the past. One of the sequels to his being able to tolerate a high degree of psychic pain for a long time was that his capacity to learn academic subjects greatly increased and with it his pleasure in learning. The point I would like to stress is that when the rehumanization process goes well, there is a flowering of creativity, very much the opposite to the spiritual and moral east wind of sadism and violence, which is indirectly or directly life destroying.

Let us consider what happens in the rehabilitation process. We have mentioned mourning for the savage deeds enacted while in the brutalized state. In addition, there is mourning for all the savage things done at all in concrete terms, and a milder mourning for those things done in fantasy only. The bearing of the psychic pain of self-blame (rather than self-pity) increases the capacity of the individual to contain painful states of mind, rather than to evacuate them into action, that is, to off-load them into someone else. Quite a number of criminals never reach this state of mourning and its sequel, creativity, and thus to better containment of impulses that can be mellowed in the harbor of the mind instead of resorting to action as a kind of short-circuiting of reality. Fantasy can be functional as a substitute for action rather than as a prelude to action as the recivilizing process goes on. Some people who fail to reach this state get bogged down in manic reparation. The good deeds or good actions are carried out, without their necessary prelude, which is mourning, regret, and sadness, for one's bad deeds, including the less painful mourning for one's malignant fantasies. This is essential before full humanization can be regained.

The group situation may potentiate brutalization processes or, in certain circumstances—depending upon its structure, leadership, and aims—can resist the dehumanizing process or even edge it in the direction of rehumanization. The purpose of the group is crucial: as is said in the scriptures, "When two or three are gathered together in my name" (i.e., God's name), there is a sanctified group. If, however, the aim becomes sadistic, criminal, or murderous, group solidarity leads to a demonization of the activities of that group. In residential schools, whether educational or punitive, the group phenomenon of bullying or mobbing* can often be found.

*The mobbing syndrome denotes a particular gang mentality.

Mobbing flourishes where one or two schoolboys are aggrieved and burning with destructive resentment. If these boys have leadership capacities and if general school morale is low, the leaders may find a following very easily. The group then carries out its activities in a secret yet persistent way.

We do not have the resources to provide individual psychotherapy for all participants in mobbing. Not all of them need it, but the leaders of the mobbing activities, and certainly the more traumatized of the victims, will need therapeutic intervention. The group dynamic situation is very important among schoolboys and schoolgirls. One is reminded of the behavior of packs of dogs and wolves. The peer group, particularly of schoolboys, is similar to these hunting associations in that there is a leader, a great deal of group solidarity built around shared aims, and remarkable stability. Attachment to the leader, though strong, does not necessarily involve any great abnormality of personality among group members.

In dealing with certain groups, including some very violent ones, the following therapeutic procedures can be significantly successful. First, the group member has to be detached from the delinquent group and reattached to a nondelinquent group. The dynamics remain similar, but the aim of the new group is different, being essentially nondelinquent. Various religious and some therapeutic organizations appear to work in this way. Alcoholics Anonymous is a good example. In schools, particularly residential ones, such possibilities should be available, for example, on the sports field, as well as in such activities as orienteering, drama, or even photography.

Thus we must deal with the mob leader, the conductor of the gang of persecutors. This individual may well be expressing some of his own psychological disturbances in the mobbing activities. There may be a mild or severe sadistic perversion, or he may be perpetrating actively what he formerly was forced to suffer passively at some stage of his life. This latter condition is less difficult to remedy than the state of perversion. Pleasure and excitement fix and perpetuate the practice of a perversion. In dealing with the victim of mobbing, we may find a youth who has some major or minor oddities, or he may have a degree of masochistic perversion that reciprocates with the sadistic perversion of the mob leader. This factor renders the condition difficult to remedy without imposing social and geographical separation—that is, without expelling one of the central core of mobbers.

Mobbing is a form of scapegoating. One individual (occasionally more) is singled out for persecution, which sometimes consists of ostracism ("being sent to Coventry"). Sometimes the persecution comprises verbal attacks of scorn and abuse, sometimes practical jokes with elements of cruelty, and sometimes outright physical attack. Essentially, the victim is pinioned, locked into a situation from which he or she cannot readily escape. Submission often causes the attacks to intensify, and retaliation may have the same result. Seldom open, much of the excitement for the mobbers lies in the conspiratorial atmosphere that is generated.

Those who become victims are people with oddities, physical or mental, but in the main it is people who are different in interests, origins, or appearance: in fact, anything that makes them part of the out-group rather than the in-group. The mobbers conform to the mores of the self-established group. They pick out what they have had inflicted upon them, or feel that they have, and do something (only more intensely) to the victim.

Whether mobbing runs a benign course or a malevolent one depends on how the perpetrators of the cruel behavior tolerate regret and guilt about their treatment of the victim. If such guilt can be borne, there is often an improvement of behavior toward the victim. There may even be some attempt to put things right. This "going into reverse," so to speak, is more common in individual bullying than in mobbing because there is something inflexible and unreparative about the group and group solidarity. Guilt seems to be *divided* by the number of group members, whereas cruelty and violence seem to be *multiplied*.

Children sent to boarding school who have gotten off to a poor start as far as their early relationships are concerned are more likely to form the core of open or well-concealed disaffection. One of the ways in which this is manifested is in the "mobbing syndrome." I conjecture that the common denominator between the leader of the mobbers and their victim is disturbance during early life. The persecutor and the persecuted probably have a reciprocal relationship. Secure young people with satisfactory intrapsychic and external parental figures are likely to be involved only loosely with the mobbing group. They are likely to be able to detach from it more easily. One cannot ascribe everything to nurture, although nurture is very important. Sometimes one encounters a youth who has contrived to nullify all good experience and—despite what sounds like a good upbringing—behaves as if possessed by evil. More usually there is an interaction between nature and nurture. Sometimes associated with a destructive character are signs of trouble within the self of the individual. These take the form of psychosomatic and hypochondriacal illness, accident proneness, and a failure to accomplish anything except troublemaking. This kind of individual readily turns to persecuting others, and mobbing is one of the means of doing this, by embroiling others in the activity. Temporary relief is afforded to the disturbed youth by making someone else suffer in his stead. The process can be regarded as an evacuation of a disturbed state of mind into a victim. More unconscious than this is the phenomenon Klein (1946) called *projective identification*, a state of feeling that is unconsciously communicated to another person. As a result of this, the projective identificator usually feels relieved (for a time) and the projective identificatee feels possessed by those feelings. What is communicated is always fairly simple—fear, for example, even a fear of death, anger, laughter, sexual excitement, revulsion, and nausea. The point I wish to clarify is that these strong feelings can be, and often are, "put into" other people. The recipient, it must be stressed, who has to cope with these feelings, may not be able to do so, and is liable to fly into action to express or deny them, or to savagely return them to their donor. In violent criminals one sees that what is returned "with interest," so to speak, also contains elements of the self and the problems of the recipient; thus conflicts escalate by being compounded. School staff must be aware of what goes on so that they can facilitate a de-escalation, not contribute to an escalation, of a situation that has already got out of hand.

So far, the *two*-person relationship has been described in some detail, and indeed it is the central core of the mobbing situation. Other people are drawn into their "magnetic field" like satellites, which is how a mobbing group gains cohesion. Unless the core relationships can be unscrambled, that particular mobbing group will tend to reassemble. How the mobbing group is mustered requires further understanding and much more research, particularly into the way in which ethological factors build up between the hunted and the hunter as the aggregation of satellites transforms the hunter into a hunting group in ruthless pursuit of its quarry. One is reminded of the way in which the Nazis dealt with the Jews, and of the Mafia. This problem confronts all of us, and the Italian term for the Mafia, *Cosa Nostra*, would be applicable even to the much milder problem of mobbing.

One cautionary note may be apposite. When a group phenomenon is associated with heightened prestige among its members, it is important to deglamorize it in the course of its eradication. When the heroic or prestigious aspect can be eliminated, membership tends to fall away.

The man who, at the end of the eight years of a life sentence that he served in prison began to write poetry, had killed a man who had done him no harm. In psychoanalytic terms, how would we describe this prisoner–patient's task? There must be transformation or many such transformations from the paranoid-schizoid position to the depressive position; from a sense of aggrievement that other people have it in for him to a sense of responsibility; from a state of unintegration to one of integration; from part-object to whole-object relatedness; from an incapacity to symbolize to one in which symbols can be used instead of being concretized into the thing itself in a symbolic equation.

This prisoner–patient, who won a prize for his poetry, had shown previous signs of intrapsychic and interpersonal reparation. These began in a tentative way and later developed in scope and significance. His poetry started off at the paranoid-schizoid level and eventually reached the depressive position.

Dispa
I saw a very small fly
Out of the corner of my
Murderously gleaming eye,
Determined that it should die.
Really no need to ask: "Why?"
Because everyone swats I,
Naturally I swat the fly.

Nun
O gentle maid so clear of voice
Why hast thou made such fateful choice?
What need have I to know thy name
When thou hast left this life's quick game?

Your elder nuns approve of thee,
They smile to see thee walk with me,
But would they smile and beam and nod
If they could know I have no god?

You humble me with gentle grace
And this grey world's a brighter place
Because you smile and make soft talk
With me on our too short a walk.

Of pride there is no single trace
On thy serene and clean-scrubbed face.
When did you gain your golden cross?
Was thy God's gain my bitter loss?

I gaze in awe at swelling breast,
Fear not for I'm not Virtue's test,
But with what blinding faith imbued?
What raging passions there subdued?

Do you retire to frugal cell
Avoiding deep and private hell,
Yet finding that where e'er you go
'Tis still yourself you need to know?

You cannot get to know thy self
By seeking that withdrawal shelf,

For tortured soul it with thee goes
As surely as thy soap-shined nose.

I thank thee for thine aural calm
That soothes me as sweet love's own balm,
And hope thy choice thee brings release
From all those thoughts that leave no peace.

One thing I'd like to know of thee:
When thou art lost in reverie
And all the world's enwrapped in thee,
Wilt thou give just one thought to me?

Eurus

I walk a stony garden
Where once a rose did bloom;
My heart begins to harden,
And barren thoughts dark loom.

This gritty path I'm walking
With petals once was strewn,
And people daily talking
Unconsciously in tune.

And all was lightly fragrant
Where she did breathe the air,
That now sore chills the vagrant,
Wan spirit in despair.

Now all I see are pebbles
That did reflect her light;
And minor key it trebles
Where once the tune was bright.

Around the drab bricks keening
There blows an eastern wind,
Its harpings have no meaning,
Not bearing message kind.

The marigolds in season,
And heartsease all dark blue,
Nor lilies shew me reason
Why rose has gone from view.

Though all these flowers rarely
May blossom in my sight,
There's none can grow so fairly
As rose of sheer delight.

Perhaps another gazes
On rose I looked upon,
Perhaps another raises
The spirit that is gone.

The garden grows but bleakly;
There is a vacant spot
Where rose entwined so meekly
A gently binding knot.

She came a revelation
That ne'er was wont to stay;
I muse in consolation:
"All roses blow away."

Parody, Hymn, The Two Fatherlands
I vow to thee Neaera
All earthly things above
Entire, but though imperfect
The service of my love.
The love that asks few questions,
The love that stands the test,
The love that ever alters
And grows to be the best.
The love that never falters,
The love that pays the price;
The love that makes though daunted
The final sacrifice.

But there's another loved one
I cut off long ago,
Most dear to them that love her,
Much grief to them that know.
We may not hear her laughing,
We may not hear her sing,

Her phantom lives in my dead heart
That knows her suffering.
As silently as silently
Her ghostly bounds increase,
Her memory is evergreen
And leaves my heart no peace.

The poems show his progress as well as some hiccups suggestive of a quick relapse into the paranoid-schizoid position, from which he was able to rejoin the path toward his rehumanization. It will be recognized that the course of debrutalization was not a chameleonlike transformation, but had to be "burnt through," as if a spiritual east wind had frosted the shoots of his renewed humanity.

Another prisoner who wrote poems avoided the intensity of his depressive feelings, although he started to mourn and deeply regret his killing of a man (not a particularly nice man, but one who, until goaded to do so, had done him no harm). Soon he identified with his victim, and, though he became a lot better, balked at "the fierce dispute betwixt damnation and impassioned clay" (Keats 1978, p. 225). Two poems of his are nostalgic, and show an appreciation of beauty and nature, but do not touch the kernel of mourning and regret for harm done in fantasy or, in this case, in fact, by the self. Instead, be began to be very depressed, with more than a hint of suicide in the background.

To accomplish the transformation from a state of brutalization to a state of debrutalization so that civilized behavior toward one's fellow human beings is the rule and practice cannot take place in any but a flash-in-the-pan episodic way except by the paranoid-schizoid to the depressive process. In this transformation there has to be a development from excuse for oneself and blaming of others to blaming oneself for aspects of one's brutalized behavior that have damaged or hurt other people. This is essentially a mourning process. Its end point is reached after many fluctuations, but it ends (it is hoped) with the full acceptance of self-blame through the use of reality testing and in making reasonable allowances for other people who have not reached the same state of balance.

We have considered the sublimatory and reparative actions of some severely brutalized persons serving prison sentences. In addition to this kind of brutalized person, there is a much larger number of people who pursue a policy of brinkmanship for most of their lives, having begun the process during early adolescence or even earlier. The same basic psychodynamic rules are valid in these people.

It cannot be stressed enough that the processes of debrutalization or recivilization depend on the presence and rehabilitated ability to use "good" internal objects and good experiences derived from those objects on whom the brutalized person depended, and from whom he or she has been estranged. In fact, brutalization implies a loss of or detachment from good objects. The person who really never had good objects during his or her development cannot be said to be brutalized. They had never been civilized anyway.

Group brutality certainly intensifies violent, sadistic, and uncivilized practices, but the fact is that there are group or gang leaders with ingrained, often very severe, character disturbances. Many of the gang members become attached to and follow the leader. Detachment during rehabilitation and reattachment to a nondelinquent group with subsequent loyalty to the nonbrutalized leader is often successful.

11

Latent Murderousness

People who take part in organized violent crime and who aim at gain from crime do not fall under the category of latent murderers: somewhere in these people's minds, though possibly not in the foreground of their conscious thought, is the possibility of killing and its counterpart, that of being killed. The persons I wish to consider fall into two main groups: first, those who are unaware that they harbor murder inside and discover it catastrophically in the course of a conflict; and second, individuals who know that they have something murderously destructive within themselves but devote conscious and determined efforts to keep it under control. In a particularly difficult situation or state of mind—mourning for a lost loved one or in a state of delirium, for example—the murderousness may burst out of its restrictions and controls and the deed done. Such people tend to reinstate their controlled selves and give themselves up to the authorities.

In *The Show of Violence*, Werthem (1927) regarded murderousness as a "ticking over in low key" inside the personality of the self (the psyche) until detonated beyond its controls and limitations. It then invades the rest of the personality. Before a catastrophe takes place as a result of the eruption, all the efforts of the individual had been used to keep control over the situation. The eruption itself, termed by Werthem *the catathymic crisis*, results in all the energies of the individual being directed at completing the murderous deed. He added that after this a slow return to some sort of intrapsychic equilibrium usually took place. Of course, the external situation had now been radically changed. In many cases controls over murderousness can hold firm or, if in disequilibrium, can be reestablished; in other words, they do not automatically follow the course described by Werthem and resolution takes place.

Clinical Examples

Group One

A young man aged 20 killed a woman of similar age. He was about to have sexual intercourse with her: his first sex experience. Suddenly she turned on him, having encouraged him up to that point, and poured out a torrent of abuse in vulgar terms against his family and, in particular, his parents. He was numbed by this vitriol, then exploded into action, picking up a piece of iron he saw on the ground and striking her once upon the head. He quickly reverted to horror, guilt, and remorse. In his previous history he had never been violent and was unaware of this violent side of himself.

Group Two

Two brothers, one known to his village as the genial one, were scything the grass around the edge of their father's grainfield. The brother known as the complaining, nasty one provoked a quarrel. Suddenly, the long-suffering genial brother took a swipe at him with the sharp scythe, killing him. He subsequently gave himself up to the police. What we do not know is whether the genial brother was filled with the nasty brother's nastiness by projective identification, and then acted out the psychic content by which he had been possessed. Alternatively, did the nasty brother's nastiness slowly overwhelm the genial brother's geniality to reveal a murderous underlay in the latter?

In general, psychically healthy people can detoxicate hurtful and damaging experiences so long as the traumata do not take place too thick and fast so that there is no time for a detoxification process to be effective. In some cases there may be *no* restoration of emotional equilibrium, so that the situation worsens and becomes highly dangerous, often ending in murder.

Not all cases of such kind end in murder.

In example three, a 34-year-old man who had had a very disturbed childhood had also been subjected to severely traumatic events during service in World War II. His childhood had been marked by paternal brutality and maternal ineffectiveness, and by the time he returned to civilian life he had developed an almost paranoid sense of injustice, on behalf of himself as well as others. A senior colleague ("father") gave him a harsh assignment over which no negotiation was permitted. Our subject felt consciously murderous impulses and followed the man for miles in a fog, clutching a weapon. Like Hamlet, "to be or not to be" ebbed and flowed in his mind a thousand times until, when it finally ebbed, he felt massively depressed. He limped home and committed suicide.

The fourth example had a happier outcome, and is a case I have cited elsewhere. A young man decided to try to win a prize for a short film. He recruited his wife and his secretary as actresses and himself as the actor. The photography was done by a friend, in color and with sound. The story was gruesome. The wife in the plot was murdered and dismembered and her husband had a fatal accident as he was about to elope with his secretary. The photography was not quite clever enough to disguise the butcher's meat and animal bones representing the wife as she was loaded into suitcases and sunk without trace in the muddy waters of a local river. Nevertheless, the fantasy that drove him to make this film had a repercussion in that he became impotent.

> Psychotherapy showed him that the concreteness of the visual fantasies of the film and the underlying thought processes had resulted in guilt and feelings of horror. Many months later I saw him and his wife together; their relationship had recovered fully and he had been twice promoted in his work.

What had happened was that he had mourned on account of his murderous fantasy, however much it was rationalized previously by his blaming the pursuit of a prize (which he did win). This illustrates an important point, namely, that mourning—a mini-mourning—is necessary to repair intrapsychic damage entailed by a murderous fantasy constellation. For a murderous impulse or a cluster of such impulses, a more substantial mourning is required. For the premeditated killing in external reality, of course, the situation is both severe and of long duration, if indeed terminable at all.

What renders a person unable to restore psychic digestion once it has ceased to work satisfactorily seems to be due, at least in part, to an inability to perform the change in attitude involved in the transformation from a paranoid-schizoid state of mind to a depressive state of mind, and to hold the state of mind at the depressive position for significant periods of time. In Bion's terms, the container is functionally inadequate and therefore, without extra help, cannot deal adequately with its content. Let us turn to Bion's (1963, 1970) reading of Freud's (1911b) essay on the two principles of mental functioning. Freud described the pleasure principle (which is also the pain-avoidance principle), and contrasted it with the reality principle. Bion elaborated the description by adumbrating the case of the person who could not tolerate frustration and who therefore tended to unburden himself of accretions of stimuli. This inability to learn from experience leads to a further unburdening of the self: so chronic does this activity become that the "headquarter self" is more and more depleted. Such a person becomes less rather than more able to cope with the hazards of life. Moreover, the transformation from the paranoid-schizoid to the depressive position becomes more and more difficult. Bion reminds us of the fact that at the paranoid-schizoid position, one is dealing with part objects and concretization rather than symbolization. In other words, a more primitive apparatus is necessarily being used to deal with a task requiring a much more sophisticated and efficient one.

So far we have considered general factors in disturbed persons related to the death constellation. These are widespread within the personalities of such individuals. There are, however, others who possess areas of specific vulnerability but also a healthy part of the personality. In these cases, unless the area of disturbance, that is, the Achilles' heel, is touched upon, one can be reasonably sure that no murderous escalation will occur. The Achilles' heel image introduces the notion of trauma, which, instead of having been worked through, remains unmetabolized. Sometimes it remains in that state for years. The phenomenon is like that of allergic hypersensitivity: if further exposure to the same protein occurs once one has been sensitized, there may be a catastrophic response in the form of anaphylaxis. Hypersensitivity, if recognized, can be treated and then there can be a desensitization. When an emotional threat to the well-being, perhaps to the life, of an individual takes place, a similar focalized hypersensitivity arises. Also, I am concerned with that part of the response of the individual under threat that can be described as a violent attempt to preserve his or her own life. It may mean attacking and killing a supposed or an actual assailant.

The detoxication or, in allergy terms, the desensitization consists of being treated and relieved of a specific paranoid sensitivity to a certain kind of threat, in this case a threat to one's own life. The danger for such people lies in the paranoid attitude of kill first when threatened, and ask questions afterward. If this attitude can be subjected to the transformation from the paranoid-schizoid position to the depressive position, oft repeated, before a murderous attack on anybody has taken place, the situation becomes a great deal safer.

In example three, we saw somebody who killed himself first after a lot of rumination, and did not reach the detoxication stage. It is, however, possible to reduce murders and other attacks if detoxication occurs. In a study of some twenty-five armed police facing paranoid armed persons holding hostages, it became apparent that they had discovered a way of retaining a state of good psychic health single-handedly. This was by facing a sincerely suffered mourning in themselves, commensurate with the threat to their lives that the actions of their assailants had created. Their method involved a repeated paranoid-schizoid to depressive position working through. This must have taken place many times during the long history of war and human conflict, but apart from religious statements and those of some poets, the methods involved have not been highlighted until comparatively recently.

To return to the theme of a pattern of action that has been represented intrapsychically, it may be likened to an ideogram that springs to mind sometimes many years after the circumstances that caused it had been laid down inside the self of the individual.

> One man, not by any means a practicing criminal, as a 3-year-old child saw his father, a policeman, apprehend a robber who fired a shot and ran off into the darkness. The father fired a shot after the culprit, bringing him down with a relatively minor wound. Nearly a quarter of a century later, this policeman's son experienced a similar incident and automatically fired a shot at the retreating robber, but on this occasion the robber fell dead. Distress, not triumph, resulted, as the man who fired the shot was not pervasively brutalized, though a facet of brutalization had caused the brutality.

I came to understand that the danger in the original situation was that fear and excitement were compounded together with implicit trust in the father figure, who could deal with the danger, bringing down the robber without killing him. The later incident involving a death was carried out by means of an identification from the son's remote childhood past and applied crudely to a contemporary, inappropriate situation in a way that did not fit the circumstances. These included the position and role of the little boy/man who fired the fatal shot. I would like to stress one aspect of the case: shooting the robber was regarded as the thing to do in the circumstances, and this indicated a focalized, automatic brutalization that for a quarter of a century had slumbered inside the psyche of the killer. There may be truth in thinking of what we have called brutalization as *rebrutalization*, after some steps toward a developmental humanization had been made. Generally, in focalized areas and overrestricted issues, this development of humanization in such people is maintained in a precarious manner. The question is ultimately whether the situation is one of original murderousness and gradual humanization, or whether there is a state of childhood innocence that acutely or gradually gets criminalized. Another possibility is that both processes occur at the same time, and it would then depend upon how we as individuals handle this double process, comprising one step toward full humanization and another toward brutalization.

This view becomes more plausible if we take into account fantasy only. Melanie Klein in 1928 refers to the cruel and savage attitudes in fantasy made by very young children in their attacks on their mothers, fathers, the breast, babies, and father's penis. As Klein wrote in a later paper, "Criminal Tendencies in Normal Children" (1927), some of the fantasies of young children reveal situations that would appear to be ominous as far as future behavior might be concerned. But she stresses that most children undergo favorable developmental changes, and they grow out of such fantasies.

A very different analytic authority, Edward Glover, stated that criminality was the result of a failure in the taming of man, who initially is a half-wild animal (1960). Killing is not called murder if it is not carried out on other humans or on a personal or factional basis. Killing, however, is carried out on an enormous scale on other living creatures and is largely unopposed if it is not carried out with cruelty or, more recently, on endangered species.

The overall likelihood is that we each have a murderous capability, even a proclivity. Apart from wars in which there is a massive unleashing of the impulse to kill, most of us experience a decisive reduction in such fantasies during childhood and later. But this does not mean we should ignore murderous tendencies, which are powerfully discouraged by nurture, as part of our endowment. These originated to protect our lives and our development.

In the *Oresteia*, Athene, the goddess, is made to say by Aeschylus words and exhortations that discouraged the in-group from resorting to murder within its ranks. The distinction was made between the killing of the enemy, which is encouraged, and murder within the home group. This was 2,500 years ago. Murder of the out-group labeled "the enemy" continues to be encouraged in certain circumstances, such as wars. Extending these circumstances is passionately discouraged. For example, when Field Marshal Montgomery remembered that every British soldier should kill a German a day, he was asked, "Even the padre?" He replied, "Yes, even the padre should kill one a day and two on a Sunday." This was heatedly refuted by the authorities.

In these complicated intrapsychic and psychosocial circumstances, it is small wonder that there are confusions and failures. We may assume that murderousness is in our nature and that it is strongly discouraged socially. Some people have little difficulty in dispensing with murderousness by growing out of it; others do not grow out of it. The process of taming may be resisted in part or as a whole. Further efforts to tame may provoke a negative therapeutic response or a positive response with weak patches. It is when basic murderousness has broken through that these weak patches reveal themselves and help is necessary. Self-help may force a death constellation out of consciousness, so that the individual becomes unaware of its presence. This was the case with the young man who suddenly killed the young woman who maligned his parents.

Latent murderousness is about as safe as a volcano known to be active but in a noneruptive period. It cannot be relied on to remain inactive. As far as the human condition of latent murderousness is concerned, internal (that is, intrapsychic) factors, or external ones, can be the reactivating agent that sets into motion a sequence ending in actual murder. The relationship of these events to a psychotic personality organization is variable and often difficult to delineate because the catastrophic deed itself alters the intrapsychic as well as the external situation. Insofar as there is a breakdown of reality testing and loss of what Bion calls *alpha-function*, the sequence is riven by psychotic processes. Nevertheless, it would be a mistake to take an unduly pessimistic view regarding future treatment: equally we do not make saints of people who are afflicted with a state of latent murderousness. We are concerned with the amount of detoxification of a death constellation that can make the acted-out resort of unburdening the self of it most unlikely to occur. Roughly speaking, these ways of unburdening the self are by projection into somebody else where the murderousness is then enacted. It can be by introjected action of a suicidal nature, by unconsciously determined fatal accidents or by psychosomatic illness of a life-threatening kind. The murderous aspect may be enacted by, for example, putting it into an animal such as a rottweiler or a pit bull terrier, which may then attack people, or each other. Similarly, there is the ritualistic tragedy of the bullfight, big-game hunting, and other blood sports. There are life-risking sports that express and externalize danger to life by taking it as a challenge to the self, which then becomes as skillful as possible in avoiding death, often by increasingly narrow margins.

Intrapsychically, the individual with latent murderousness is at risk. Many if not most who have this condition commit neither murder, nor suicide, nor a fatality on the road. Some people handle the situation better than others. Our task is to help a person who presents with this condition of latent murderousness to manage it more safely. Not all loaded guns go off, and although unloading the gun is highly advisable, disposing of the gun may not always be necessary. More important is that *the controls should be intrapsychic* and not externally imposed if we are to deal adequately not only with murder, but with murderousness.

It must be stressed that in pursuing the latent death constellation of a murderous rather than suicidal kind, there may be a temporary increase in its activity. In other words, an increase in the risk of its being expressed in some active form during the early stages of treatment is possible. Some deeds of heroism, especially in war, appear to have this kind of connection. There appear to be at least two kinds of behavior. One is the reaction formation, in which external courage is used as an assertion of exactly the opposite feeling dominant within the psyche. Paul Scott (1985) wrote about the other in his book *The Mark of the Warrior*. His hero was a young man whose brother had been killed, allegedly through the folly, envy, or cowardice of an officer. Subsequently, in an officer training unit in India, the hero showed complete determination to achieve the objectives of the training task, and died in the course of it, as if it were in battle. There seemed to be several ingredients compounded together: (1) incomplete mourning for his brother; (2) identification with him; and (3) a rivalry to show him up together with a reprisal against the officer whom he blamed for his brother's death. There was also an arrogant determination to excel. This example is given because of the complexity of the compounding factors. It is linked to those persons who do not display overt murderousness, but who have the potential to kill or be killed in the course of an achievement of aims. Sometimes, it could be said, they make the ideal military leader. The central message of Paul Scott's book was the death on a training exercise. Developmentally there existed an imbalance between life and death instincts in this gifted young man and this was tilted toward death under stressful circumstances.

Very different was the case of a highly competent Indian NCO whom I interviewed in 1944 after a tough battle in Burma. He would call himself frightened, not brave. After the Japanese had advanced and overrun the mountain artillery battery in which he was working, the soldier climbed a tree and remained there. Noticing that the Japanese had pursued his retreating comrades and not touched the artillery or the ammunition, he came down from the tree and fired one of the guns repeatedly at the pursuing Japanese, totally disrupting their pursuit. For this he was awarded a Victoria Cross (VC). Contrast this with the hero of *The Mark of the Warrior.*

The intrapsychic situation in those who harbor latent murderousness varies widely. Those who have been traumatized so that they are either goaded toward killing "to get even again"—by evacuating by projective identification the death constellation into someone by whom they had been "abused" or someone reminding them of that person or persons—may experience a fluctuating balance between the murderous part of the self and the victim role chosen for the self. A person who set out to kill and ends up by killing himself would be an example.

A murderousness long incubated and held inside the self may finally burst out (cf. Werthem's catathymic crisis). The individual with "the mark of the warrior" in certain circumstances can kill, but assumes the victim role if he fails to achieve his objective. In this category a pathological relationship to death and the death constellation seems to be woven into the character structure and appears to be a more integral part of its possessor. Treatment should be directed toward altering the intrapsychic balance by activating and sustaining a mourning situation, that is, at the depressive position. In persons whose disability turns out to be intractible, dynamic psychotherapy can help them manage their lives without detonating catastrophe.

The Indian sergeant who disrupted the Japanese and won the VC did his job well, and remained alive, by doing what was necessary and possible at each stage of the ordeal, without heroics, and, as a result, without fatal consequences.

At least two questions remain. One, do any persons with latent murderousness get better from it without murdering anyone? The short answer is Yes. Two, do any resort consciously or unconsciously to measures that help to remedy the situation, keep further action at bay, or reduce the murderous state of mind?

In individuals with this intrapsychic patterning of latent murderousness, it is frequently found that they have ways to mourn the fantasy, and the impulse, before it is set in action. Mourning for the fantasy is minuscule compared with mourning for the impulse and the infinite mourning necessary after murder has been committed. The personal capacity for psychic digestion and metabolism necessary for mourning develops to some extent in each of us. In potentially very violent people there is a hitch in that development, which can be remedied subsequently by dynamic psychotherapy, or by certain kinds of maturation of the individual, even without therapy. Two choices (by which I mean unconscious choices) are open: (1) evacuation into action or (2) psychic digestion and metabolization that leads to the detoxication of murderous fantasies and impulses. While this sounds simple, it is actually extremely complicated and depends on the quality of the self or the psyche as a container. This in turn depends on what the self is already populated by from earlier experiences and whether those experiences have been metabolized—in which case they are safe—or not. We also need to consider what has been added to the psyche in the past and more immediately, and what psychic digestion or psychic indigestion has ensued. If there is a chronic state of indigestion, the patient, to some extent, is always at risk. Psychic digestion is greatly helped by adequate mourning, particularly if this covers both fantasy and impulse, and any token action that might have taken place. It is a very different thing when the mourning, which *is* necessary, follows the deed of murder. In addition, a capacity for psychic digestion and metabolism—and a capacity to look at and evaluate the self reasonably correctly—is exceedingly advantageous.

PART III

12

Assessment and Risk

In prison, the lifer has had time to look at himself, with or without psychotherapy, and may have changed over the years. The change may be insignificant or significant. Sometimes change is based on truth; sometimes it is a long way from truth. It may even consist of a confidence trick in which more often than not the lifer himself is among those conned. How can the situation be assessed, including with the person who denies having killed somebody even though he or she has been found guilty at trial?

Aftercare of lifers is a formidable task. It can be extremely interesting and in some cases rewarding, particularly if the lifer is willing and even keen to work with the probation officer or social services person assigned to the case. The story of the crime as told by its perpetrator is nearly always a cover story. The constellation from which and in which murder is generated is like the iceberg—only a small portion is visible. The rest is below the level of consciousness. Murder occurs concretely in most cases when it has been committed many times previously in daydreams, nightdreams, and sometimes in unconscious fantasy that has never become conscious. Sometimes, of course, it is committed in conscious fantasy and action.

When the intrapsychic constellation has a strong sexual linkage, there is likely to be a process that repeats itself, not necessarily and concretely in active murder, but in some expression of the death constellation: for example, masturbation with a murderous fantasy that coincides with orgasm. This means that the murder in the mind takes place at the moment of orgasm. These are particular cases and not all that common. When the fantasy in the mind ceases to afford gratification and relief, the murder may be acted out concretely as a last resort.

Sexuality, even when the actuality of a pregnancy is neither possible nor desirable, is fundamentally about making a baby. Sexual perversion (even without an overtly murderous act or token) is usually about killing a baby or, when it exists in a mother, is about a no-baby. Sometimes the wish is to make a devil baby—Rosemary's baby!

What makes a small minority of people act out and kill another human being? Perhaps we should ask why so *few* people resort to murderous action. We all know that with the appropriate sanction, an inducement to kill persons belonging to a race or nation designated the enemy will lead most people to kill, though a minority find that they cannot bring themselves to do it. The issue is presented as one of "kill them or they will kill you." The experience of or belief that the action is in self-defense is a powerful facilitator. Threat involving the arousal of fear for one's life often provokes an attempt to deal with that threat by killing it in someone else. The aggressor is turned into the victim. This is a powerful reversible perspective.

Sometimes the threat is not to the life of the person threatened but to his state of mind. An example is the young man who killed a woman in the mistaken belief that she was the mother of the girl he wished to marry. In prison, the amnesia he developed concerning the crime cleared up, but only with difficulty. He became distressed at realizing not only that he had killed, but that an innocent person, not the enemy who had confronted him with an unbearable situation, had been robbed of life. Another example was a man who replicated Othello's delusional jealousy: a loyal and faithful woman was killed because her killer felt that her putative infidelity had been a threat to his survival. The Iago character can also exist within the murderer himself, and it did so in this case. The whole delusional constellation can be generated in such a man who kills his loved one as a result of internal sources, not the least of which is his own tendency to be unfaithful.

Risk is difficult to assess. There is risk so long as there has been no adequate mourning for the dead person killed by the lifer. Three such lifers met for a short holiday after they had been released on parole. On the surface, two were in good shape; the third I did not know and therefore cannot give an opinion. They proceeded to recount a story to each other that caused all three to roll about with laughter, about a killing machine to deal with the problem of race relations. It was not funny and showed that killing was regarded as a legitimate last resort. I do not think that any of the three will kill again, but this example shows that there is risk as long as murder, that is, killing, remains a justified option in the mind. Actual murder takes place when too much pressure is experienced by the individual at risk before he or she has had the time, opportunity, or capacity to digest it and detoxicate it psychically.

What about the majority of people? I think it unlikely that most people are at risk of becoming murderers under pressure of personal circumstances. What could happen if powerful and respected authorities approved of such action is another matter.

In the case of adolescent murderers, for example, sanction is invariably given unconsciously by one or the other parent, and is picked up by the child and then acted upon. Official (external) "sanction" and intrapsychic sanction play distinct roles in murderousness.

The young man described above who killed by mistake had an underlying weakness of ego structure; thus severe disappointment could not be tolerated without his resorting to violent action of a retaliatory, revengeful kind. What I did not mention was that when he was 5 or 6 years old he had suffered a most serious injury, a careless accident, without ill-will or intention. This may have been the grievance that had not and probably could not be psychically digested or metabolized. He thought that the mother of the girl he felt he loved had forbidden the relationship because of his disability. This might have been true. Then came the break with reality: he became convinced that the woman he saw actually was the mother, despite her protestations. Something best called an intrapsychic catastrophe took over, and he killed her violently.

In practical management terms, a parolee with this kind of personality is unlikely to commit murder unless he finds himself in a crisis to which he is especially vulnerable. Time spent in working through and, for the probation officer, containing such massive anxieties can be and often has been lifesaving. The man I quoted who killed after the manner of Othello was basically more stable, but with a war history during which he had been through a number of violent episodes. These were stored away intrapsychically and not properly digested. In this case early childhood experiences probably acted as a sensitizing "dose" and the later ones strengthened the "allergy." Then came the shock, which involved a number of factors:

1. His violent experiences were glamorized.
2. He was not contained. The debriefing following his war activities had been cursory.
3. Like Othello, he had been culturally displaced; despite what seemed like an adequate adjustment, there was an element of make-believe that rendered it a pseudo-adaptation, not an adaptation.
4. The woman he killed was his container, the best he had ever had, and he thought that he had lost her. Due to his own vengeful, paranoid, and, as it turned out, delusional action, he *did* lose her.

During therapy in prison, some favorable changes did take place in this man. He became less of an "externalizer" and did more for himself inside himself. I have been in touch with him since (he has been paroled), and have noted that if things go wrong, he becomes accident-prone so that he himself is hurt. He no longer hurts others. (I have found this to be a good prognostic pointer in parolees.) The next stage of improvement is to be able to bear psychic pain until it can be worked through, without concretely contrived physical self-punishment. It may be impossible to reach this stage, but after all, what we are likely to get with those on lifetime parole is safety rather than perfect psychic health. It is doubtful whether complete psychic health can be achieved by someone who has consciously killed a fellow human being on his or her own behalf. This need not turn out to be as pessimistic as it sounds. Living with past misdeeds in mind may be painful, but if sustained, it leads to development and maturation together with a reparative way of life.

Some of the most moving and impressive experiences I have had in this work concern recovered lifers on parole, one of whom said, "I can stay successful and relatively at peace with myself only if I spend about three-quarters of an hour to an hour each day on my own, thinking and feeling sad about what I have done." In other words, a small number of them express the capacity to keep in touch with the mourning for the victim who cannot be repaired and restored in the external world. This is making the best of a bad job. If it can be sustained, I think that risk is minimal. The opposite is true too: in persons in whom there has been no mourning or totally inadequate mourning for the victim, I would not regard the risks as being negligible, though it is true that it is a very difficult risk to assess. The "just failed" situation is evident to everyone, but the "just not committed" crime is rarely known about, except to the person who has been impelled toward it. Many such potential murderers have said to me, "But I was able to not do it. It was a near thing but something within me changed and stopped me." One man became sorry for his intended victim, dried her tears with his handkerchief, and let her go. I think that the death wish is so universal that it is worthwhile to wonder why it is so rare for it to be acted out in full. I would conjecture that people who have a capacity to mourn the victim of the fantasied deed never need to kill.

It may be asserted that probation officers are not trained to deal with complicated psychodynamic issues. I think this may be true, but they also often have tremendous capacities and experience. The probation officer can sometimes see essential issues without being clouded by too much technical or theoretical detail. In many cases I have seen, the probation experience has been crucial in facilitating progress and guarding against catastrophe or simple deterioration, which is in any case a personal disaster for the criminal concerned.

An important variant of this pattern is when it is reversed, that is, when the authority figure, parents, police, educational or religious authorities, or social service person projectively identifies with the individual who was and possibly still is prone to act out, possibly murderously. The projection can be malign or benign. Sometimes a delinquent component or part of a case worker is projected or evacuated into the person who himself is much at risk. This mechanism—difficult to describe clearly, but very commonly used—is powerful and unconsciously dynamized, and can be a most useful tool in our armamentarium if we learn how to use it appropriately and constructively. The person with whom we are dealing responds to what he experiences as being understood and tolerated, though in no way is there agreement with or any condoning of the crime he has done or may do. The transference relationship from client to worker is thus crucial, and in a very complex way it is *that* relationship that enables the contemporaneous situation to be understood and any danger signs recognized. Also, as long as there is movement in the interpersonal situation between client and therapist, any acting out is likely to be a signal only, a plea for help rather than an escalating catastrophe.

13

Engagement and Treatment

The care for and therapy of a person on lifetime parole is difficult. It is late in the day. The deed has been perpetrated, probably many years previously. The man or woman on parole has been stirred up, calmed down, reassured, and worried, and one can reasonably expect to find some well-established defense. This defense is likely to be directed against psychic pain and to protect personal sovereignty over the self, that is, defense against intrusion into areas of privacy. Part of the defense derives from the suspicion or belief that information obtained will be used against its owner—not the same as, but similar to, "taken down in writing and used in evidence."

The first task is to establish some rapport, empathy, and—later—trust, and to sustain and consolidate it. In 1971 I wrote a paper titled "Risks to the Worker in Dealing with Disturbed Adolescents." What I still agree with in that paper is the need for continuity of relationship with at least one person. I designated three categories: the "guardian," for example, prison warden, the "carers" of which all of us are representatives, and a "continuity person." This person need not necessarily be highly trained, though high levels of training are no bar to the effective functioning of a continuity figure. Guardians may fit into the role very effectively after the guardianship phase is over. I have known quite a few wardens and prison medical officers who maintained a continuity role by means of letters and occasional meetings with a prisoner, including some on lifetime parole. The caring and continuity roles can be carried out by the same person and at the same time. To get to know the lifer while he is still in custody and then to see him when he is released on parole is a good continuity function because, after a number of years in prison, the lifer is usually at risk for a period after his release. One of my lifers immediately stole two tins of concentrated soup from a supermarket after his release, thus showing how he wanted to be in the soup again and get back to prison (which had been benign, at least as far as he was concerned). A few years later he went to live on a kibbutz, which in his mind constituted a benign open prison!

In "getting in touch" with the parolee, it is important to be able to estimate the form the murderous or death constellation is taking at that particular time. What are the defenses against it like? Consideration of the strategy or tactics of coping with the life parolee is important. Questions arise. Is it necessary to intervene with a defense that renders the parolee comfortable but the situation dangerous? Will he settle down? What kind of company is he keeping? What are his psychosexual relationships like? Is he drinking too much, and if so, how? When ruffled—angry or humiliated—what goes on in his mind? Is it fantasy, murder, or something more limited? At a deeper level it might be possible to get clues from his dreams. Above all, however, is the question of where he stands in relationship to *persecutory* or *depressive anxiety* (the terms used first by Melanie Klein).

Persecutory anxiety as mentioned often in earlier chapters, is based on a fear of attack or aggrievement after an attack, real or supposed. It is the form of anxiety found throughout the animal kingdom. Sometimes it drives its sufferer to attack the supposed persecutor. In nature it often ensures survival for the threatened individual. Persecutory anxiety begins at birth and grows for several months as long as only parts of mother and others are recognized. At some point during the first six months, as a result of growth and development of the perceptual apparatus of the young infant, the main object—mother or her surrogate—is perceived as a person rather than as a number of part objects. Some observant mothers can cite the exact day this first happened. The situation ebbs and flows, but gradually the presence of mother as a whole person becomes desirable. Before that time, reactions are remarkably primitive in that the absent primal figure (mother) is regarded as bad, and the present one, giving food or care to the baby, is regarded as good. This primary splitting is healthy and is a differentiation, not a pathological process. The good, giving mother is loved, the bad, depriving mother is hated. Then a process of integration occurs; mother is perceived as a whole person with good and bad aspects, and the primary polarization of good and bad is no longer tenable.

To reach the state just described, there is the developmental crisis Melanie Klein called the *depressive position*. The essence of this conflict is that the baby is afraid that his hatred of the bad, depriving mother will have damaged, even destroyed, the good, loved mother, both aspects belonging to one integrated figure—mother. This conflict heralds the onset of a different kind of anxiety, namely, depressive anxiety as opposed to persecutory. This kind of anxiety is not to be confused with the clinical illness of depression. It is a normal and healthy development. Failure to negotiate the depressive position is associated with relapse into a state of mind dominated by fantasies of persecution.

Persecutory anxiety, clearly, is about experiences felt to be threatening—about aggrievement and about looking after the self, if necessary at the expense of everyone else. Depressive anxiety, on the other hand, is about responsibility, guilt, and concern over harm by the self to one's good objects, in the early stage of life mother or her surrogate. Depressive anxiety is about the object and is not an entirely selfish state of mind concerned only with the subject. This pattern has an internal representation. It is concerned with the well-being of the internal mother or the intrapsychic representation of mother; later, other people of the nuclear family; and, as the years go on, people from a wider social field.

Bion graphically represented the conflict and the vacillating movements between the paranoid-schizoid position and the depressive position by the now familiar P/S ↔ D. Throughout life, and particularly at times of change or stress, a major renegotiation of the conflict between these opposite kinds of relationship with their opposite kinds of anxiety is necessitated. It can be understood how an adequate renegotiation of the depressive position can strengthen and help to stabilize a person, while a poor renegotiation weakens and destabilizes the person. Some people emerge from a mourning process following a bereavement strengthened and deepened—more human—while others never recover from a bereavement in which mourning processes have been avoided. Some people become bogged down, perhaps for life, in persecuted self-pity.

In addition to major renegotiations of the depressive position, there are considerable minor fluctuations between P/S ↔ D. The pattern has changed in many lifers whom I have studied over long periods (twelve to fourteen years on the average). At first the lifer makes tentative sorties from P/S toward D but is repelled by the pain and relapses into a resentful, aggrieved state, blaming others and excusing himself. In favorable cases, however, this slowly changes so that the approaches to D are tolerated longer—long enough for reparative activities to become manifest. In several instances this has taken the form of giving blood. One lifer said to me, "After I have shed the blood of another, to give my own to others is the very least I can do." Some make things; others write. One of my current patients took exams ending up with university entrance qualifications and winning a Koestler award for poetry.

The task of dealing with lifers on parole is to facilitate the movement from P/S toward D and to help to contain the discomfort of the process. It happens to all of us, but why should it be so difficult in criminals, particularly violent ones who have an ominous intrapsychic death constellation? Without going into the details of causation, I would like to go back to what we dealt with cursorily earlier in this chapter.

During the very early months of life when primary splitting or differentiation takes place (or should take place), the giving, gratifying, present mother normally is loved, while the absent, depriving, frustrating mother is hated. The width of separation or divergence between the loved object and the hated object depends on the characteristics not only of the mother, but also of the baby. The more impassioned the baby, the wider the separation between the loved and the hated mother. Instead of being loved and hated, feelings escalate and the mother is idealized and denigrated. The final degree of polarization is when the good mother is deified and the bad mother is demonized. It will be evident that the wider the polarization in the splitting, the harder the task of bringing the split objects together in the depressive position, though some individuals make valiant attempts. Some fall by the wayside. Some do both. I am reminded of an army officer in the Far East who took an intense leadership and tactical course. He was capable of being first class and yet of being quite a criminal. His evaluation said, "This officer is likely to get either a high decoration or a court martial." He got both. I could give other examples in which conduct was either/or, but never integrated in an ongoing, stable way.

As far as dealing with lifetime parolees is concerned, there are heart-warming experiences and abysmally disappointing ones: the high decoration/court martial situation occurs quite frequently in the same person. Our task is to make the best of a bad job. This aim is not to be despised.

I now wish to address a different aspect of the task, namely, the risks to the worker. Physical risks are there, but those are dealt with fairly easily. Paranoid (delusional) states directed against the person who treats the lifetime parolee should be addressed and faced separately and not allowed to escalate by being ignored. If the situation does not respond to this intervention, a change to another person might be considered. Colleague help in consultation should enable the individual to cope with any of his own blind spots in relationship to a particular parolee.

Psychic risk is more subtle. A lifer who has reached the parole phase without intrapsychic attitudinal changes toward his or her particular homicide, and to the question of respect for life in general, may evacuate via projective identification and fill others with psychically indigestible projections at the expense of his or her own mental health.

14

From Fantasy to Impulse Action: Is This Reversible with Psychotherapy?

When I was asked many years ago to give psychoanalytical psychotherapy to convicted prisoners serving prison sentences, I was impressed with the marked tendency in these men to move from fantasy to impulse and thence to action. This differed fundamentally from Julius Caesar's "Veni, vidi, vici" in that the lack of thought and judgment that characterized the prisoner's rush to action had not led to victory but to conviction and imprisonment. What was the main underlying mechanism?

Freud (1911b), in "Formulations on the Two Principles of Mental Functioning," differentiated between those who rushed to action to unburden themselves of accretions of stimuli and those who could tolerate frustration. By stimuli he meant circumstances that burdened the individual with psychic pain. Those who are better able to bear the frustration of psychic pain for long enough perform a vital task, namely, that of reality testing. During reality testing the likely consequences of any action taken by them can be considered. In addition, two other things happen. One is the capacity to tolerate the pain; the other is that modifications of any subsequently chosen action will have had time to be thought out and tried out in fantasy. The enormous difference between the rush to action and the ability to wait cannot be overestimated.

There is an exception to this distinction. The calculating criminal, who can bide his time and often operates in association with others of like mind and behavior, behaves differently. Due to factors ranging from constitutional to traumatic to early nurture of a criminogenic kind, these criminals have established an allegiance to a criminal or else severely narcissistic organization within themselves. That this intrapsychic constellation is dominant means that a loyalty to bad objects and bad aims has developed.

By bad, I mean the intention of doing harm to other people. These people are usually not ill in the way that those labeled "neurotic" criminals are. There is little internal conscious conflict. They take calculated risks, and while serving prison sentences usually cannot explode into action that would get them into further trouble. An exception to this is when those involved in drug dealing themselves become drug-dependent, undermining their adjustment and allowing impulsiveness to erupt into violence. Drug dependency is a self-inflicted, self-generated illness.

Many straightforward career criminals choose not to work at deep, personal psychotherapy, but do respond to a changed loyalty away from the delinquent leader to a nondelinquent, caring person who clarifies their reality sense and grows to be trusted. This constitutes a changed attachment, in this case to a person who can shepherd them to a state of controlled delinquency or nondelinquency.

Looking closely into the psychic structure of "gang" or "pack" criminals, one finds at least three different kinds of personality: the "attachment person" described above; the person with a powerful intrapsychic pathological organization more suffused with death than life (this individual, if intelligent, tends to become a gang leader and, if not bright enough, the "hit man"); and a mixed person with cruelly criminal encapsulations within his psyche, but with some identification with noncriminal activities, compassion, and a sense of justice veering toward geniality rather than punishment of others.

A clinical example of this third type is a young man who was, in effect, facing both ways: toward criminal violence and an escalation of it, and toward geniality and compassion, friendliness, and kindness to others.

At the time of a particular dream, he was ill in the hospital; he told me the dream on the day I visited him:

> Two stray black cats in bad condition wandered into the ward kitchen in search of food. The staff nurse fed them and then they made a home round and about the kitchen and the nurse's room. The staff nurse, and to some extent her fellow nurses, fed the two cats regularly. Gradually, however, their behavior changed. One black cat became more and more friendly and affectionate, rubbing itself round the ankles of the nurse and purring. Meanwhile, the other black cat got into much better physical condition but at the same time became more unfriendly, snatching its food and then growling and showing its claws. After eating, it jumped on top of a cupboard and glared down at the staff nurse and any person who came near it.

Both cats were black, but with kind treatment they behaved differently and the differences tended to increase. One cat was tamed into friendliness, but taming in the other turned into paranoid resentment and increased savagery. Both cats represented the two-sided nature of the dreamer, and his character illness may well have stemmed from a seemingly unbridgeable gap between these two sides of himself.

This state of affairs prevails in certain criminals. The nearer the approximation to the savage and untamable black cat, the more difficult it is to get a satisfactory response to dynamic psychotherapy. On the other hand, the more the individual resembles the friendly black cat, which showed that it could learn from a good experience, so he or she has a much better prognosis if given dynamic psychotherapy.

Detachment from the criminal group is necessary, as is reattachment to a noncriminal one. Anyone who has become brutalized in the course of "service" in a criminal group requires rehabilitation, that is, debrutalization. This process necessarily takes time. Some moral but nonmoralizing religious groups can, and do, perform crucially important work in the process of debrutalization and reattachment, for which they provide the alternative group. It must be emphasized that it is internal (i.e., intrapsychic) change that is sought. Some violent persons do not undergo this internal change but do improve to an extent, showing themselves able to conform to accepted behavior and to social and legal requirements. These people, however, suffer from continued tension and strain. They sometimes relapse seriously.

Melanie Klein's (1927) paper, "Criminal Tendencies in Normal Children," considers those children, boys and girls, who have highly destructive fantasies, attacking mother, father, and/or siblings, and wounding, poisoning, castrating, murdering. They feel very guilty about these fantasies. There may be impulses too, but sometimes the repression by an already developed and cruelly strict superego operates first, before the impulses can be acted out. The fundamental law of talion operates here: as a person treats his objects, external or intrapsychic, so he feels treated by those objects. Quite often he or she feels that the punishment by his objects will be more savage than the activity by which they have been provoked, that is, there will be retaliation and punishment, mutually potentiated.

As Freud (1916) wrote in his first brief paper on "Criminals from a Sense of Guilt," the guilt resulting from the criminal's fantasy is sometimes so great that a criminal action is triggered and the subsequent punishment serves to mitigate the guilt. But Freud pointed out from his clinical observations that whereas the fantasy was of a major crime—parricide, matricide, filicide, or mutilation of his nearest and dearest—the ensuing crime actually committed was a mere token. The punishment for the lesser crime committed in external reality assuages the guilt for the major one committed in fantasy only. This fundamental finding of Freud's contradicts his view that criminals have a poorly developed superego. Melanie Klein took our understanding further, stating that criminals have an *over*punitive and extremely strict superego, but the pain caused by it acts as a goad rather than guide. It is a persecutory superego.

Our theme is the passage from fantasy to impulse to action. At a fantasy level we all have criminal tendencies. How is it that only a minority of people go on to experience impulses and a smaller number still go on to take action? Moreover, a minute percentage go on to major crime, such as murder, though many more reintroject the murderous fantasy and attempt or commit suicide.

What, in addition to growing experience and the mellowing of impulses, can bring about a successful resolution of this sequence so that it does not end in dire and irreversible action? At least, is it possible to help criminals to reach the stage that happens in most people?

I was impressed by some potentially criminal individuals who developed a psychotic breakdown, but who did not act out the criminal impulses by which they had been possessed before breakdown. By contrast, I came across some psychotic individuals who, when in an uncontrolled state, were able to commit a major crime that appeared to be one they would not have committed had they been sane at the time of the crime.

This raises a question. If some people use psychotic breakdown as a defense against serious crime, and others use it as a means of committing a serious crime but complain that they were not fully responsible for their actions, how can we explain that these two situations are antithetical? Could there be an absence or nonfunctioning of some transactional process that results in some people going one way, others the opposite way?

Could it be to do with projective identification, discovered and named by Melanie Klein (1946) in her seminal paper "Notes on Some Schizoid Mechanisms"? This was taken further by Bion (1967a) in his short paper "On Arrogance," and this may give us some help. The essential feature of this paper is that Bion encountered in some borderline or psychotic patients a widely scattered triad of features: arrogance, curiosity, and stupidity. He considered these signs of an earlier, primitive disaster. He concluded, after considering the available evidence, that the disaster consisted of a mother or mother surrogate who would not or could not accept, predigest, and feed back to the infant in improved form its projective identification.

This could also be due in part to the infant who could not use what was fed back to him in improved form by the mother, who accepted his communication by means of projective identification and, after detoxifying it, returned it to the infant, resulting in the non-functioning of a vital component of mother–child interaction that precludes a setting up in the individual's inner world of an internal projective identification, digestive apparatus. This leads to a marked deficiency of the structure needed for reality testing. Arrogance can be regarded as a somewhat manic defense to mask this intrapsychic deficiency. Curiosity consists of a relentless seeking for something—an object or experience unknown but expressed by the subject in terms of a continued search. Stupidity is derived directly from the deficiency or absence of some aspect of the internal psychic digestive system.

I have used Bion's hypothesis in relation to a number of convicted criminals, including some serving life sentences for murder, and in the light of their communications I believe that Bion's views on this matter help us understand how it began. In psychoanalysis or in prolonged psychoanalytical psychotherapy, it is sometimes possible to redress this early deficiency. By tolerating, understanding, and containing the projective identifications of the criminal patient, the experience of the therapist or analyst enables the delinquent or criminal to introject the containing and detoxifying aspect of the therapist. The patient may eventually develop an effective do-it-yourself apparatus, intrapsychically. In the therapy of hardened criminals, however, the therapist may be set up as a pleasant museum piece rather than as an effective container and digester of projective identifications.

There is also the major risk that a newly developed internal do-it-yourself structure, which if used properly could help reality testing and containment to take place, will not be used. In such cases it becomes apparent that a sort of internal gang is operating, fostering and promulgating the destructive, cynical part of the self. When stimulated by improvement or potential improvement, the gang makes a savage counterattack and takeover bid for the whole of the self of the criminal. One is reminded of Faustus, of the wicked, uncaring criminal voice in Coleridge's "Ancient Mariner," and of the social, national, and international malignancy of the Nazis. How, in the therapeutic situation, can this be worked through and overcome? I observed that those who benefited least from dynamic psychotherapy were those who could not mourn their situation and that of their victims. A manic response seemed to develop in which mourning was bypassed, stultified, or annulled as soon as it became painful.

Sometimes acting out complicated the therapy, acting out that ultimately was an attack on the therapy and the therapist. It was also an attack on change, certainly any change for the better. On the other hand, those who in a follow-up study had been able to face, tolerate, and work through a mourning process were able to cope with life outside prison when they were released on parole or unconditionally. Some criminals managed to sustain some mourning in the intermediate situation, but at a certain stage bounced out of it, leaving the process incomplete. For the mourning process to progress favorably, a good deal of psychic pain must be tolerated.

What happens in fairly healthy, nondelinquent people? How do they deal with their criminal fantasies? As mentioned earlier, a number of adolescents and young adults who suffered criminal dreams, fantasies, and occasional brinkmanship behavior showed features similar to those shown by major criminals, but on a minor scale. One criminal said that he could plot his moods sequentially as though on a temperature chart: happy and genial, irritable, angry, depressed, angrier, persecuted, more depressed, hopeless, murderous.

If a mini-mourning situation can be carried out by the individual who has criminal tendencies and impulses not yet translated into action, the intrapsychic situation will stabilize and generally no criminal action will ensue. If the mini-mourning is undertaken for some time but not completed, the likely consequence is actual criminal action, though much mitigated, sometimes only a token action. If no mourning takes place, the criminal action is likely to be a straight acting out of impulses. If a paranoid current operates powerfully, the action is likely to escalate. An example of *mitigated* severity is that of the previously discussed adolescent boy whose brother, a member of a gang that killed a man in the course of robbing him, had tried to prevent the murder. In accordance with the law at that time, the brother was executed along with the person who did the deed. The younger brother felt he could not contain his vengeful feelings. He wanted to kill a policeman because his brother had been killed for not killing. What he did, however, was to steal a pair of boots from a shop and get himself caught. Then, fortunately, he was put under the care of a gifted probation officer who helped him recover without further delinquent acting out.

Then there is the young criminal who said that he committed a sexual assault, in his mind, on a young girl of a certain age and felt awful about it. All he had to do to mitigate the awfulness, he said, was to find a suitable victim and actually commit the offense. Then he felt better, but only for a short time. Few criminals put the matter so clearly. This man was of high intelligence, but had no internal projective identification-containing apparatus. He had suffered from a most disturbed, constantly uprooted, and traumatized early life in which no containing person was available.

In another young man of high intelligence the situation was different. He became physically ill when about 6 with a crippling, painful, chronic illness. He was a complaining, naughty child, but his mother was devoted to him. When he was 7 his mother developed cancer, and before he reached 9 she had died. He began to act out in a delinquent way, and his criminality escalated in severity. His crimes had to do with stealing, and were in line with his previous criminal fantasies. These were contained at first by his mother during his latency years, but her death led to their intensification, as not only was there little ability to contain them, but there was also an added revenge motive. The baby self of this boy experienced his mother's death as wholly unreasonable, and his subsequent crimes were directed in the main against large, anonymous organizations making and containing something essentially feminine, frequently warehouses of female underwear. The crime that led to his last sentence was his breaking and entry into such a factory. He went to sleep there, and was found on a Monday morning fast asleep with his head resting between the two brassiere-covered plastic breasts of a model!

Another man, a clothes fetishist, also specialized in women's underwear. In the main he stole from clotheslines, but if no garments were available, he began to steal from the young women themselves, knocking them down and taking off their undergarments. When arrested, this young man said to the policeman, "Thank God you have caught me: I might have gone on to do something much worse." What he was referring to was the full fantasy constellation, which included the killing of the female. So far he had acted out only a small part of the fantasy; thus some modification had taken place but not enough for there to be no external delinquent action at all.

At worst, however, the state of persecution in which the individual acts out criminal impulses in the idiom of previous fantasies becomes almost inevitably intensified. Thus the situation in the inner world can get markedly better so that there is no acting out of criminal fantasies and impulses. It may get somewhat better, so that the crimes committed are modified until they become tokens of the original fantasies. Fortunately less common is a potentiation of violence, a paranoid souring-in-cask, rather than a mellowing. For example, as discussed in earlier chapters, a 21-year-old man stated that the reason for his crime was that the victim mortally offended him by lightheartedly raping his fiancée. It was the fiancée who reported the rape to him, but the alleged rapist stated that it was in fact an easy seduction. The young girl withdrew her emphasis on rape when she saw how murderously angry her fiancé had become. I interviewed the young man several times. He told of a disturbed childhood against which he was chronically rebellious. Later he worked with animals, describing them in glowing terms. "They never forget a friend and never trust anyone who has ever been unfair or unkind to them." Clearly he identified himself with the animals. His turbulent, aggressive behavior provoked the police to attempt to curb him. He then resorted to a miscellany of drugs so that his already flimsy controls were further eroded. It was at this time that he met the young woman with whom he fell in love. Naturally their relationship was unstable. Then followed the action, recounted above, that drove him into a paranoid state, and this seemed to get worse with each passing week. When he eventually met the young man by whom he had been cuckolded, he was seething with murderous fury, and killed him with great violence. Here is an instance of a murderously violent intrapsychic situation worsening and not becoming psychically digested, as is more usual.

The mixture appeared to be compounded of:

1. Righteous anger becoming self-righteous fury
2. Catastrophic loss of self-esteem
3. An unquestioned identification with animals with an emphasis on unforgivingness
4. The whole system of controls being sabotaged by drug-taking experiences
5. Self-blame for the "rape" resulting from some real or supposed neglect of his fiancée by himself. His guilt became too persecutory to be sustained and instead increased his resentment against the "enemy."
6. Retrospective attempts to maintain self-justification.

This example serves to underline the complexity of some of the difficulties encountered during therapeutic attempts to reverse the fantasy–impulse–action sequence. This is what happens in most cases when the starting point is a compulsive or an impulsive tendency to lead a life punctuated by criminal acts. Among the signs of approaching transformation from a more to a less criminal way of being is an increase in introjection and a decrease in projection and acting out. There is also an increase in containment and a decrease in noncontainment. At this time psychosomatic symptoms tend to increase, and are signs of the increased capacity for containment of conflictual situations, but this containment incurs a good deal of stress and psychic pain that tend to be somaticized.

A further encouraging event is the ability to turn to a creative, sublimatory activity. In certain prisoner-patients I treated there was a move toward construction activities so that use was made of, say, training to learn a trade such as bricklaying. Some wrote poetry. Another man wrote a series of short stories. One man carved figures in wood that charted his growth over two years as these representations of persons grew in depth and complexity. This kind of happening, I think, was a sign of a relatively successful negotiation of the depressive position. I must add that the poetry I allude to was far from escapist in content, and dealt very much with guilt, remorse, and finding a way ahead. Dangers at this stage of change are of a sudden, acute relapse into a paranoid-schizoid state accompanied by an absolute rejection of psychic pain. When this occurs, the risk of suicidal attempts is not to be underestimated. Worse still, a repetition of a murderously vicious attack on an arbitrarily chosen victim becomes a real possibility.

15

Reparation

Reparation for a crime that has been committed in the mind can only be healing to the individual who performs such a process. Its first stage is mourning. If there are no ongoing urges to commit the particular crime, then mourning for what has been perpetrated only in fantasy is not a particularly complicated process. The other end of the scale of criminal deeds is murder of a person by intention. The premeditated murder is particularly serious, and a great deal more deep and prolonged mourning and regret for the taking of the life of the victim is to be expected than seems to be necessary after a sudden crime, or a *crime passionelle.* One reason for the premeditated murder to be regarded as more serious legally and psychically is that, in the premeditation, the act of murder has probably been committed in the mind many times before its eruption into concrete, irreversible action. In the domestic murder the victim is usually the person toward whom deep feelings of murderousness are felt. If murderousness is felt toward someone, including a family member from whom the potential murderer may have long been separated, the person chosen as the victim may simply happen to fit the murderous psychic constellation.

This constellation is present all the time, but can be brought into action even many years later, rather like a volcano that, though long inactive, can burst into violent eruption with fatal consequences (Williams 1959). The parallel with the volcano is that the dangerous potentiality remains, despite long quiescence. This means that the causal constellation is unresolved. Can anyone say that there will be no more murderous violence? Can anyone state confidently that this volcano is extinct? Regarding human beings, the murder constellation is not extinct unless adequate mourning for the murders committed in the mind has taken place. In those who have actually killed, the mourning has to be lifelong. This is painful, as is shown in those who have had psychotherapy, but far from crippling if the situation can be faced as an ongoing state of affairs. Also, there are degrees of responsibility. The fatality due to an accident or carelessness is not of the same order of magnitude as the purposeful, long-brooded-upon taking of the life of an innocent victim used as a scapegoat for someone else.

What of intrapsychic transactions? The transformation from the paranoid-schizoid to the depressive position (which can be likened to an endless encounter with the game of Snakes and Ladders) has to be undertaken indefatigably. At the same time, using Bion's concept of container and contained, the capacity to contain painful states of mind without rushing into action to expel or evacuate them has to be developed.

If we return to Freud's (1920) concepts of the pleasure principle and the reality principle, we see how acceptance of the latter hinges on the capacity to tolerate painful and unpleasant situations within the self rather than yield to the impulse to evacuate them, thus unburdening the psyche of accretions of stimuli. If these intrapsychic situations can be tolerated without rushing to action, then the mulling over in the mind can be successful as a substitute for action rather than as a prelude to it.

Clearly, the capacity to do this depends on an intrapsychic apparatus to do so. That depends on the experience, accessibility, and functionally operating state of good objects in the individual. I have drawn attention to the lack of an adequate projective–identification-accepting mother or mother surrogate in the early lives of most convicted murderers, and of those with a marked tendency to murder. The other two factors of the syndrome are stupidity and curiosity. Before this aspect of the illness can be ameliorated in the analytic or psychotherapeutic situation, a great deal of work has to be done either to refurbish or create for the first time a mental apparatus capable of containment and reflection. This oversimplified description essentially refers to a psychic function that enables a detoxication process to take place in the mind. It deals with those impulses and attitudes arising from within and from without: these may be frustrations, goadings, and misfortunes arising from outside, or the ordinary or extraordinary exigencies of life.

This is easy to write about, but not at all easy to put into operation in psychotherapy or psychoanalysis. However, in each person so treated, one can make some progress. Provided that things are proceeding relatively well, at some point in the therapy one observes that reparative activities begin to appear and to run in sequences. Sometimes there is a general increase in geniality. This can be seen in the prisoner who helps troubled fellow prisoners. There may also be signs of increased creativity, such as growing or making things, writing, and taking advantage of educational facilities provided. Progress, of course, is punctuated by setbacks when formidable obstacles cause paranoid-schizoid/depressive-position transformations to reverse and become bogged down at the paranoid-schizoid end of the spectrum. Also, and in a spectacular way, a leap forward could occur to meet an immediate challenge. In a case mentioned elsewhere, the man who suffered from compulsive incendiarism prevented a prison officer from being seriously injured, but was badly hurt himself. He had been affected by a surge of depressive anxiety, not persecutory anxiety, which characterizes the resort to incendiarism. When released, he wondered what the future held for him, but as time went on he realized he was no longer under a compulsion to light fires. On a visit to see his children, he became aware of a new, softer side shown to him by his wife. Soon afterward they decided to remarry. He contacted me and I was heartened to see the change in him. He had never killed anyone, and his guilt and reparation had been worked through to some extent during the psychotherapy he had from me. His independent judgment provoked by the attack on the prison officer, followed by effective intervention, showed him a more objective and fair way of looking at situations. Finally, his intervention demonstrated a capacity to stand up for a principle. The episode was a dramatic psychoemotional development.

Usually the evidence of a capacity for reparation is slower and less dramatic, but the transformation from the paranoid-schizoid to the depressive position is the crucial process on which all else is supported. Not all activity that appears to be of the reparative kind has the same degree of authenticity. Sometimes there is reparation that is glib, short-circuiting mourning and regret over harm done by the self to others. This kind of reparation, which Segal called *manic reparation*, does not have the authenticity of true reparation in which there has been no evasion of the pain of mourning. Manic reparation eventually reveals its patchiness and its unfinished facets. Among the poets, Coleridge is an outstanding example of a person who resorted to manic reparation. Biographers have shown "The Ancient Mariner" to be an almost autobiographical account, demonstrating Coleridge's struggle to deal with powerful and complicated forces within himself. By stressing the example of reparation initiated by manic elements, I wish to stress that manic reparation is not necessarily associated with emotional shallowness or superficiality, but rather that an intrapsychic process fails to sustain a developmental course.

So far we have been dealing with reparation for deeds carried out in external reality. The crimes have been the result of a failure to detoxicate a state of mind and a resort to action. There are other possibilities that one sees in clinical work. The impulse-driven fantasy constellation may be held within its donor and modification takes place.

In persons whose fantasies of a criminal activity are not backed up by powerful impulses, there is often an element of enjoyment in the fantasy, which may be a recurring one worked out in detail like a piece of crime fiction. There may be little or no tendency to go on to make it into an actual crime. A big problem today, however, lies in the addiction by many people to violence in the form of fantasies, videos, stories, and so on. The death constellation is expressed in ways that superficially seem to be harmless, and in many, if not most people they are. For a small minority, however, they are psychically dangerous. A father-abused baby grew up to become the killer of a man representing his father; he was addicted to violent cartoons. He was bewildered when his victim died and did not get up and walk off at the end of the "game." His addiction had produced an intrapsychic situation in which mourning for a murderous fantasy was avoided. The buildup of the impulse was short-circuited into a near-masturbatic murderous fantasy, and life went on, apparently satisfactorily. This was, however, based on false foundations in that there was little or no emotional life, growth, or development.

In another patient with criminal fantasies but no criminal action, the murderousness was expressed in masturbation to homosexual, murderous, and perverse fantasies. It became clear during a number of years of analysis that mourning for the use of the perverse, paranoid, homosexual fantasies as an essential component of masturbation enabled him to retain a pleasurable component while keeping the situation relatively safe from escalation into catastrophic action. The whole sequence was used as an instrument of homeostasis, with no relinquishment and no frightening action, but instead a sort of emotional limbo. Some reparation must have been sustained because he acquired more geniality in relationships with other people. One manifestation of this change was an increase in a benign sense of humor. Apart from that, it seemed that the developmental process was enshrined in a museum of arrested experience.

What happens if an individual is, and remains, unaware of his or her murderous, destructive, fantasy systems? The likelihood is that the individual becomes more inhibited without knowing why, other than the fact of associated anxiety. For example, a very moral, entirely law-abiding man had a nocturnal emission without any manifest dream content being remembered. Eventually, when the dream content did have a visual counterpart, it consisted of the cruel exploitation of a young person, which made him feel ill for days. Eventually he recovered; he had mourned the content of his intrapsychic sexual life and fantasy, and was in fact better for the surfacing of this most forbidden part of the fantasy. What kind of mourning takes place, or has taken place, because of forbidden murderous, cruel, damaging, or grossly exploitative fantasies? Again, the length, depth, and painfulness of the mourning vary, having to be more thorough and more painful if the fantasy has included an addictive attitude toward the perverse constellation and subsequent pleasure from it. When there is yet an additional perverse and harmful fantasy constellation, it is easy to get into a prolonged cat-and-mouse interaction, with reparation and then fresh depredations against the erotic object of addiction. Sometimes this sequence is openly masturbatic, sometimes only subtly so.

16

The Micro-Environment

Recently I came across a large pond that had been artificially constructed many years ago by men who were excavating gravel. When they came to the end of the gravel, a large hole was left that quickly filled with water. Thereafter an impressive micro-environment slowly developed, eventually reaching an ecological balance. There were trees around the edge, an array of plants, and a wide variety of freshwater creatures from water voles to frogs, fish, and dragonfly larvae. An oasis had formed that facilitated the settlement and breeding of diverse forms of life under conditions that favored growth and development. It was less exposed than the world around it. Although it was comfortable enough, eventually it must have been restrictive to some creatures. I began to reflect on the similarity between this micro-environment and that of the family. There is often the same protection from the outside world, interactiveness, ecological balance, and, ultimately restrictiveness. When the balance has been disturbed by forces acting within the micro-environment or impinging from the world outside the environment, homeostatic processes are set in motion to restore the balance. In the case of the family in which self-healing has failed, a point is reached when they are referred for or seek therapeutic help.

The voices audible in the field of family therapy theory often appear to be saying different things. Yet is what they say so different? And who is saying what? There are the ethologists, the systems theorists, and the psychoanalysts. Traditionally the Tavistock Clinic has occupied a position between the intrapsychic emphasis of the psychoanalyst and the interpersonal emphasis of the sociologist. Kurt Lewin, the expounder of field theory, clarified this approach. Later John Bowlby at the Tavistock veered increasingly toward the ethological view. How can we pursue a study of the problem working from our individual points of view and keeping other approaches in mind without losing our scientific poise?

A parallel would be to consider the various ways of looking at the pond as an entity in itself—at its surface, at the creatures at different depths, at different seasons of the year, or in the setting of the wider environment. Following this parallel in the case of a family, it is difficult to see any reason why the different ways of looking at and studying a family should necessarily be incompatible.

My co-worker, who also happens to be my wife, and I approached the C family from a psychodynamic stance as we are both psychoanalysts working from the Kleinian viewpoint. This means that we regard factors dating from early life as being of paramount importance. The depressive position, persecutory and depressive anxieties, splitting, and that primitive method of communication to which Melanie Klein gave the name *projective identification* are the central elements of our everyday work. This does not mean that we underestimate the importance of classical mechanisms of mental functioning such as projection and introjection.

> The L family was referred to us as private, fee-paying patients by their general practitioner, whom I knew because of previous referrals to me. The family consisted of father, 42, mother, 40, son 18, and daughter, 16. The son, S, was the index patient. The complaints about him were that he was un-

manageable: sweet as honey one moment, a devil incarnate the next. Stories of his escalating violence when he got into one of his "bad" sequences made my wife and me anxious lest there might have been an epileptic basis to the disturbance. This would not contraindicate our undertaking family therapy, but we might have been working against an undercurrent of neurological disability not necessarily accessible to verbal therapeutic and family interactions. So out of touch with any learning from experience did S feel at times that we negotiated with the GP to have an EEG to check for the possibility of neurological malfunction. Both an earlier and a new EEG record were minimally abnormal, but in a not very specific way. As the family therapeutic meetings proceeded, we gradually realized that the abnormality was a precise measurement of the lack of integration and maturation characteristic of S.

How did the sessions begin? Mr. L, the father, an intelligent, loquacious Jewish businessman, nearly always started off by recounting a long story of the depredations of S, how his impossible demands became violent and destructive when they could not be met. S would listen intently to all that was going on, agreeing or sometimes shaking his head if he thought what was said was wrong. If anything touched him emotionally, he would shout abuse at either parent, his sister, or at either therapist. S would attempt to divide the authorities in a way typical of the oedipal child. He would set father against mother, or mother against father. He would try to set my coworker against me or me against her. In general, however, he tended to be softer and more propitiatory toward males and harsher toward females. Retreat on the part of his mother or sister would lead to escalation of nastiness because hostility was reinforced by contempt and, in a manic sequence, mockery would follow.

Remonstration rapidly led to violence. On one occasion S flared up against his sister, J, who responded defiantly. S got up, wrenched her arm, then sat down again, saying, "That'll teach you." J was in tears for a long time. If things became even more threatening, father would get up and control S, who, after a scuffle, would settle down, sometimes even weeping like a young child. S sometimes struck out at his mother, leaving her in tears, too, and even threatened my wife, who continued to interpret S's unbridled aggressiveness without flinching. Before this confrontation could be worked out between them, father intervened.

We became aware not of murderousness, but of a complete lack of caring about life, including the lives of other people, and were anxious about what would happen in the next session. My wife made our anxieties explicit, but there was no time to pursue the subject adequately. At the next session there was gloom and fear. After parking his car, S had opened the door to get out and a drunken motorcyclist had struck the door, skidded, and fallen heavily in the road, striking his head on the hard road surface. He died within minutes of an intracranial hemorrhage. S was prosecuted and found it impossible at that time to feel sorry for the dead man; he was bogged down at the paranoid-schizoid end of the anxiety spectrum. The family's reaction was only slightly more concerned, but mainly protective toward S. My wife and I were shocked and sad, and wondered how much this was an overdetermined situation akin to, but not identical with, acting out, or how much it was an entirely fortuitous disaster to which the L family in general and S in particular were responding in their characteristic way.

When the court case was over, the family relaxed, and there was a good deal of rather macabre jokiness. At this point we pointed out the shared attitudes of the family: other people really did not matter at all, except insofar as they were useful to the L's. When family interpretations were made, there was an immediate scurry to load what was experienced as blame or accusation onto S. My wife and I realized that S was repeatedly being set up as the executive agent of the family's violence and aggressiveness. The elements of family interaction in the session consisted of accusations used as missiles:

mockery and devaluation with the aim of denigrating a family member or either therapist. Soft-soap, wheedling, and threats were the elements used in dealing with the therapists, but self-accusations were experienced as if coming at one or another family member from the therapist.

Gradually, the picture that took shape was of an Atlaslike father carrying the family world on his shoulders, coming to the therapist in an attempt to ease his intolerable burden. From mother's viewpoint the picture was of a masterful but querulous and clever husband, a lovely big-dolly daughter, and a monster—a nice-looking but dangerous devil son, rather like in the film *Rosemary's Baby.* At the same time the mother's picture of herself was of a clueless, elegant, naive, and infinitely worthy woman striving to cope with her family under impossible circumstances. In addition, she was vainly attempting to meet the social demands of a prosperous Jewish social environment. J's complaints were strident, wholly directed against her brother, but in the first year and a half of therapy, she would spring to S's defense if she felt him to be under attack from anyone else.

We, the co-therapists, later designated grandparents, were nearly always set up as critics, but not in a straightforward way. My wife, who is about the same age as Mrs. L, was endowed with anger and disapproval; I, who from the point of view of age could well have been the grandparent, experienced a mixed response. I could see what dreadful things S said and did, but at the same time I responded to a certain comic quality in his behavior. The response would have been appropriate had I been watching a play, but S's burlesquing had a serious and potentially dangerous side. I used to feel quite embarrassed when I found myself smiling or even laughing at what was going on, but when I looked across at my wife I saw she was angry with me. I later realized that I was being taken in by the shockingly amusing aspect of infantile behavior, a result of S's regression. My wife, on the other hand, was increasingly disturbed by her disapproval of S's manic current with its mockery and cruelty, another aspect of his behavior. In discussions after the sessions, we concluded that we were being programmed with mixed messages, probably by means of projective identification, so that we became possessed by confusing feelings. This complicated response may have been related to the family confusion about the feelings experienced by various family members at a given moment in time, with an implied taunt being added in the form of the question: "How do you cope with this?"

This situation took us some months to get over and after we had managed to get into step with each other, we noticed that the family began to work in the sessions, and even to do some work in the intervals between sessions. S listened to everything, but was more prone than the other family members to externalize what he learned from the therapeutic sessions, and to apply it to the others rather than to himself. The other family members also behaved like this, but less so. Father intellectualized most things; mother felt accused of being a failure and wept copiously. J, when she felt accused, accused somebody else, usually S, but at times she quarreled with mother or father, or with either of the two therapists. She had a high-pitched, yappy voice, and her already childishly good-looking face took on a petulant, babyish expression. What was troublesome was a serious quantum of unreasonable aggression and violence that floated about. For the convenience of the rest of the family it tended to settle on S. He in turn was susceptible to this projection into him of awfulness.

This projective identification, in which the object or projectee experiences what has been put into him and the subject or projector is freed from an unbearable state of mind, can be and often is reversed, so that what has been put into someone is returned. This is what S seemed to do, returning much of his own violence in the process. I must emphasize that projective identification is not the same as projection. In projection, a state of mind of the self is ascribed to someone else, not put into that someone.

S's projective identifications and special status gave him a sense of self-importance. As in a children's game, he liked being "It." By It, I mean that he was singled out by the family to act on their behalf as a receptacle for, and perpetrator of, the shared family violence. But as well as being It, S was persecuted and aggrieved. The enjoyment of being It is perverse, and alienated S still further from truth.

We began to interpret the way in which the family violence and antidevelopmental aggressiveness was put into or upon S and how, despite all protestations to the contrary, in some respects it suited the family for this to happen. It relieved them of guilt, externalized their sense of responsibility, and gave them a cherished grievance together with a sense of their own virtue. It also suited S, who was vain and exhibitionistic, and who bathed in the notoriety of every tense and reproachful family situation. This clearly is the perverse manifestation. He also was able to feel, with some justification, persecuted and set up as a scapegoat by both parents and his sister. This, it must be stressed, was a healthier aspect of him.

The course of family therapy did not run smoothly, but rather proceeded from crisis to crisis with intervals of comparative calm. Against this backdrop of improvement and relapse, changes of a more ongoing nature began to show themselves. Notable among the situations that seemed to be important was the sibling rivalry between the two young people, characterized by a tyrannical, controlling attitude on the part of S toward his sister. Both young people seemed to have an infinite expectation of service and devotion from their mother, but J did not attack mother with the same fury as did S. He sucked out goodness and appeared unable to benefit from that goodness. When the parents rebelled or refused him, he became violent and destructive. At least Mr. L shared his son's view of women as slaves to be exploited and ill-treated, though his view was expressed in a more muted way and in more diplomatic terms.

At any job he had S behaved well at first. He had a particular fantasy of himself as a prosperous real estate agent and appraiser, but at times he had to be content with working in a clothes shop for men. When he had gotten used to a job, to the staff and to the terrain, he would become increasingly arrogant and querulous, even nasty, especially to one or other of the women who did secretarial work. Eventually he would be asked to leave, and having saved no money he would once again become a total charge upon his father. Gradually it dawned upon us that S's identification with his father consisted of an imitation of his father's attitude toward other people, especially toward subordinates at work. What S did, however, was to caricature and distort his father's attitudes and behavior. In this there was an attempt to *be* his father, but also at the same time an attempt to subvert him. He did not do this to my wife, but he did do it to me; to give him his due, he put up a creditable, comic impressionist act of being me, well up to television situation comedy standards. What was unproductive in all this was the way in which the caricaturing (which was, of course, part of a manic defense) stultified learning.

When S was angry and destructive, paranoid processes predominated. When caught in a manic psychic current, he was mildly grandiose, condescending, and quietly mocking. Both states of mind defended him against psychic pain. He was never anywhere near the depressive position, and any brief reparative activities consisted of manic reparation. There was little ability to learn from what was going on in therapy until he gradually became able to own some of his own negative aspects. The first steps toward this improvement followed S's being relieved of some of the projections which more truly belonged to other members of the family and which they heaped upon him. Repeatedly, the work done in the family therapy sessions was undone in the gaps between the sessions, like Penelope's tapestry. At times the violence floated around in an unstable state until it landed on some family member. There was always something of a relapse during holidays, or when the parents went on holiday and left the children to cope on their own in the family home.

Any family member who happened to be physically ill suffered from psychic disturbance. This happened to S when he had his tonsils removed and when he had a severe attack of influenza. J too was disturbed when she had glandular fever. (She was childish rather than delinquent, while S was childish *and* delinquent.) Father developed gallstones and was advised to have a cholecystectomy. Following the operation, when he was doing light work and was worried about hypertension, a misunderstanding took place: Mrs. L, indulging in a bit of mischief-making, contradicted what Mr. L had said to J. Mr. L flew into a sudden, violent rage and threw his whole meal, together with the plate, at his wife's favorite picture. He then proceeded to throw everything everywhere, wrecking the room. This piece of behavior was recounted in detail in the next session by Mrs. L, while her culprit of a husband listened sheepishly. S made a takeover bid for my therapeutic role and interpreted with less caricature than usual. My wife drew attention to the way in which the mantle of violence had now fallen upon Mr. L and wondered what would happen next. She speculated how long it would be before the violence was forced back into S. We had not long to wait.

The next session began in the old familiar way. S had lost his job and broken up the drawing room at home. A contributing factor had been intolerable jealousy aroused when J announced she was going to marry B, her boyfriend. It appeared that the marriage was to be some years in the future, but S had felt upstaged by it. He had had a succession of girlfriends. The relationships had not lasted because they found S to be quite intolerable. Their vocal expression of disapproval of S's unacceptable behavior, instead of acting as a guide to moderate it, goaded him to further violence and that finalized the rejection.

(Before giving an account of the last few sessions with the L family, I would like to recount one more example of how the violence shifted yet again. J spoke rudely to me, and her mother remonstrated with her, but was then answered even more rudely. With no warning, Mrs. L stood up, crossed in front of me, and hit her daughter hard four times. My wife drew attention to how the violence had now settled on Mrs. L, who carried it on behalf of everyone else.)

> S settled into a new job. Things seemed to get quite a bit better. Then we were told that Mr. and Mrs. L were going away on holiday together, leaving the siblings to look after the house and themselves. We offered to make ourselves available to see S and J together during the parents' absence. This offer was not taken up. At the next family meeting it was clear that there had been disturbances. S had become interested in a young woman and, according to J, had scarcely been in the house and had given her no help during the parental absence. She said that he had been a parasite and that she had done her best to do all her own work and to act as mother in the home. He said that J had been more than diligent, excessively fussing and demanding of his time and attention. J had got into a state when S had brought home his girlfriend late at night, though he had not taken her to bed. On the return of the parents J had complained and they had scolded S. He became destructive and they said that he must leave home and find a place for himself. S left home, not for the first time but the third, but on this occasion he went out and found his own place (previously his father had found a place for him). Meanwhile he had broken up furniture at home and had had a nasty, upsetting fight with his father. It was very alarming and we wondered whether things were back at square one.
>
> We were, however, aware of the plea implicit in S's destructiveness, which ran as follows: "As long as I remain embedded in this family I will never be able to behave responsibly and control the destructive little boy part of myself." We said this and the parents and J were outraged, but S, seriously and sadly, agreed. During the interval between sessions S had

shown regret for his behavior, apologized, and had attempted reparative activities that did not have the manic quality of former times. We felt that something different was happening.

At the next session J began by saying that she was not coming to any further sessions because there was nothing wrong with her and she came only to do S good. S retaliated by treating her as if she were the little child, calling her "Piggy," which infuriated her, and patronizing her in an outrageous way. Toward the end of the session, when both therapists were wondering if there might be a way of interpreting an undercurrent of tempting but frightening incestuous sexuality that might have determined, or at least worsened, the troubles when the parents were away on holiday, the next event took place. J, goaded beyond endurance, got up, rushed across the room, and bashed S several times about the face and shoulders. As she did this I thought she looked like an outraged wife or fiancée whose spouse or lover had been unfaithful to her. To our surprise, S was not violent but, instead, tried to control his sister as gently as possible. He looked awkward and embarrassed and eventually half picked up his sister, half pushed her onto the consulting room couch. Before letting her go, he lingered over her in what looked more like an embrace than an attack. I thought of Romeo and Juliet. We interpreted along these lines, linking what had happened in the session with the difficulty that had arisen during the parents' holiday. We pointed out that they had been left together to play the well-known game of mommies and daddies—this was exciting and very frightening, particularly to S, who, it had been reported, had made various quasi-sexual advances to his sister when they were little children.

J did not come again, but events moved rapidly with S, who after some weeks announced that he wanted to get married. He had told his girlfriend about his difficulties and asked whether the therapists would be willing to see him with her for one interview and then to find him someone who would help him with his own problems. He was worried lest he should wreck a good relationship. We did see them together and we also saw Mr. and Mrs. L as a married couple. S was referred to a colleague. The outcome of the treatment of this family was a recovery.

What happened in the therapy of the L family? The attempts to denigrate the therapists, to draw them into the Charybdis of the family whirlpool, are usual features of family behavior in therapy, as is the circulating object or characteristic, in this case a constellation of violence. Let us now look at the problem slightly differently. To return to our pond, what I omitted to say is that such ponds in gravelly areas have a natural life cycle. When deep-rooted bushes and trees pierce the impervious seal of the pond floor, which happens ten to twenty years after the formation of the pond, the water drains away and there is dry gravel below. Many aquatic creatures die; some are able to move elsewhere. A new and differentiated micro-environment develops in the swampy residue of the pond. Nuclear families also last for about twenty years. The L family was confronted with the prospect of the death of its own micro-environment, and the various members could not face it. Instead, mother connived and even encouraged the regressive behavior of both adolescents. It will be remembered that early on in the therapy J was very childish, and even when she got a boyfriend she was looking toward marriage only in the far distant future. S was inconstant and querulous in all relationships. Even his work was really play on a grand scale. Father performed his role as an indulgent, complaining manager of the family business, of which the nuclear family itself was a troublesome branch.

The factors that delayed growth and development consisted of:

1. The shared unconscious need to defend against the death, that is, the breakup, of the nuclear family and collusion over the idea that children do not grow up, leave home, and get married.
2. The manic defense based on the formulas of "I'm all right, Jack" and "What's in it for me?" (These very terms were actually used at times by different family members.)

PART IV

17

The Individual and Organized Crime

The remarkable feature of organized crime is how relatively stable social structures are established, and how most criminals who are involved manage to achieve some stability within them. One wonders why the members of a criminal gang or subculture choose to obey the rules of the delinquent underworld and do not try to conform to the much more tolerant rules of ordinary established society. One reason for exchanging subjection to the rules of one regime for another that is harsher is that the aims of the criminal subculture coincide far more with the personal aims of those who drift or are drawn into its hegemony: its aim is power and often material gain.

It would be fair to postulate that a delinquent subculture has a social structure that in some way matches the personality structure of a large proportion of the individuals who gravitate toward it. About a third of the prison population, perhaps 40 percent, at any one time consists of men who show minimal neurotic or psychotic features, yet who are devoted to a life of crime, often adhering strictly to certain terms of reference beyond which they do not venture. Their ordinary behavior, including toward their wives and children, usually cannot be said to indicate symptomatic behavior or personality disorders. One is forced to notice, however, that there is little or no evidence of emotional conflict over what they do by way of criminal action such as might be encountered in the neurotic criminal. There are no violent eruptions or incontinence of instinctual impulses, such as those that characterize the behavior of the impulsive psychopath. Nevertheless, it may be that when the personal histories of the criminals are traced back as far as their recollections can reach, exceptionally painful experiences have occurred. There may have been ill-treatment, bereavement, a long physical illness, or a crippling accident that seems to have given the individual a grievance that has enabled him to regard himself as one of life's "exceptions." Freud (1916) described such people in "Some Character Types Met with in Psycho-Analysis." The paper is divided into three parts. One part deals with people who regard themselves as having been wronged or underprivileged from the start: King Richard III, for example, because of his deformity. They regard themselves as excused from the laws and restrictions that operate in the case of ordinary people. In the second section Freud describes people who are wrecked by success, people who, to achieve success, have fulfilled wishes that were forbidden not only by society but also by an important part of their own personalities. He cites Rebecca West in Ibsen's *Rosmersholm* and Lady Macbeth as examples. In the third section Freud describes "criminals from a sense of guilt" showing that in some cases the guilt precedes the delinquent act, and through externalization of the guilt by means of the action, both the criminal impulse and the need for punishment are gratified. Incidentally, the external punishment for the token crimes committed was far easier to bear than the conscience punishment from within for what really was a much more serious crime, such as parricide or fratricide. The more serious crime was carried out only in fantasy, with only a slight spillover into a token minor crime in action.

For reasons that may be evident, as in the case of "exceptions," or those with secret destructive impulses (greed, envy, pathological ambition), or those who are ruined by success, or for reasons not discernible at all, the delinquent sets himself up against the ordinary rules of the society in which he lives, and allows himself to do certain things that are forbidden by the law. He is also frowned upon by society, so he is alienated from the ordinary social environment in which he lives. Working in isolation is difficult. The delinquent becomes a fugitive and the feeling of persecution that develops internally is matched externally by a buildup of hostility and force against him, which increases with every one of his depredations. Paranoid feelings often tend to increase in the delinquent. These are painful, and it is all too easy for him to blame his emotional distress on the establishment, and in particular on the forces of law and order. The response to this is an increased feeling of isolation, alienation, and enmity from society and its standards, and this process involves the criminal in what amounts to a progressive illness. (We can also call it brutalization.) It must be emphasized that he is not visibly ill and does not acknowledge that he is ill in any way. He may go on to meet up with other members of the criminal subculture. This often occurs during or after his first prison sentence. The relief from loneliness and isolation resulting from a sharing of aims, the mitigation of feelings of guilt by group involvement in crime, and the comfort of a structural framework to replace the lost conventional framework have a ready appeal for the individual delinquent. This social structure, the criminal organization, reflects his own personality structure and provides for his delinquent needs. What are the main characteristics of this kind of personality structure?

The criminal character is essentially a primitive one. Instinctual impulses are strong, whether they be of greed, sex, envy, or hatred. They are countered by conscience figures that tend to be savage, brutal, and punitive, thus matching the impulses it is their function to curb, mitigate, and mellow in the light of reality. The very severity of the conscience figures, made up as they are of parent images internalized in the course of emotional development, renders them more or less useless as guides. Because they are so persecutory they act as goads. The secret of the malevolence of these conscience figures lies in their power, which as Freud stated in "The Ego and the Id" (1923), stems from the energy of the instinctual drives themselves. When, in the course of early emotional development, an individual is able to negotiate the depressive position, the splitting of objects into good and bad is reduced. The good and bad are brought together and their polarization is diminished. This primary splitting into good, present, reliable, gratifying persons (mother at first) and bad, absent, depriving, punishing figures is important as a firm base from which further developments can take place. Its maldevelopment results in developmental and antidevelopmental processes getting muddled up. The consequences of splitting are not only intrapsychic.

Unless full importance is given to the defense mechanism of splitting, the danger is that a picture will be given of a society sharply divided into the brave and fortunate people who have negotiated the depressive position satisfactorily and the recalcitrant or unfortunate ones who have not done so. It will be recognized at once, of course, that this is not a true picture of what goes on. There are all kinds of gradations and variations in the spectrum between the two extremes of a negotiated versus an unnegotiated depressive position. The former is not a magic portal allowing access to success in life. Some negotiation of the depressive position, however, is the sine qua non of satisfactory emotional growth and development, and of a capacity to benefit from and learn from life's experiences.

To return to a further consideration of splitting: when the conflict between the two opposing tendencies (idealization and hostility) becomes too great for them to be embraced within the same psychic spectrum, one becomes detached from the other so that they can then pursue divergent paths independently. The end product is a Dr. Jekyll and Mr. Hyde split. In psychopaths there may be multiple split-off selves, operating independently and defying integration into one relatively mature and adequate personality. In psychosis in general, but particularly in schizophrenia, splitting is into more minute fragments. A person with this kind of fragmentation is not usually capable of taking and holding an effective role in criminal organization. He is too riven by emotional cross-currents to be reliable.

A person who has made poor progress in negotiating the depressive position in infancy, later, when anxious, tends to rebel against the authorities which he feels are picking on him. He does this in various ways, but when the ways are antisocial and persistent, they usually come within the category of criminality. His activities evoke further reaction from authority figures who become designated as the "establishment," so that his rebellion spreads from the home to school or work and from there to the forces of law and order. When he has been through the courts and possibly sent to an approved school or correction facility, he meets people of his own kind; if he is individualistic and incontinent of aggressive impulses, he may find it difficult to form social linkages and groupings even in a community of young criminals. It is sad to reflect that after some steps in personality integration have been taken, the young criminal may be better able to take part in forming a delinquent group with the other criminals he has met in the remedial institution. While he has become more integrated, his criminal aims—based on persecutory anxiety, a feeling of being different, of society owing him something (of being outside the law)—dominate his whole activity. By improving he can pursue his criminal aims more actively and successfully. The advantage of probation is that it tends not to have this effect because of its emphasis on a one-to-one interpersonal relationship between delinquent and probation officer. I do not suggest that all young delinquents improve in their capacity to form meaningful human relationships only to put such an improvement to subversive use via delinquent aims on a group basis, but often this does occur. We have to be careful in designing our remedial institutions so that this difficulty does not manifest itself, not least because it will be the group-oriented delinquent who tends to carry over his institutionally developed group skills into the service of a delinquent criminal organization.

The next step is to consider the dynamics and structure of the delinquent group. Generally it is composed of individuals who develop feelings of being picked on more readily than feelings of responsibility, and this colors and conditions the development of the group. There has to be leadership and the leader tends to be the individual who looks as though he will be the person most likely to be effective in helping the group to achieve its criminal aims. Splitting and projection take place, and each successful job leads to further splitting and projection. Respect and admiration develop toward the leader, while scorn and aggressiveness are directed against weaker members of the gang. The structure is based on the projection up the hierarchy toward the leadership of all positive attitudes and down the hierarchy of all the negative ones. It is not so different from what prevails among the medical and nursing hierarchies of some of our most respected general and teaching hospitals. The essential difference is that of the aims of the hospital on the one hand and those of the criminal gang on the other. The gang structure (and the nursing staff structure) is authoritarian, strictly stratified into a pecking order and based on power principles. Might is right, and the aim or objective of the criminal gang must be reached at the price of whatever ruthlessness is necessary. Feelings of compassion, conscience qualms, or a tendency to compromise with society, including its rules and standards, are regarded as a threat to the security of the gang and dealt with harshly and punitively. One of the serious consequences of a delinquent organization is that in group sharing of criminal activity there is also guilt sharing for wrong done to others. Unfortunately, there is also a tendency for competition to arise over criminal effectiveness, which always involves ruthlessness and, often, brutality. Therefore crimes perpetrated by a given delinquent group tend to escalate in severity. The splitting and polarization work so that the "out-group," that is, society, is regarded as persecutory or is devalued or in some way apotheosed as the enemy, while positive attitudes held on an authoritarian basis are reserved for the "in-group." By denying the humanity of the out-group and designating it as the enemy, alienation and brutalization take place. At each step in the processes described there is a further departure from the ordinary cultural norms of the society in which the delinquent gang is operating and less and less identification with the aims of the nondelinquent society.

Discipline is maintained within the gang by means of grouping together for gain and mutual protection. The enemy may be members of any nondelinquent organization, but in the exploitation of society at large, that is, in the practice of their predatory role, a clash between delinquent groups often occurs. Savagery erupts and may follow a logical sequence of increasing violence reaching murder. It is strange how a rival gang is designated as the out-group as far as violence is concerned in a competitive field, but as the in-group when informing the police and the judicial authorities. In a gang the use of violence as a means of coercion is an accepted principle, just as it is accepted in a war by the majority of citizens. This follows logically from the authoritarian structure—the "might is right" principle. If by any chance depressive anxiety comes into the picture and is acted on by one or more members of the gang, it constitutes a threat to the security of the gang and is ruthlessly put down. If it continues to operate, it is the beginning of the disintegration of the gang.

Some penal institutions have latched on to the principle of gang structure, and unruly, violent, atavistic offenders who formerly caused much anxiety—and, not infrequently, considerable personal injury to the staff—are curbed by their fellow prisoners under suggestive guidance from the staff. An inmate is brought into relationship with a prison officer by a combination of understanding, punishment, and reward. The prison officer, or someone in the hierarchy, then takes the place of the gang leaders. The "converted" convict is then, if so instructed, willing to curb and control any new and troublesome prisoner. The word *converted* is incorrect because there has been no change of heart and no personality development, only a change of *attachment*, and this has been used (possibly without the staff knowing the dynamics of the procedure) to establish some control over otherwise menacing and violent characters. The foregoing procedure is essential as a first step in dealing with the individual who is not particularly unstable in the sense of having a florid symptomatic behavior disorder, but who is a devoted member of a delinquent organization.

Psychotherapy as such is out of the question. The man himself would refuse it and would state that he was not a "nut case."

Instead, means of initially altering the allegiance of the man must be devised. Only then may he find increased dissatisfaction with himself such that he begins to feel uncomfortable. There may even be an efflorescence of depressive anxiety, but more usually he bogs down in persecutory anxiety, with the real risk of a violent acting out of delinquent impulses with the conscious or unconscious aim of nullifying a remedial procedure. If this does not take place, and any crises are negotiated without a savage and complete relapse re-emphasizing criminality as a way of life, the prognosis is not at all bad as far as this kind of delinquent is concerned. This kind of person does have the capacity to sustain interpersonal relationships because his basic character structure has become somewhat stabilized, albeit on a delinquent basis. Treatment is, of course, difficult; too close an identification of the therapist with the establishment can risk realienation of the delinquent in treatment, whereas without clear identification with the standards and principles of society the relationship is likely to be accepted but without alteration of aims. The subject may even believe that the therapist is a con man too: one prisoner, about to be released after a brief period of psychotherapy, said to me, "Can I do anything for you, sir?" I looked a bit bewildered and said, "What do you mean?" To my astonishment he said, "Can I beat anybody up for you?" While the criminals were in custody, the practices of this particular penal institution paid good dividends as far as peace and tranquility were concerned, but they practiced their gang patterns of behavior during their incarceration and on release, their behavior was no different from their pre-sentencing behavior except that the criminals were better organized. What is most difficult to convey to the delinquent, particularly to the delinquent who has been part of a delinquent organization, is the idea of a democratic system in which an individual can be subjected to group experiences that lead to growth, maturation, integration, and the development of a personal sense of responsibility and relatedness to other people. What often sabotages the democratic system is what is projected into its representatives, especially those identified with the establishment—for example, officers at various levels of command and responsibility within the remedial services.

It is obvious that the lower grades of the penal hierarchy tend to be more vulnerable. They are nearer the social stratum of their charges and their educational and intellectual equipment does not give them much help as a rule. Most important they spend a lot of time with the prisoners, who often pressure them into feeling isolated in a hostile milieu. Hatred of them is more direct and evident and there is often a physical risk. Consciously and unconsciously, prisoners put the staff in a difficult position by filling them with many of their own feelings—anger, hatred, cruelty, fear, and the most dangerous of all, cynicism. When possessed by powerful, unpleasant, and often bewildering feelings, the penal staff tend to resort more and more to authoritarianism. Characteristically, they take up defensive positions behind the protection of the rulebook. A few officers become identified with the prisoners, and occasionally are seriously compromised by what they do for them. A heroic minority manages to cope with the cynicism of the criminal, and with the various other unpleasant feelings put into them. They retain their humanity toward the prisoners, and at the same time remain perfectly loyal to the terms of their employment, to their own principles, and often to the standards most highly prized by society. This minority has a beneficial effect on the prisoners who are fortunate enough to be in close contact with them for relatively long periods of time.

An extension of the tendency of criminals to create the kind of group structure that they want or need takes place inside the penal institution. In some ways, a callous, cynical, brutalized authority and establishment suits the criminal from a criminal organization better than what he would term a "soft" (and what we would call a democratic) regime. The criminal can feel in the strict and authoritarian, even brutalized, setup that he is absolved from any personal responsibility to be other than callous and cynical, and he feels more relaxed in this context. He can then contemplate exploiting any mistakes and weaknesses shown by the administrative hierarchy. In other words, an institution based on persecutory anxiety is a place in which there is custody and stasis, but no development. No transactions within such an institution are worthy of being called "therapeutic."

There is a great difference between tolerance and appeasement. The former is based on depressive anxiety, and its near relations are love and compassion stemming from the life instinct. Appeasement, however, is based on persecutory anxiety, and consists of a frightened victim yielding to unreasonable demands in the hope that the appetite of the assailant will be quenched before all is lost. It is usually ineffective. In the criminal gang we are dealing with individuals who are not necessarily suffering from symptomatic behavior disorders, but who by their practices and allegiances have become brutalized. To have any impact at all, the remedial regime must be firm, but to avoid further alienation and brutalization, it must be tolerant. Boundaries must be drawn, but drawn to provide enough life space geographically and psychologically for maneuvering around and reality testing. At that juncture, in the course of what can truly be called therapeutic, a new phase of growth and development can take place. Thus the process of brutalization is put into reverse. The rehumanization process inevitably involves the individual in making an approach to and preferably also some inroads into the depressive position.

Fundamental procedures such as the ones just outlined are expensive in time, money, and effort, although perhaps less costly than lifelong management of a criminal. In some cases they fail, and even in the majority the results are not perfect. Legal and medical authorities tend to become impatient and skeptical when progress is slow. In addition, we do not know enough about the treatment of the delinquent, particularly, the person who is a member of a criminal group, gang, or organization. The resources employed to treat the neurotic criminal and (if any services are available at all) those with symptomatic behavior disorders have been all too meager. Of the total criminal population, about 60 percent suffer from neurosis and symptomatic behavior disorders. The hard core of criminal personalities thus have had virtually no treatment. Of course, the boundaries between these groups are not rigid. One gangster, who would have been regarded by everyone as a criminal personality without symptoms, has shown characteristics of a symptomatic behavior disorder with a marked proclivity to outbursts of violence during his long sentence.

When one treats *symptoms* of illness, progress may be slow, but it is nothing like the slowness that usually occurs when the character or personality of an individual is being treated. Once the disturbance is in the fabric of the personality, so to speak, therapy is always a protracted and arduous business. Trouble can flare up at any point, causing the therapy to be abandoned. There is a credit side to all this, however, in that members of a delinquent organization who have had the courage to stay the course and recover from brutalization and the many side effects of their delinquent personality have a real effect on other delinquents inside or outside the delinquent organization. In dealing with the career criminal, there is often a particular moment when he is willing to accept help with a view to altering his personality. If the opportunity is taken at that time, the prognosis may be far from hopeless because under these circumstances he can acknowledge that the treatment is for him and he invests his will in it.

18

Victims and Victimology (I)

There are individuals who evacuate seemingly unbearable states of mind into other people or into another person and then attack that person. In so doing they attack the part of themselves that has been evacuated, the part they have been unable to digest and metabolize as part of their impulse or fantasy life. After offloading it they feel relief, but this is a temporary respite, as they then feel they will be attacked by the person into whom they have evacuated the dangerous, unmanageable part of themselves. The counterattack may be by the person in receipt of the projection, or by the part which is in the projector himself or herself. This part is felt to be angry at having been gotten rid of.

Some potential victims who have been treated this way retaliate violently on their own behalf. Some, however, seem to be born victims who unconsciously, or consciously and perversely, welcome ill-treatment, even to the point of becoming murder victims. There is a distinction between the perverse masochism of finding pleasure in pain and/or the threat of pain and serious damage—in other words, a more and a less serious category. An example of the latter is the young man who persuaded some youths to crucify him in a public park. Fortunately, he was freed; only much later was it revealed that he had asked to be crucified. Some expressions of masochism, and indeed of sadism, are extremely complicated. What is happening cannot be únderstood until the unconscious fantasy constellation is pieced together. Usually the individual addicted to a particular kind of action knows only a part of the constellation, most of which is going on below the surface in the unconscious mind. Whenever in a repetitive sequence of action there is a dividend of pleasure, it takes a lot of therapy and a good deal of understanding in depth before that dividend can be renounced.

Many murderers find (or choose) their victims by means of a complex process. This applies particularly to premeditated murders. But as many workers have observed, murder occurs in external reality when it has occurred before, often many times, in phantasy. The victim may be the person encountered who most reminds the murderer of the person he has killed before in his mind. This does not apply to persons who challenge or goad the killer so that the choice depends, in these instances, on behavior rather than appearance. A special case is when, because of similarity or a delusion, the victim is drawn into the murderer's situation and murdered because of an experienced identity with the intrapsychic object of hostility. Another form is when the killer projectively identifies with a person by means of an omnipotent phantasy in which he splits off a hated or feared part of himself and kills it in the person whom he has chosen to be the receptacle for this part of himself.

The Ancient Mariner in Coleridge's poem knew at once into whom he could evacuate his distress. Having attacked the Albatross (the white breast) as the originator of his misfortunes, he soon discovered that he had killed the "good object," not the bad one. The family group consisting of the Ancient Mariner and the rest of the ship's crew were all punished "magically." They died, and the Ancient Mariner alone was sentenced to a life-in-death. This was made clear in the mirage, or hallucination, of the phantom ship with its two occupants, Death and Life-in-Death, who were seen dicing for the ship's company. They were sentenced to death while the Ancient Mariner was sentenced to life-in-death. The bad, killing mother, the hallucinated figure of Life-in-Death, was the slow killer rather than death, the quick death-dealer. The Ancient Mariner himself, that is, Coleridge, followed a mourning inadequate in length or depth, largely because it was not completed, because he evacuated his distress whenever it grew to a certain point of intensity. However, there was some mourning and when it had reached a certain point and he was able to recapture his love for some living creatures, the Albatross dropped from his neck and fell deep into the sea.

True repentance publicizes remorse, acknowledges the need for mourning, and sets the mourner free. I think the essential feature, psychically, of this part of the story was that mourning should have gone on, but instead, as soon as the Albatross sank into the sea, the Ancient Mariner (Coleridge) felt that the task was done. But it was only half-done. We must remember that the Albatross was killed by the Ancient Mariner with his crossbow, his murderous crossness as a baby, as a child, with which he attacked both the external mother and the internal mother, the ship standing for the external mother, the babies, that is, the other siblings, the ship's crew and also his unborn siblings. He was the youngest of a large family. They were all killed as well as the mother—symbolically of course. His reparation was to bless life, but it was glib and did not suffice to cause or enable him to be relieved from the periods of agony which he found to be uncontainable. Also, by evacuating his painful state of mind he failed repeatedly to use the pain in a constructive way. This tallied with the actual life of Coleridge who, despite his brilliant mind, failed to break himself of his dependency upon opium, the mitigator of pain *but* ultimately identified in its thralldom with the "Nightmare Life-in-Death" figure, "who thicks men's blood with cold." He added these lines seventeen years after the main poem was written. Part of the problem was the way in which (described by De Quincy) Coleridge never really allowed people to know how addicted he was. I don't think he really allowed himself to know. In our own present day adolescents remain gripped by drugs, especially if there is a denial of the psychic reality of drug dependency or a lack of the willingness or capacity to publicize it, that is, to admit it and to show the sincerity of effort to overcome it. The prognosis for these people is not good. This statement probably applies to addictions in general. One thinks of the prayer about true repentance, where following that, and the following through of that, there is a relief from the guilt, a forgiveness for sins. The working through of mourning then diminishes and sets the stage for recovery. When the crime is an actual murder, the process of mourning is vastly more difficult, as I have stated elsewhere. This results from the impossibility of full reparation in relation to the internal image of the person who has been killed, that is, deprived of life by the self. Coleridge, who had murderous thoughts and some token actions as far as is known, actually and concretely killed no one, but there must have been a highly concretized, murderous fantasy constellation which I think was expressed when he threw a knife at his older brother and then ran away and hid himself overnight near the River Otter not very far from his home. He was closely identified in his mind with Cain. One would have conjectured that Coleridge's poems give evidence of a good deal of mourning for the fantasy of murder, but something in the process did not suffice to restore his psychic health:

> I pass like night from land to land
> I hear strange power of speech
> That moment that my face I see
> I know the man that must hear me
> To him my tale I teach.

I have encountered this situation in many people who have murdered another person or more than one person. The quality and effectiveness of the mourning have varied a great deal. In two of those people, after serving life sentences and being released upon license, there had been adopted an almost religious ritual of mourning from half-an-hour to one hour each day. I was very impressed by both these people and the evidence of good psychic health in them. In others, where there was an obvious or much more subtle and elusive current of manic reparation in which some of the suffering of the mourning process had been bypassed, the life situation was not nearly so good. Much of this was shown in repeated "accidental" attacks upon the self, a sort of self-victimization. This could have been due to a need for concrete punishment or there could have been an element of moral masochism in it.

It was Freud who pointed out that human beings are far more moral, and also far more immoral, than any of us believed. In adolescence there is a powerful heightening of the impulse life and later of the capacity to control impulses, but the surge in intensity of the impulse life precedes the capacity to control these same impulses. These impulses are both sexual and aggressive. There is a fluctuating balance between forces derived from the life instinct and those derived from the death instinct. It is not surprising that these two powerful and opposite forces frequently get into a state of disharmony. The adolescent who can tolerate disturbing states of mind without immediately rushing to action to unburden him- or herself of accretions of stimuli is much more likely to resolve the intrapsychic turbulence than those who rush to the kind of action that causes trouble. Such action is certain to backfire, and the perpetrators end up with a virtually unresolvable situation. I am reminded of the movie *Cool Hand Luke*, in which a fairly slaphappy young plumber gets a parking ticket and uses his plumbing tools to cut down the parking meters. During his four-year prison sentence his mother becomes ill and is dying. Refused permission to see her, he escapes. In a mounting saga of increasing crime, he eludes recapture and is eventually shot dead. His continued inability to sustain or suffer a situation, whether just or unjust, had led to escalating trouble ending in death. A quite well-known British criminal had a similar defiant history although with much greater finesse, and his life ended in suicide. It was significant that before the suicide, he said, "They will not get me." This in its turn is reminiscent of the famous Pro-Hart "Waltzing Matilda" poem and song. The hero/victim, when caught, having stolen and cooked the sheep, jumps into the billabong saying, "You won't catch me alive," and proceeds to drown.

There is no satisfactory substitute for the bearing, that is, the suffering, of psychic pain. Mental health and relative normality consist of being able to suffer and sustain an adequate degree of psychic pain, that is, of getting the balance right. This necessitates a capacity for exercising judgment. It was Bion who stated that people who complain of pain but refuse to suffer it also fail to "suffer" from pleasure. If both these states occur, which is quite common in adolescence, one encounters young people suffering from boredom, ennui. One sees them in their addiction to a Walkman, not liking or suffering the world at large, and "rewarding" themselves from their personal resources, that is, from their own inner world. Here is the matrix from which addiction to antidevelopmental activities provides a pseudo escape, for example, into alcohol, drugs, glue-sniffing, petty crime, sexuality without relationship, ultimately developing into a saga of organ pleasure on a part-object basis. There is a considerable difference between tasting these measures and becoming dependent on and finally addicted to them. The final antilife drift is into disease and death, often by suicide. First, the psyche is the victim, and then the entire self.

As far as suicide is concerned, a notice put by the Samaritans on a building near the Clifton Suspension Bridge at Bristol runs as follows: "Before doing anything, do please come and talk to us." Their office is right there, on the spot. This notice homes in on the basic need, which is to think and discuss, thereby putting some kind of buffer (in its psychical sense) between impulse and action. Bion pointed out that the relationship between two people or groups of people may be commensal, symbiotic, or parasitic. In the first, commensal, the relationship is beneficial to both. In the symbiotic, one is benefited and the other sustains no harm. In the parasitic, initially the parasitizing one benefits, but later the host is damaged to the point of death which then overtakes the parasitic one as well. In biology things are somewhat more complicated. Nevertheless, if we follow these three kinds of relationship with respect to victim and victimizer, it may be helpful in our study of victimology. In addition to feeding the baby, the mother accepts raw anxieties from the baby and processes them. In a good mother–

child relationship the mother relays them back to the baby in improved form. Bion elucidates these transactions as follows: the baby has an idea and much anxiety, which could be put as: "No breast, I am going to die." This is experienced at the paranoid-schizoid position, and can be communicated to the mother or her surrogate only by projective identification. These projective identification elements are beta particles. If mother can accept these intuitively into her own psyche and subject them to her own alpha function, they can be delivered back to the baby as alpha elements, which are capable of being repressed, remembered, or stored, and are participants in dream formation. Some mothers may not be able or willing to accept the projective identification of their infants; thus there is a lack of alpha function, a paucity of alpha elements, and a considerable impairment of the ability to learn from experience. Worse still is the mother, herself suffering from a disturbance of the capacity to contain, who takes the projective identifications of her infant, strips them of meaning so that what the infant is left with, or what is sent back to the infant, is a nameless dread. The specific "No breast, I am afraid I shall die" becomes generalized into an unspecific fear of death. In my view, this later becomes expressed as an ongoing, generalized fear of death, indigestible, unmetabolizable, and, in the worst cases, uncontainable. The transformation from the paranoid-schizoid position to the depressive position is rendered more and more difficult. The lack of a holding, that is, the prevention of acting-out situations, makes almost inevitable an acting-out sequence of either a sadistic, murderous kind or of a masochistic, suicidal kind, thus making a bad situation infinitely worse. It must be stressed that what I have just described represents a relative state. Were it to be absolute, the possibility of an improved situation in response to deep and profound dynamic therapy would be remote. Perhaps in some instances it may be so, but among the patients I have seen the outlook often appears to be a good deal better than that.

There must be some transformation from the paranoid schizoid toward the depressive position, that is, from part-object relationships based on feelings of persecution toward the whole-object relationship in which there is an ability to take on some degree of responsibility. There must be a compromise situation somewhere; otherwise there would not be very much to stop every acting out ending in murder or suicide. Having described the extreme state, it is important to emphasize that far more numerous are the mixed states, as, for example, the baby who can tolerate frustration under certain circumstances and in certain situations, and is emotionally allergic to certain other ones. If the mother can contain some anxiety but has specific inability over others—for example, feeding situations—some negotiation of the depressive position takes place, but then a persecutory situation to which the particular individual is allergic results in a violent relapse into the paranoid-schizoid position again, during the throes of which some delinquent acting out takes place.

What may happen next? If the delinquent deprivations are not subjected to a mourning process, a repetition is likely with probable worsening of them. If there is manic relish in the delinquency, its bad results or effects on the victim are glossed over glibly ("the fox likes being hunted"). Worse still is a sadistic addiction to destructive parts of the self, or a sadomasochistic game of cat and mouse. Many years ago, at a university bookshop in a Canadian university, one of my sons applied for a temporary job for two or three months. The regular holder of the appointment, seemingly an intelligent adolescent 17½ years old, had been given his month's pay, had bought a gun, and, with a friend who also had a gun, had played a game of shooting at each other in a local park. The young man was killed and his friend wounded. There were no other signs of psychosis, but the fatal interaction was based on a breakdown of the capacity to symbolize and their testing of reality was grossly impaired. Reality testing should take place in the phantasy world in the mind before being committed to action. Something had gone wrong in the paranoid-schizoid- to depressive-position transformation, ricocheting back to the paranoid-schizoid position in a form of sibling rivalry that had started off by being genial, but escalated into a murderous suicidal interaction, reactivating an unmetabolized death constellation in one at least and probably in both of them.

Murderousness: Where Is It Located?

During the adolescence of two boys whose father was murdered in one of the last murders in Britain for which the convicted criminal was executed, the older one first and then the younger as he reached adolescence attended the Tavistock Clinic for psychotherapy. I supervised one of these treatments and conducted the other one with the younger son. The main theme of their dreams was that murder was located in a weapon. This had something phallic in it, consisting either of a gun or a sword or a long stick, and so on. Now whoever had this, whether it was the oedipal father or the oedipal son, wherever it was located, the potentiality and the capability of committing a murder existed. Often in the dreams of these two young men a fight took place between one of them and the father figure. Wherever the murder weapon originated, it tended to change over to belong to the other one in the course of the threat and no murder actually took place in the dream. However, at a crucial moment, when a murder might have taken place, the dreamer woke up and the whole episode was felt to be a persecutory nightmare. During treatment, the containment of the fear of being murdered and the wish to murder was psychically metabolized to a large extent, simply by repeatedly working through, and both young men recovered. There was never a Cain and Abel situation. It was entirely an oedipal situation, son killing father, or a situation in which father kills son.

Remember the case of the ill-treated, beaten, scolded, and humiliated woman who turned from making the evening meal for her husband and cut off his penis with a knife as he lay naked on the bed, abusing her with words. His words were so cutting that taking up the weapon was the consequence of an introjection of the murderously cutting penis; the retaliation was to actually cut off the persecutory cutting penis. In a peculiar way this seemed to give the marriage a lease of tenability and vitality, although we could not follow it up so there may have been recurrences.

The phallus, or the phallic object, the murder weapon, guilt, remorse, the capacity to mourn, and sexual potency are very much linked in this oedipal kind of murder. I am thinking of a particular patient who was far from overtly murderous. In fact, he had never been aware of a murderous fantasy or impulse, but while loading a heavy tree trunk onto a truck, he was asked to work the crane that lifted up the great trunk and lower it into a safe place. He was being guided by his brother and his father. The patient pulled the wrong lever and the tree trunk fell full weight, crushing the father to death. The son who was driving the crane felt overwhelmingly guilty, and also became totally impotent in his marriage. It was for this reason that he sought therapy. It was clear that he had been given a tool, an instrument, a piece of apparatus, without any training, and had been expected to know how to use it. The father had an unreasonable expectation of him. The son failed, the father was killed: it fitted in with an oedipal pattern and the son felt entirely guilty and persecuted in relationship to his mother. This was also displaced onto his wife with whom he became impotent. There is a constellation here in which some psychic digestion and metabolism has to take place, even if there is no element of perversion in the situation, before psychic health can be restored.

19

Victims and Victimology (II)

Someone said to Oscar Wilde, "Each man tries to kill the thing he hates." Wilde replied, "No, each man kills the thing he loves." Both these statements express an aspect of the truth. The hated aspect poses a threat, is experienced as a persecutor, and is a conscience arouser. It is an enemy of one's own peace of mind and of success in life. In extreme examples in literature and in history, one finds that the categories into which the activities of a nonmitigator of murderous impulses fall are few in number. Oedipus Rex, Cain and Abel, Clytemnestra and Agamemnon, followed by Orestes and Clytemnestra, all exhibit patterns that one can discern in repeated murderous actions over millennia. Roughly, they can be matched with the states of mind of the respective villains—envy, jealousy, greed, suspicion, retaliation, revenge, or, more psychologically, paranoia. In addition, there is the confusion between a hunting approach and an amorous, courtship one, as if the two currents of human endeavor had not been sufficiently differentiated. At base, the problem in Shakespeare's *Othello* demonstrates the military dilemma: how to proceed, from within a warm, "homosexual" pattern of military comradeship, to a quite different kind of pattern, that of family relations and development. Under "attack"—a military kind of attack by Iago—Othello resorts to a military ruthlessness in his attempt to settle his domestic problems, but is tactically outmaneuvered by Iago.

Herring gulls have to learn each year the difference between a territorial threat when the males have already marked out their respective territories and an approach by a female bird with a view to sharing the territory for mating purposes and raising their young. Apparently it takes ten to fourteen days to get this issue straight and to establish firm pairing bonds. In a number of sexual offenses by disturbed people, some of which ended fatally, this confusion between hunting down and wooing seemed to be the main problem. Some of this was because hunter and quarry have a different viewpoint, or *vertex*, as Bion called it, from each other. A young man thrown out by an attractive girl slunk away saying, "It's not fair. She won't play." In the field of so-called sport, for example, fox hunting, one hears as a reason for continuing the sport that "The fox loves it as much as we do." This sounds uncommonly like projection, the ascription to another creature of an attitude of the self. A man convicted of terrorizing nanny goats—a euphemism for sexual relations with them—said to me: "It was quite untrue. They were not frightened. They liked it. At least they experienced no painful sadistic behavior."

Assailant-victim interaction has been likened to a dance of death, and in many if not most cases in the United Kingdom there has often been a complicated interaction over a long time. Straight, sudden, savage attacks on an unknown victim are different. They occur when a massive stimulus results in an angry, excited, murderous assault. Sometimes the roles are reversed and the victim designate counterattacks and overcomes the aggressor. On the other hand, victims may pursue their own destruction with what looks like the inevitability of Greek tragedy. An attractive, older man told his wife that he was going to leave her. She reacted by clinging to him, but her fatal mistake was to threaten that she would never let him go. He knew that she had information that could get him into serious trouble if she publicized it. She had no intention of doing this, nor had she any intention of letting him go. She then disappeared and was found some days later. She had been shot but had died of drowning. The husband disappeared but was caught later over another matter. She could easily have saved herself, but only on conditions she neither would nor could accept.

Another woman who was a victim designate was attacked by her petulant husband because he had been given some narcissistically wounding news regarding his family of origin. He put his hands around her throat and began to strangle her. She managed to grab an umbrella from the hall stand and proceeded to prod him with its metal point until he loosened his grip. She then beat him with the umbrella until he cried for mercy. Next she opened the front door and pushed him down the steps with her foot as the neighbors jeered. He disappeared, but ten days later the deserted wife brought a parcel containing an effigy of herself in sausage meat with skewers stuck in vital places. At the time I thought it was an ominous threat, but as the weeks and months passed by she heard and saw nothing of her husband. I gradually came to think that this was a token action instead of a lethal one. The victim designate had saved her life but not her marriage.

One of the most curious reversals was the case of Marwood, one of the last men to be executed for murder in the United Kingdom. I did not see him, so all I have to go on are the reports that he was disturbed. Apparently he was going straight after earlier violent behavior. On his wedding anniversary he was restless and eventually went on a solitary walk, unfortunately armed with his sheath knife. In Seven Sisters' Road, London, he encountered a group of teenaged boys attacking a policeman. His stated feelings were that he intended to go to the aid of the policeman, but with no awareness of any change of mind he found himself knifing the policeman in the back. If we are to believe this story and Marwood's confused identifications, loyalties, and state of disequilibrium that evening, I think the account he gave did sound like the truth. He must have switched in the way a son of mine once demonstrated: "Bad boy shot good bird," he said; then, not many minutes later, "Good boy shot bad bird." What this switch illustrates is the capacity for a change in direction of action when splitting is the predominant psychic mechanism. In the case of Marwood, there must have been massive splitting and probably an early infantile confusion between good and bad. I would conjecture that the splitting was oscillating between his old delinquent self and his new, married-man, adult identification. He started off with a flimsy adult identification when consciously intending to rescue the policeman, only to revert to an identification with the hoodlums, showing them what ruthlessness he could summon up. He was executed.

The reverse or almost the reverse of the Marwood case was that of the compulsive incendiarist discussed in earlier chapters, serving his third prison sentence. After a period of psychotherapy with me, he was able to *control* his incendiarism for a year or so after his release, but then got drunk one night and set a building on fire. While serving his five-year sentence he saved a prison officer under attack by three prisoners and spent some months in the prison hospital. At the end of his sentence all impulses to burn things seemed to have disappeared. So different was he that his wife, who had divorced him years previously, remarried him, and his children welcomed his return to the family.

It all sounds too good to be true. What happened was a massive switch across a split, enabling him to get into contact with and become the person we had always thought he could become. But where is the snag? Could he switch back? I think he could, because the incendiaristic, destructive enclave, though weakened, had not been resolved. What actually happened was that after a warm and friendly meeting with me, he had a coronary thrombosis, and the next time I saw him he was in the hospital. Apart from the threat to his life posed by the thrombosis, things generally went well with him, but I did have the feeling that the fires had gone inside him, and now constituted a threat to his existence.

20

Drugs: Dependence on an Unreliable Container

In considering an individual drugtaker, one is confronted with a need to consider preexisting psychopathy, character structure, and the development of that person. There is also the need to discern and study the modifications that have resulted from the effect of the drug(s) taken over time.

Even before the efflorescence of drug use in modern societies, authorities such as Simmel, Rado, Glover, and others, working as far back as the 1930s, recognized several constant characteristics that could be delineated and agreed upon:

1. The psychic use to which the drug is put is more important than the choice of the drug itself.
2. The underlying cyclothymic personality of the user is significant, but it is generally agreed that it is not quite like manic-depressive illness. The foregoing workers, and later, in 1960, Herbert Rosenfeld, underlined certain similarities but also differences between the drug addict and the manic depressive.
3. The struggle between life and death instincts was tilted toward death, but in the main, the conflict remained unresolved.

Rosenfeld, in his 1960 paper "Drug Addiction," states that the addict cannot be successfully psychoanalyzed without reaching back to an early phase of life during which the wide separation between the present, gratifying breast (or its substitute) and the absent, frustrating, and depriving breast resulted in a polarization between good and bad. This led to idealization and denigration and, in the most extreme cases, according to my experience, deification and demonization.

This over-wide primary splitting occurs before and during the phase of dominance by paranoid-schizoid anxieties and the paranoid-schizoid position. It imposes much more difficult problems of integration at the depressive position and hence the development of whole-object relationships as a result of reaching and tolerating work at the depressive position. The same kind of wide splitting before and during the paranoid-schizoid position and the difficulty in negotiating the depressive position can be seen in most really disturbed and violent criminals. As in criminals, the fantasies of drug addicts tend to be cruel, destructive, and violent. This tallies with Klein's work on criminal fantasies in normal children.

Drug addicts share a tendency to act out with criminals-to-be. It is because of the poor and inadequate tolerance and negotiation of the depressive position that their criminal fantasies do not become subject to a mini-mourning process. Fantasies that go on to be acted out in token or in full necessitate a more substantial and longer-sustained mourning for satisfactory developmental processes to ensue.

The process of mourning necessitates a containing mother who can accept the burden of the communication of the infant or child, hold it and do some work on it (Bion 1962), and then send it back to the infant or child in a state sufficiently improved for the infant to accept it and continue to work on it. Before the mother or her surrogate worked on it inside herself, there had been an impasse in the infant. This is reminiscent of Winnicott's concept of a good enough mother, which implies that a mother of a difficult child has to find more resources within herself to deal adequately with that particular child.

Coleridge was said to have been a difficult child, both brilliant and violent. For example, in a contretemps with one of his brothers, he threw a knife at the latter and was ostracized by his parents and other siblings. Unable to tolerate this, the young Samuel ran away from home and spent a cold, frightening night by the River Otter near Exeter in Devon. The local squire found him the next morning and took the forlorn 7-year-old back home. His clergyman father, instead of being the severe superego father he could be, greeted him lovingly and all was forgiven. This incident showed the character difficulty that haunted Coleridge's life. Laudanum, which he became addicted to, instead of easing his problem of working through the depressive position, led to a widening of splitting between an idealized part object and a denigrated one. Coleridge showed himself to be insightful, but unable to withstand the psychic pain involved in freeing himself from the tyranny of his narcotic, transient reliever of pain. Laudanum was a totally inadequate container for his anxieties.

I have observed that if one cannot help liking an addict, the transference in general, and the projective identification in particular, seem to be more tolerable. This does not mean that there is collusion between the analyst/therapist and the destructive parts of the patient. Rather, I think it is a sign that the life instinct is not entirely subordinated by the ravages of the death instinct. During a long treatment, of course, the situation can fluctuate dramatically. As Bion (1967b) stated, no one likes analytic change while it is actually taking place. Rosenfeld (1960) emphasized how each major step in the reintegration of the ego of the addict is followed by an increase in the sort of acting out that brings the risk of a violent relapse from the depressive position back to the paranoid-schizoid position with its splitting and tendency toward projective identification. The constructive use of restored parts of the self only follows a kind of underpinning of the newly liberated aspects in relationship to their normal functioning. Fluctuations from improvement to relapse, and vice versa, occur commonly during the course of a drug addict's analysis. One example of this is Patient A, an intelligent and sometimes cooperative man with a long history of opium addiction. At one point he was off all drugs and very excitable, with a restless liveliness not far from persecution. Returning from a session with me, he found words forming in his mouth: "I would rather cut my throat through to the bloody bone than let that fellow Williams make me better." This was the start of a relapse, but that too was able to be dealt with as he switched away from absolute negativity fairly soon after the event. When the balance between life and death instincts is tilted away from life to a greater extent than in Patient A, the outcome tends to be quite different. Again, Coleridge acquired a peculiarly deep insight into what he referred to as "Death and Life-in-Death" in his image of the phantom ship that appeared to the Ancient Mariner as a mirage or hallucination. When Death and Life-in-Death played dice for his soul and the souls of his shipmates, Death won his shipmates; Life-in-Death won the Ancient Mariner himself. This poem was written in 1798. In 1817, nineteen years later, when the Ancient Mariner had failed to help Coleridge break the stranglehold that opium exerted upon him, Coleridge altered the passage to:

> Her skin was as white as leprosy,
> The Nightmare Life-in-Death was she,
> Who thicks man's blood with cold. [III, st. 11]

While Patient A oscillated for some years, the outcome was good and life won. Patient B, a man with a first-class honors degree from one of the older universities, had had at least fifty trips with LSD, which had, as he put it, "blown my mind." Although he emerged apparently physically fit, he could hold down his job, which consisted of opening and closing a lock on a much-used inland waterway, only with difficulty, reflecting his condition, which was, psychically, a stalemate. Patient C was much worse. He too had taken a concatenation of drugs—cannabis, amphetamines, cocaine, morphine, heroin—and many unremembered trips on LSD. He too said that LSD was the drug that had blown his mind and his brain. I had a holding brief as far as his treatment was concerned and was able to make some contact with him while he awaited long-term therapy with one of my colleagues. After a few weeks, during which he seemed to improve (a suspect early improvement), he became totally inaccessible (while denying any drugtaking). One day he telephoned me suddenly at the Tavistock Clinic and said that if I did not get to him within forty-five minutes, he would blow his brains out. I told him that it was physically impossible for me to guarantee any time like that, but as the rush-hour traffic would be less dense coming into London, I would see him immediately if he came to me. He agreed to this arrangement after a lot of argument, but thirty minutes later his father telephoned and said that his son had blown his brains out and had shot at two friends who tried to stop him. Here was a savage, lethal counterattack by an intrapsychic, pathological organization galvanized by the death instinct, determined to annul and prevent forever any improvement. I found out later that though his condition had improved in the few weeks of holding therapy, he had lied and had been on drugs all the time. Patient B had reached a compromise situation in that he had kept his life but lost what he referred to as his mind. He had lost some of his essential humanity, as well as his ability to use his well-trained intellect, because of an inability to tolerate psychic pain against which he had developed what might be termed an allergic response.

An intensely manic response, which I observed in another Patient, D, led not to a grotesque outcome or suicide as in Patient C, but to increasingly bold actions that showed no sign of responsibility or exercise of judgment. These responses can lead to violence with others, and/or risks to the self. Patient D did in fact end up in prison for irresponsible driving offenses.

Ruthless Pursuit of Supplies of the Drug

It is this kind of bold, ruthless personality that is to be found among drug pushers, who acquire a sort of confident cunning in their enterprises. There is always a danger, however, of slippage or of a bursting beyond the boundaries and committing, for example, murder or a number of murders in the quest for drugs and/or profits from the sale of drugs.

The drug-using group phenomenon in Western Europe and America is an important development during the past generation. The adverse consequences of a group sharing in regressed behavior have had ill effects on certain types of crime, but even more suicidally disastrous has been the sharing of dirty syringes and a concomitant contamination with the HIV virus. What will happen in the next generation is difficult to predict. My experience of opium-addicted Indian soldiers in World War II in Burma would suggest that some sort of nondisastrous equilibrium might be reached. These opium-dependent men developed the usual withdrawal symptoms in circumstances in which their supplies were not available. One of them explained that he was dependent on opium, as were his parents and grandparents, but that with a fixed supply he was not ill. He challenged me to test what hard work he could do if I gave him a supply. He was right, and I discovered that in this situation there did exist an equilibrium, and that in certain parts of India it was not uncommon. What this suggests is that factors such as profound social disapproval may have the effect of raising the paranoid, furtive attitudes of Western European and American addicts.

In its severe forms, overconsumption of alcohol is recognized as a strong factor in much crime, including murder. Some years ago an article in the *British Journal of Psychiatry* stated that murder in Scotland was almost always associated with alcoholic intoxication. We get some idea of a dangerous drug *not* associated with general social disapproval from the way in which there is a tendency to diminish the blame attached to alcohol as a crime-facilitating agent, whereas there is a tendency possibly to even exaggerate the effect of other drugs in the etiology of crime.

Truth and a capacity to sustain it during the experience of psychic pain has a crucial and in my opinion decisive effect on the prognosis, especially in response to psychoanalysis or other psychodynamic therapies. Patient A was a person with violently intense impulses, often destructive and sometimes reparative. He could lose contact with truth, but would regain it and sustain the pain both of abstinence from the drug and of facing the need for ongoing reparation in relation to his damaged good objects, intrapsychic and interpersonal. This could be expressed in a number of ways. Despite the pressure of persecutory anxieties and the urge toward action to quell persecution, he retained a compassionate heart and thus a capacity to give and receive love. Patient C had a disturbingly variable drug-dependent mother with whom he was closely identified. I think that she constituted for him what for Coleridge was the seductive, menacing nightmare Life-in-Death figure who "thicks man's blood with cold." Patient C could not detoxify the internal image of his mother. A little dynamic psychotherapy mobilized some positive features in him, but also reactivated the full menace of the nightmare Life-in-Death mother image in his psyche. He then proceeded to kill, to annihilate her in his mind, and posed me with the impossibly Herculean task of getting to him in rush hour in too short a time. I think that I was apotheosed as the father, the somewhat inadequate father, trying to help, but with the task of combating a tidal wave rather than a rough sea.

Turning from the basic preaddictive personality to the pharmacotoxic effects of drugtaking, there is a great variation, for example, between the immediate, almost orgiastic, relaxation after an intravenous injection of heroin—which seems temporarily and for all too short a time to quell all emotional needs—and the effects of LSD. LSD opens up a bewildering, kaleidoscopic panorama of sense impressions—uncontrollable, vivid, sometimes enjoyable, and sometimes terrible. It is as though the lid of Pandora's box had been torn open so that the individual undergoing the experience has had his or her mind blown open, as two of the patients actually said.

The idea, at least the conscious idea that motivated the drug taking of some of the Romantic and early Victorian poets, was to enrich their capacity to write poetry by opening up their intrapsychic resources by means of the drug. At first this did seem to happen, but just as a phase of depression, sometimes depressive nihilism, follows the transcendental experience immediately after the drug, so the disillusionment accumulated in time to again become "the Nightmare Life-in-Death who thicks man's blood with cold." There are hints that Keats had tried out drugs through some of his references—"Or emptied some dull opiate to the drains/One minute past and lethe-wards have sunk" in "Ode to a Nightingale"; in "La Belle Dame Sans Merci" he describes a beautiful infatuation with a terrible letdown until he ends, "And I awoke and found me there/On the cold hillside."

This could have portrayed symbolically the phase of idealization of hope that the magical substance could work, and then the frightful disillusionment and the slide into loneliness and despair. The more terrifying aspect following the magic of the initial drugs experience is stated clearly in Coleridge's "Kublai Khan," written immediately after an opium-induced sleep:

> And weave a circle round him thrice
> And look on him with holy dread,
> For he on honeydew hath fed
> And drunk the milk of paradise.

The decline in quality of life and work affects both output and capacity, and every human relationship, first in the more refined aspects, then in the everyday decencies. Little wonder that in a curious kind of noncaring despair dirty syringes may be used and sometimes HIV infection invited to complete the slide toward death. Even Patient A drifted near the destructive brink at times when, in an angry, self-reproachful state of mind, he would dissolve the morphia tablets in water taken from the lavatory pan. Had it not been for antibiotics, he undoubtedly would have died.

The issue of "getting off drugs" is made difficult because the whole self is required to sustain the work needed. The P/S → D transformation has to be made repeatedly. It is an unconsciously induced process, as one woman patient, herself addicted to barbiturates, stated clearly by stressing: "I sometimes feel persecuted, and sometimes depressed, but whole. Both states are painful, but I do not choose which to be. It just happens." A drug like methadone, in the small number of patients I have seen who used it to withdraw from opiates, stops bringing dreams. Unconscious communications also seem blunted, almost shut down, in fact. They seemed to go into a kind of emotional limbo.

Use of such means could be justified in the course of getting off drugs. In a state of progressively intensifying need, without resorting to drugs, an analysis can in some circumstances proceed with the analyst serving as a replacement for the drug; thus the addiction is transferred to the therapist and away from a chemical substance. This is a hard and exacting task, as workers and writers about drug addiction emphasize—hard for the analyst/therapist, the patient, and the people who have to deal with the patient outside the treatment situation. The patient is likely to recover with gain, not loss, in total human quality if the situation can be sustained. I have never seen this state as a result of any kind of treatment other than psychoanalysis.

When one reviews the work on drug and to some extent alcohol addiction, there is general agreement among the earlier workers regarding the intolerance of frustration that increases as the stranglehold of the drug gets tighter. Simmel, Rado, Glover, and later Rosenfeld agreed on the underlying cyclothymic rhythm of which the drug-taking individual is intolerant, the precarious balance between life and death instincts (which in most cases gets more and more tipped toward the death instinct as the addiction increases). Rosenfeld, however, pointed out that the origin of the character prone to addiction was much earlier, namely, as stated briefly at the beginning of this chapter, at the phase of primary differentiation between the good, gratifying breast and the bad, frustrating breast. This gives an early and adequate point from which the relatively healthy individual and the person prone to or liable to become addicted deviate, so that the gap widens with each subsequent challenge that is evaded or met in an antidevelopmental way.

In general, drugs are taken for one or more of the following five reasons.

1. Conformity to the practice of a group of people, for example, a peer group

2. The relief of physical or psychic pain
3. The quest for an ineffable experience of pleasure
4. Control by the individual of a wide amplitude of mood swings from depression to elation (the drug-taking tends to be reinforced on the way down the slope from elation to depression, ultimately substituting a different rhythm of moods Rado called the pharmacogenic rhythm for the cyclothymic rhythm the individual found so difficult to manage)
5. The pursuit of magical substances

Ultimately, addiction is a state initiated by an intolerance of frustration; this takes us back to Freud's (1911b) paper, "The Two Principles of Mental Functioning," which promulgates a tolerance or intolerance of frustration as the decisive factor in the development of reality testing and ultimately of reality sense. Bion (1963, 1967b, 1970) elaborated and extended Freud's views about the pleasure principle and the reality principle, and the development of the ability to suspend action while a situation is tried out in fantasy in the relatively safe harbor of the inner world. This enhances the capacity to learn from experience. People who are easily caught in the toils of an omnipotent substance, a drug, seem to be particularly susceptible to this developmental obstacle. The thrall of the drug involves initial satisfaction of orgiastic intensity. Its aftermath, which is painful and extremely difficult to tolerate without further resort to the drug, compounds the original difficulties, becoming the "Nightmare Life-in-Death," or, as Keats said, "La Belle Dame Sans Merci."

Problems of Treatment of Drug-Takers

The inability to tolerate psychic pain, whether due to paranoid or depressive anxiety, creates a tendency to act out. The most available form of acting out is relapse into further drug-taking. It is also tempting to make suicide attempts or, less frequently, to commit homicide. Accident-proneness is common. Self-inflicted wounds are widespread. Not caring about or even deliberately injecting oneself with dirty needles is commonplace. In therapy, as improvement increases guilt and remorse, so is there then a savage attack on the improvement as a causal factor in heightening psychic pain. Symptoms are likely to increase, and sleeplessness can be troublesome. The patient may be unable to work. Rosenfeld states that the problem originates extremely early, that is, in the first few months of life, and that not until these early anxieties have been revealed and worked through in the transference can the patient make a durable advance toward recovery. On the way to this state, however, there can be serious disturbances of judgment that may be generalized or highly specific. One of the medically qualified patients I treated was working in a therapeutic unit for insulin coma therapy for patients suffering from schizophrenia. It was noted that he got into difficulties in stopping the comas more frequently than is usual on such a unit. Only later was it found that this particular doctor was himself taking narcotics by injection almost every day. Simmel referred to the identification, during analysis, of the addicted patient with the analyst, and told how one of his patients went on a lecture tour as Dr. Simmel. One of my patients signed my name on the prescription for the drug of his addiction, believing I was addicted to it too.

Nowadays there is a tendency to spread the use of drugs or a particular drug not solely by a pusher trying to make money, but by a person proselytizing ambivalently. This recruitment procedure is designed partly to inculcate, partly to increase the group, and partly to attempt by projective identification to evacuate the individual drug pusher/addict's own state of emotional imprisonment by the drug into someone else. Most of the main writers on the management and treatment of drug-takers/pushers have stated that the personalities are cyclothymic but not quite manic depressive. The mood swings are not exactly typical of manic depressive illness, although they can show some similarities. In one person I treated, a manic phase became so high as to render it frightening and the opiate was taken to stop the excitement, which threatened to get wildly out of hand. As the patient described it: "Everything became too bright and I became aware that my judgment was impaired, so I stopped it by taking a large dose of morphia." The amplitude of the swings between the elated and depressed states was persecutory. He felt completely thrown by the mood changes, and the drug reportedly quieted the turbulence and restored some kind of psychic equilibrium. Too much of the drug was usually taken, of course, and a downswing followed. Nobody seems to doubt that drug-dependent or -addicted people are difficult to treat and pose a grave problem to anyone who attempts to treat them by means of psychoanalysis, but if Rosenfeld's recommendations are carried out, especially regarding the analysis of very early anxiety situations between the paranoid-schizoid and depressive positions, the analysis stands a chance of success, especially later during the approaches to the depressive position.

It is important to stress that amenability to sustained improvement finally depends on the capacity of the patient to tolerate frustration, tension, and psychic pain without rushing for the magical relief of drugs. This ability is contingent on the capacity of the analyst or therapist to understand, contain, and clarify the anxieties of the patient over a long period. I believe that the patient has to establish within him- or herself an adequate structure intrapsychically, based on identification with the analyst/therapist. There is evidence in these patients that this was not adequately achieved in early life, and its establishment later is no light task for the patient, or his or her therapeutic catalyst.

21

Countertransference in the Psychotherapy of Violent Prisoners

A prison provides a firm, external containment barrier against escape in a physical sense. Outside prison, family ties may be nonexistent, weak, constrictive, or punitive. In therapy, one comes across problems arising in the patient or in the psychotherapist or psychoanalyst arising from within themselves. Problems can stem from a therapist's mistaken responses to a patient's problem, lack of understanding on the part of the therapist, or lack of willingness or ability to tolerate necessary degrees of psychic pain on the part of the person being treated.

The patient may become paranoid and refute the work the therapist is trying to carry out. The therapist may assume an arrogant, patronizing, or didactic attitude unacceptable to the patient. Or the superego aspect may be overstressed so that the patient despairs or rebels. An overemphasis of moral aspects in a judgmental way can be antidevelopmental and certainly antitherapeutic. Sometimes a total rebellion is displayed by a retaliatory orgy of criminal or other antidevelopmental activities. How do these perpetuate a state of mind? The function of the following needs to be taken into account:

1. The destructive part of the self
2. Any sexual perversion present in the index patient
3. A tilt toward death in the balance between life and death instincts
4. The effect of envy, conscious or unconscious

Treatment management needs to include psychotherapy, which will usually involve supervision or regular consultation with colleagues. Further treatment considerations will need to take into account the roles of:

1. temporary in-patient facilities
2. caregivers, guardians, and continuity figures
3. organizations such as Delinquents Anonymous, dangers of positive aspects, *training* for criminality rather than its control
4. the probation services
5. If the pathology is located primarily in the individual, individual therapy is recommended. If a family or social pathology predominates, family or group therapy is indicated, at least for one phase of the treatment and/or rehabilitation.
6. Case history as it unfolds. Cynicism, narcissistic character organization, reversal of values, avoidance of psychic pain, refusal to mourn bad deeds already done, are among adverse factors. Offloading onto other criminals, criminal proselytization, paranoid attitudes.

Countertransference in the Psychotherapy of Violent Persons

Is violence, as Bismarck referred to war, an extension of "diplomacy"? Does it result from an inability or limited ability to contain violent feelings and impulses? Is there a tilting of the balance from the life instinct to the death instinct? Is there a chronic or acute preponderance of paranoid attitudes? Does the individual spring from a family, and possibly a wider milieu, characterized by a rush to action rather than an ability to negotiate? How different is the outcome of issues subjected to the process of reality testing from those over which there is an immediate unburdening of the self, of "accretions of stimuli"? Freud (1920) calls this the pleasure principle. I would reword it somewhat and call it "the flight from psychic pain."

Two of Melanie Klein's discoveries, discussed in previous chapters, are helpful in understanding what happens in intolerable states of mind, in countertransference terms. One is the P/S ↔ D transformation from aggrievement to responsibility and regret. The other is projective identification (Klein 1946) in which parts of the subject are split off and mentally put into other people, especially the therapist. These projective identifications can be used to influence the object, as an evacuation into the object to proselytize or to parasitize the other person: more healthily, after residing in the object for a while, they can be taken back by the subject or given back by the object.

Bion (1967a) stresses the long-term effects of a mother (or her surrogate) who, by depriving the baby-child of a normal receipt of amounts of projective identification, inhibits development in the child so that he or she becomes incapable of coping inside him- or herself with what otherwise would become projective identification or acting out. In the absence of this apparatus, the individual continues to evacuate states of mind he or she cannot cope with. Paramount is the evacuation into the psychotherapist or analyst. This may lead to a refutation or blocking by the therapist of the therapeutically necessary transmission of projective identification by the patient. It may lead to a detonation into the action that the patient becomes impelled to carry out, but instead puts it into the psychotherapist, hopeful of receiving back understanding. If the psychotherapist *can* work on the projective identification and then relay it back to the patient in a safer, modified form, an important therapeutic transaction will have occurred. In the course of therapy, this transaction will need to be repeated many times in response to a host of projective identifying communications.

Things can go wrong. The psychotherapist may *act out* what has been put into him. The projective identification may be refuted in a superego-ish way and the patient then feels not only misunderstood, but reproached and criticized. Worse still, the psychotherapist may miss the fundamental meaning of the communication at a time when a large part of the patient may want to control or modify his actions. There can then be a resentful intensification of an impulse to perpetrate a delinquent act, maybe with escalating violence.

Another risk to the psychotherapist or analyst is that he or she is stimulated, tempted, or goaded into his or her own delinquent tendencies—not as a result of what the patient has put into the psychotherapist, but through a kind of unconscious rivalry with the patient. Fortunately, this is not common. This acting out may be sexual and an expression of the life instinct, while that which the patient has put into the therapist by projective identification may be suffused with the death instinct, so that a favorable but unwise reversal may occur. More seriously, the patient has not been understood in a conscious way: the meaning of his actions is therefore not clear to him.

Another manifestation of countertransference is an opting out on the part of the psychotherapist via a state of bewilderment, excessive anxiety, or, sometimes, disappointment leading to therapeutic nihilism. Among such feelings can sometimes be one of dislike for a prisoner or violent patient because the crime he or she has committed touches on a specific area of sensitivity for the therapist, a sort of Achilles' heel. Quite often the need for further personal psychoanalysis becomes evident to the psychotherapist/psychoanalyst and sometimes the therapist's need is clear to colleagues. At other times supervision suffices to open up a logjam or roadblock of the personal emotional development of the therapist. I myself have experienced both. After a meaningful and taxing therapeutic transaction with a violent criminal patient, the worker should allow time for his or her own psychic digestion and metabolism to restore equilibrium. I once emerged from a prison to rush to a meeting at the Tavistock Clinic. A rather aggressive van driver blocked my way for no good reason and I pressed my horn aggressively and in a prolonged way. He stopped and got out of his vehicle; I inflicted upon him some abusive language. Then, when he became violently enraged, I realized that I had identified with the violent prisoner whom I had last seen and was acting out, that is, evacuating a disturbing and disturbed state of mind on the van driver. So much for immediate and acute transactions. There are more chronic and insidious risks. These can be recognized in one's fantasies and in dreams and identifications with prisoners or the authorities. Roughly speaking, there are two groups of reactions: one lies on the side of the impulses and the other on the side of the control of impulses, that is, the superego, law, and the demand for good behavior.

One kind of delinquent, and a very diffuse kind to treat by psychotherapy or psychoanalysis, is the person who has excessively strong impulses and at the same time a punitive, persecutory conscience. Freud's view was that psychopaths have weak consciences; Melanie Klein drew attention to the fact that, on the contrary, they have very strong consciences. It is a persecutory conscience and often unbearably cruel, and it sometimes acts as a goad rather than a guide. In therapy the psychotherapist may be seen as overstrict; only after much psychotherapy does the prisoner realize that it is he or she who is overstrict—exactly as he or she imagines the therapist to be. The opposite of setting up the psychotherapist as a moral, possibly idealized superego figure is when the prisoner/patient attempts to embroil the psychotherapist in some sort of delinquency. At the milder end of this is the request to the psychotherapist to post a letter, or something like it, when he leaves from the prison. The strict boundaries of the prison regime can be used as a very claustrophobic experience or, contrariwise, as a safe containment of impulses that can provide some security, which, in a number of therapeutic transactions, can facilitate the developmental processes without risk of their self-sabotage. One prisoner/patient who had progressed well while in prison found upon release that the loss of boundaries posed him with great problems of containment. Though himself not Jewish, he became the all-purpose handyman in a kibbutz, thus replacing his strange feeling of uncontainedness with the nonpersecutory boundary of a benign, open prison, or so it seemed to him. He had a dream that, had I recognized it, would have forecast the situation. In this dream lockers opened on both sides, one side looking inward to a benign, restrictive environment in which all wants were satisfied (this, of course, would be the womb). But there was no reverse direction, and if escape was attempted, the atmosphere deteriorated markedly. Release was possible only when the secrets of "managing" a series of strong rubber bands, which became dangerous when they were stretched, had been solved. I think this refers to the fact that he was a contingency criminal, dangerous when stretched; then the intrinsic characteristic was to let go by behaving like a catapult. Also, sadly, it had resulted in his being put inside for a stretch of time. The boundary of the prison worked in two ways: by acting as a limit-setting procedure and also as a pressure cooker so that issues could be worked on in a smaller, artificial world enclosed within its perimeter. The way ahead therefore would seem to be the making of each prison, or at least a large proportion of prisons, into versions of therapeutic communities. This would be expensive in terms of resources, but far less so than the totality of the cost of crime, much of which is unnecessary. What I have been recommending has to some extent taken place already.

In a paper I wrote in 1971 ("Risks to the Worker in Dealing with Disturbed Adolescents"), I tried to define some of the roles of workers with disturbed adolescents, some of whom could be described as criminals already or criminals in the making. Guardians, caregivers, and continuity figures were designated. The workers were thought to be able to fulfill two of the roles but all three only sometimes. For example, a prison governor, essentially a guardian, can also be a continuity figure. A caregiver, that is, a prison hospital doctor or nursing officer, can be a caregiver and a continuity figure. When not in a residential institution, a probation officer may take on all three roles, but changes in his or her role must be worked on openly in the presence of his or her charge.

The guardian figure sets boundaries and limits, and contains anxieties. He also gives directions and orders. The caregiver deals with personal or group issues that need to be sorted out. The continuity figure provides a sense of ongoing involvement, as in a family. These three roles, well articulated, lead to a satisfactory degree of stability. They lend stability to the organization and security to the persons who reside within the perimeter or who depend upon it. In the tortuous realm of crime and delinquency, stable—that is to say honest and sincere—workers provide a matrix or a cultural medium in which personal growth may occur. It does not always happen like this. There can be destructive attacks, sometimes stemming from envy, sometimes with conscious malice and sometimes entirely unconsciously motivated. I once went to see my prisoner/patients and found that all rapport seemed to have gone. On the previous occasion, I had been on relatively good terms with them and I asked several of them what had happened. They said, "Oh, the other psychiatrist has been getting at us." I thought of my colleagues and considered that this was highly unlikely. Then I said, "Well, tell me about this other psychiatrist." They said, "Well, you see it's the doctor that's doing time for doping dogs." Well, it wasn't too difficult to debunk the authenticity of that person, who had attempted to undermine our work.

In coping with and endeavoring to provide a developmental experience for delinquents and criminals, one must not expect smooth progress. Attacks on the process are inevitable. These can be handled on a one-to-one, personal, therapeutic level, at a group level, and/or at an institutional level. The aim of attacks, at least unconsciously, is to destroy the will to help, to abdicate from growing responsibility, and to drift back into a sense of aggrievement. In other words, the blame can be shifted onto the system, the organization and/or key workers within it. That it is sabotage, however, is evident. Between two persons, the therapist and the delinquent patient, interactions are much more discernible and can be interpreted. The insight-giving or insight-developing process may be gained by interpretation. However, in a residential community other factors, such as the example that staff give by their own behavior, are of great importance. At this point discipline, which originally meant leadership by example, is of paramount importance in that there is in the residential community an opportunity to observe the example set by staff members. What takes place is an identification with them or with a particular emphasis on one or more staff members, and does not consist of "a dose of conscience medicine." This is introjected at an ego level unless the patient is very rejecting of what gets into him or her in this way. In most cases the positively developmental elements tend not to be demolished catastrophically. If they are, the attacks are usually recognizable by the peer group. Caricature is a common way of ridiculing one or more staff members, and sometimes the recognition of what is happening gives the staff members themselves opportunities to change.

It was Glover (1960) who labeled criminality a consequence of failure to tame man, a half-wild animal. Taming consists of investing the selves of those of criminal personality with a different philosophy and a new system of life, and ideally of their being integrated with it and continually becoming it. But first the criminal core based on aggrievement and retaliation has to be detoxicated.

Some individuals and groups set out to resist change by the use of negative factors by which favorable changes can be inhibited and avoided, or set into reverse. They behave like unwilling prisoners of war, or prisoners of their good objects. This attitude occurs because of a paranoid, suspicious outlook or because of a loyal identification with bad objects. This may be near the heart of brutalization. One is reminded of Macbeth in Shakespeare's play: "Badness, be thou my good." This was largely to carry out the instructions of his wife, who later got cold feet and killed herself, while Macbeth became more and more brutalized, though disturbed and hallucinated, and clearly psychotic.

A differentiation can be made between criminality and response and obedience to bad objects, bad parental or authority figures, and the ebullient criminal activity that bursts out of the individual: "Satan finds some mischief still/For idle hands to do."

A third kind of criminality is personal, selfish, either arrogant or vengeful, or a mixture of these factors. Little wonder that staff working with these powerful perpetrators of crime can be at risk:

1. from criminal proselytization
2. from projective identification of criminal activities into them

3. from being goaded into counterattack involving resort to criminal means (e.g., some of the complaints against the police)
4. through muddling the worker
5. through the concretization of a fantasy constellation (compare, for example, the Loeb–Leopold case portrayed in the film *Rope*)

Let us examine these factors in more detail:

1. Criminal proselytization acts by exciting and suggesting that substitutes for criminality are not the real thing. Fascist propaganda is of this type; also, there is the effect of the media, video nasties, which may be held as symbols in the minds of most people but are concretized into "action nastiness" by a small but dangerous minority of people who live out the fantasies.
2. Projective identification is an unconscious mechanism. In this area the worker or somebody else (another inmate, for example) finds him- or herself experiencing thoughts, fantasies, and/or impulses by which he or she has become "possessed" in some way. Moreover, there may be some internal drive toward acting these out: for instance, the case of the violent prisoner and my own subsequent fracas with the van driver.
3. Goading into action is a challenge that is often provocative, cruel, unwise, and usually unnecessary. It can occur on a group basis, between individuals, or between a group and a scapegoated person. It is directed as a rule against all goodness, or on the principle of all goodness being retained by the provoker and all badness being designated to the scapegoat. Sometimes the provoker is soundly defeated, of course, although that too may be disastrous: for example, the aggressive, cruel, abusive husband whose wife became possessed by her husband's aggression and who then rushed in from the kitchen and cut off his penis.
4. Muddling the opponent, the aim of guerrilla warfare, occurs to some extent in civilian life. It can happen in less lethal ways in schools and colleges so that learning is sabotaged. Trouble starts in one part of the lecture theater, then another; then there is a flare-up elsewhere in the same gathering until the main purpose of the group is eclipsed.
5. The direct concretization of a fantasy (owing to the unwillingness or inability to mourn for a crime committed in fantasy only) leads

to crime that is not due to excitement but to unfaced, therefore evacuated, regret. The difference between this motivation and the greedy, domineering, excited crime is that enacting the crime gives gratification, relief rather than acquisition or revenge. It is linked with but not precisely the same as committing a crime out of a sense of guilt, as written about by Freud as long ago as 1916.

22

Criminality and the Claustrum

When I first began to attempt the psychodynamic therapy of convicted criminals, including the consequence of their being convicted for murder, I was struck by the fact that some of them showed a genial and apparently healthy side to their characters. This was associated with behavior toward other people and toward themselves that could be regarded as healthy. Nevertheless, in each of them there appeared to be a split-off, encapsulated, cruel, perverse, and often evil side that I came to regard as primitive and savage and that had remained unmellowed during the course of emotional development. This aspect tended to erupt episodically, like a volcano, and when it did so, a sometimes murderous crime or series of crimes ensued. Meltzer's (1992) work and views on what he calls "The Claustrum" offer a conceptual framework by means of which it is possible to gain insight into the phenomenon of murderousness. Few tasks are more important than the reduction of its menace toward other people, victims, and the brand of Cain that marks the owner of such proclivities, which often defy therapeutic modification. In *The Claustrum*, subtitled *An Investigation of Claustrophobic Phenomena*, Meltzer stresses the ubiquitousness of projective identification.

Some years ago I began to relate the persistent constellation of murderous fantasies, impulses, and actions to the idea that death had not been digested psychically. A usual reason for this has been the absence or inadequacy of the baby–mother interchange of projective identification. Following Bion's (1967a) paper "On Arrogance," I viewed the situation as having consisted of a projective identification refusing or blocking mother or mother surrogate, or else a baby or young child who could not or did not accept and use what was relayed back to him or her by the mother or her substitute in her response to the projective identification into her of Bion's, "No breast; I shall die." This is not the place to describe the many possible reasons for the ineffectiveness of the interaction, but the results of its failure may promote the development of "no-go areas" as far as psychic digestion and metabolism are concerned. These phenomena tend to remain the same over long periods of time and, like other pathological character organizations, strongly resist the analytic process as far as change and development are concerned. (See Rosenfeld [1987], "The Impasse," and Steiner [1993], "Psychic Retreats.")

Following are two accounts of individuals who have committed murders or have or have had fantasies of doing so. We shall see how sometimes the fantasy/impulse constellation has long simmered within the mind of the individual, militating toward action, sometimes functioning as a substitute for action, sometimes as a prelude to such action, that is, the enacting of punishment on the self as murderer.

Patient X

X, mentioned briefly in earlier chapters, was aged 26 when I was asked to see him with a view to giving him psychotherapy during the life sentence he was serving for the murder by strangulation of a 60-year-old woman who had asked for a lift in his truck. He had had the idea of rape and murder in his mind. The elderly victim told him that rape was out of the question; he killed her (almost immediately regretting it) and left her at the roadside in a dry ditch.

X had a criminal record of rape and attempted rape, and had spent many of his twenty-six years in a reformatory or prison. During the interview he was serious, puzzled by his recurrent behavior, honest, and anxious. He told me that for some unknown reason refusal of his sexual advances made him feel murderous, but that he could turn away from a murderous impulse in certain circumstances and be kind and helpful instead. Significant factors in his early history were that he was the eldest of two boys and two girls, and was evacuated during the early part of World War II to a farm far from home while his parents remained in London. His companion in evacuation was his brother Donald, next to him in sibling order. This brother was the good boy, attractive to the evacuation couple in loco parentis, while he, X, was singled out for criticism. He came to think of himself as the "ugly duckling," a notion based on low self-esteem, not an objective fact of nature. During these lonely, unhappy months, X planned to run away from his uncongenial foster home/prison, and on a hot summer day he did so, scantily dressed and unfed. A hue and cry ensued. He felt that the whole village was hunting him. Eventually, to escape, he had to run through a tightly matted bed of tall nettles, but as he did so, he fell into them and was recaptured. Although he was not badly treated by his captors, the innumerable nettle stings caused a severe allergic reaction, much worse than the painful return to his foster home. His mother was summoned to the farm and when she was due to go home, he successfully begged to be taken with her to the much less persecutory situation of London during its bombing.

As a youth X made investigatory sexual advances to each of his sisters in turn. Eventually, the sisters decided that because he was kind to them, they would together ask him to desist and would not report him to their parents. Home was in an East End area where delinquency was endemic. X did bad things and good things. He was organized in either activity, and while his childhood passed relatively uneventfully, adolescence brought a crop of problems concerning learning, sexuality, and obedience to or transgression against the law.

X got a job as fireman on a local steam train service. The engine driver, whom he had admired, made homosexual advances to him, pursued with some cruelty. Precisely what happened I was never able to ascertain, but I think that both anal intercourse and fellatio might have taken place. The cruelty with which the abuse was enacted seemed to have gotten into X, and during the course of a fifty-minute session with me, he could swing from male to female and back to male identification several times. This change was evident in his face. I might say, "Now you are having a feminine fantasy," or "Now you are having a masculine fantasy with some cruelty in it," and it was invariably right because he confirmed that he did switch in his identification with remarkable lability. Even his voice changed: he spoke one octave lower in a male identification than he did in a female identification.

Not long after this he made several attempts to rape young women. One of these was an assault on a 30-year-old woman who said, when he started to struggle with her, "You are a silly young man. Why do you attempt to invade me like this? If you ask me nicely, how do you know that I would not say yes?" Eventually they did attempt intercourse, but he was so afraid that he might be impotent that she helped him to complete the act, and then invited him to spend the weekend with her. His paranoid anxiety mounted at this invitation and he fled from her into his own solitude. She, in a state of pique, gave his description to the police, who arrested him. He said that he deserved the prison sentence of about three years, and didn't argue about it because his intention had been rape. This sense of justice regarding what he did and what he had intended to do characterized him throughout his criminal history. When he felt he was unjustly treated, he was exceedingly angry and resentful; when he felt he had been justly treated, he accepted his punishment, indeed almost welcomed it.

The next attempted rape was of an 18-year-old girl who was

coming down a hill on her bicycle. He put a stick into the spokes of her front wheel. She fell off into the long grass beside him at the roadside. He attempted to rape her and when she began to cry he was torn between two impulses: one, to go on with the rape, the other, to console her. The latter prevailed and he explained that when she sobbed as he was holding her against him, he could feel her heart beating through her thin clothes. This reminded him of his sisters whom he loved. He decided not to pursue the attempt to rape her and told her so, helped her to get composed, dried her tears, and said, "You are now free to go." He apologized to her and she said, "But you'll get caught and punished." He replied: "Well, that is my fault and my business. You didn't ask me to do this to you." They parted on reasonably good terms, but as they were doing so a police car came along and a police officer asked her why she was so ruffled. She told them, and X was arrested, subsequently receiving a four-year sentence that he did not resent, or at least stated he did not, because he felt he had deserved it. Whether, in the provocation, there was an assertion of his masculinity rather than the threat to him constituted by his femininity was difficult to discern, but I think this did figure in some way.

His total identification with the role that pervaded him at any given moment was one of his principal characteristics. Whatever he identified with, he pursued to its limits. I recall him working through some of his anxieties about the fugitive escape from the evacuation home/prison in a very feeling and vivid way. I left him in quite a state at the end of the session. When I went to see him a few days later, I was told he was confined to his cell because he had swollen up like a balloon. I went to see him and found him blown up with angloneurotic edema. He had pretty well psychically repeated the trauma of the nettle stings. I made interpretations along such lines to him in his cell, and by the end of the discussion the swelling had gone down visibly, and he made an eventual recovery over the next twenty-four hours.

At some point X became attracted to the process of learning. He had always been sensible, logical, and able to understand, but was poorly educated. Prison afforded him the opportunity to remedy this and he embarked enthusiastically and successfully on any courses he could take, eventually piling up an impressive list of good grades. This was no mean achievement. Of note was the speed with which he picked up Spanish in one year, even writing a sonnet in the language during the following year.

The situation he repeated in the course of therapy was one in which he was unfairly treated, and then reacted violently to being so handled. One day I heard he was on a charge and was being sent before the governor, whom I knew to be a fair person. X had had a fracas with a prison officer. Each said that the other pushed him. I saw both together and was struck how alike they looked. Here perhaps was a sibling situation like that with his brother Donald. I wrote a note to this effect to the governor, who replied: "This may be so, but I have to support the prison staff." A minimal period of loss of privileges was the punishment, but the governor was impressed with the character of X and a few weeks later restored his privileges. Shortly after, X was given certain responsibilities and allowed to move freely about the prison.

John

John, aged 15½, also discussed briefly in previous chapters, was a quite different kind of person. The doctor who referred him to me had made arrangements with a well-known charitable organization to pay for several years of psychoanalysis should it be thought necessary, as was probable. John had gone in great distress to his parents, complaining that he was unable to work because of his total preoccupation with murderous, homosexual fantasies directed against just-pubertal boys who had certain required characteristics. They should be slightly plump, have smug, well-cared-for faces, and be wearing clothes with shiny, silky surfaces. This had a fetishistic quality that was to prove important later. He had two kinds of fantasies. One was to attack the boy with a knife, which he would stick up the boy's anus and twist, causing death; the other was to do a kind of projected hara-kiri, that is, he would come up on the boy from behind, grasping the knife with the right hand and holding the boy with the left. He would then use the knife to make an up, along, and down rent in the abdominal wall so that the victim's guts fell out and he would then die. One of these two fantasies was the prerequisite of satisfaction during masturbation. John's worry was that he thought he might get so desperate that he would have to commit the crime, rather than be able to fantasize it, if a boy excited him sufficiently.

John was a studious young man with a sense of humor; yet there was a continuous, underlying tension in him that was appropriate to the fantasies and impulses he suffered from. His younger brother would fit into the category of victim, but the brother was handicapped by a birth injury and had never challenged John as regards intelligence, proficiency at schoolwork, and so forth. He also wasn't especially good-looking and didn't wear the kind of clothes required of the fetishistic victim of John's fantasy sexual murder. The two boys were the only children of a businessman father and a mother who was a trained schoolteacher. They lived in an outer suburb of London and seemed to have a satisfactory if rather dull way of life.

It was clear when we began that John had no clue about psychoanalysis. After a month or two of association that one could scarcely call free, and interpretations I felt were appropriate, he suddenly looked at me and said, "When is treatment going to begin?" The containment of his anxieties that was taking place, crude though it was, was sufficient to enable him to take his exams without undue distress and to pass satisfactorily. He went on to advanced levels with a view to going to university, possibly to study history.

I discovered that John's fetishistic object of desire had evolved in stages from the first transitional object, a smooth scarf that used to be regarded as essential to his well-being, especially necessary to be in his hand when he went to sleep. It had gone through a number of evolutions, although still existed in itself, until it became a masturbatic object of desire. Behind this lay the idea of the youth. It seemed that the anticipation of the brother had brought part of this constellation into being, but that with the brother's very considerable handicap, it had to be displaced onto somebody else. Sometimes it was a boy at school in the same class, or a class or two junior, and sometimes it was a fascination with a young adolescent he saw in the street. Although there had been a phase during which father, straight out of the armed forces, had apparently been rather brutal to John as a young lad, it did seem that he had settled down to be an understanding parent. John felt his mother to be the hostile parent who did not understand him.

John's internal situation fluctuated quite a lot. The homosexual way of life that he maintained in his fantasies seemed not to be fixed, and at times he became fond of and sexually attracted to one or another of his two girl cousins, one a little older than himself and one a little younger. These feelings neither crystallized nor grew, and he returned to the original kind of object of stimulation, which was entirely homosexual. He got on quite well with women at university and later at work. As Keats would have it, "the fierce dispute between damnation and impassioned clay" seemed to be mitigated to some extent by drinking, and later he developed the habit of consuming a bottle of wine a day.

In the early days he felt that if anybody offended him, including his sexual objects, that person should be murdered. Anybody who affronted him, belittled him, or lowered his self-esteem was liable for the same kind of attack. This attack was a bit different in that it wasn't so sexualized but was more in the nature of a revenge for injury. It became evident that John did not want to rid himself completely of the capacity to murder, should it become necessary, and this was based on some sort of delusional appraisal of the situation. Should it become necessary to kill somebody, then he would have the ability and he didn't want to forfeit his ruthlessness. It must be stressed that he did not *want* to kill, only to be *able* to kill. A necessity to kill would result from overwhelming sexual temptation; a blow to his self-esteem, which would be catastrophic; or financial or social ruin.

He also feared injustice, and I think this linked to the feelings of injustice in his home, specifically the treatment of him by his mother. She found him difficult to understand and contain, but there was more than a small element of refusal to contain him. I had thought for some time that he exaggerated this problem, but after he had been in analysis for two and a half years, there was a crisis in which he felt very guilty and persecuted and thought the only thing to do was to kill himself. I am not sure how determined and sincere this intention was: he came into the consulting room looking very ill and readily confessed to having taken an overdose, mainly of aspirin, in my waiting room. After getting him taken to the local hospital where his stomach was pumped out, I telephoned his mother and asked to arrange for him to be picked up from the hospital as it would be impossible to preserve the analytic situation if I had to do it. She went into a long, angry, explanatory speech about his always doing things like that, always causing crises when she had something on. For instance, that afternoon she had a church sale to go to. I pointed out the seriousness of the situation and she said, "Oh, well, ring his aunt. She will come." I told her to ring the aunt herself and arrange for it, and she did. An understanding, containing woman arrived later that day with the young man, who now looked like an unhappy little boy. The contrast between the seriously uncontaining mother and the good containment of the aunt was striking. I think he was not exaggerating about his mother's treatment of him, although one doesn't know what damage he did to her as a container.

Let us jump over many years, in some of which he had no therapy or help of any kind. He returned to therapy because of the increased activity of his fantasies and the feeling that he needed to be contained. He saw me once a week, paid for himself, and did moderately well at his analytic work. However, it did seem that he was determined to have an interminable analysis and to keep me as a container until I either died or stopped work. He would then want to find someone else to act as a container. This situation defied interpretation for a long time. Nevertheless, he was quite successful at his job and was able to lead life with minimal acting out. His difficulties were also mitigated and mellowed by a good sense of humor. In his earlier days at school, he had a tendency, if he ran into difficulties in a given subject, to give it up. Nevertheless he managed to get into the University of London and read history. Over the years there were small episodes of acting out. On one occasion he tried to touch an adolescent boy on the genitals. On another, to prevent himself from doing the same thing, he tripped over a stair with a tray full of glasses and drinks. This caused a ruckus and deflected attention from the tension state he was in. On another occasion he saw an exciting-looking Indian youth and hit him hard in the back. No other similar situations occurred to my knowledge.

His sense of humor was ironic and sometimes very funny. He had once been mugged and robbed of his wallet and other valuables. He went along with this with a considerably increased reality sense, not fighting an impossible fight against three large young men who could have knocked him out or possibly killed him if he showed resistance. He then called out to them, "I have a bottle of wine. You've taken everything else I value, why not take that as well?" They didn't quite know how to handle this situation. Eventually they said, "No you can keep that, we've got what we want."

While he was a university student, he took up mountaineering and rock climbing. I think this was because he was afraid not only for his own skin, but of having the opportunity to endanger his companion or companions, which was outside the strict desiderata for murder he had adopted. These restrictions would constitute defenses against action of a murderous kind.

PART V

23

Antidevelopmental Processes in Adolescents

In the playing of war games, excitement is sought, practiced, and developed. The process is depersonalized and there is little or no responsibility taken. Addiction to war games, sexual games, or cops and robbers games without any sense of sadness and guilt is pathological. Even if token sadness and guilt are felt, a kind of psychic poise or balance may be restored. A man who had shot and killed another (who himself had been provoked into threatening him with violence) said that he bore no ill-will against the man he killed. He had been acting out a cops and robbers video that he had watched compulsively and to which he had become addicted. He felt horrified at the actuality of the crime and I have no reason to doubt the truth of his reaction. When his victim did not get up and walk off at the end of the game, he felt shattered. Another man, younger, who had not yet emerged from adolescence, had tried to enact the sexual drama of a rape that ended in murder. He chose the wrong victim, a good-looking woman who was a practiced expert in unarmed combat. He approached her only to find himself sprawled on the ground six feet behind her. He repeatedly attempted to overpower her, each time with the same result.

As he slunk off into the bushes, he found the words forming in his mouth, "It's not fair, she won't play."

These two examples are by no means unusual. Such happenings are encountered when there is conflict between the wish to kill and the wish to play. One of the difficulties of murderous and violent sexual portrayals in the media is that the boundary between play and criminal action of a destructive kind is blurred. Behind and complicating an addiction of the kind described is a disturbance of psychic digestion. This arises early in life and is based on one or more of a number of factors:

1. An intolerance of frustration, of not being given what one wants, paramount among which is relief from psychic pain. This includes child abuse as the victim, nasty food, hatred of school, and so on.
2. The absence of or inadequacy of the mother or her surrogate insofar as the containment of the projective identification of the baby is concerned. A developmental omission or lack will occur in the use of the mother's alpha function on the beta particles put into her by the baby's projective identifications, and the relaying back to the baby alpha elements suitable for storage, for repression, and, above all, for learning from experience (Bion 1962). Normally this facilitates the transformation from the paranoid-schizoid to the depressive position—from part-object to whole-object relationships intrapsychically and, by extension, to whole-object relationships in the outside world. Resentful, savage, persecutory feelings are replaced, partly at least, by more genial, reparative attitudes, and a developmental process proceeds. In extreme form, one encounters, in one person, a Dr. Jekyll and Mr. Hyde in negative juxtaposition with each other. A mother with this variability is positively criminogenic.

   These considerations are clinically important because a dynamic psychotherapeutic approach that does not extend to work through the conflict of container and contained and the paranoid-schizoid and depressive positions—and the transformation from one to the other—is likely to be helpful only to the more genial, developed, and integrated part of the patient. It may render the savage, destructive, primitive part of the same patient more isolated and make it much worse.

3. A series of traumata that assail the baby or young person so that psychic digestion is overwhelmed—for example, being sent from mother and home to a home for young children, and being abused there. Bereavement, accident, or severe life-threatening illness are other examples. Separation or divorce of parents, or breakdown, especially a psychotic one, of one or both parents, presents a difficult situation for the child.

   A paranoid illness in the mother of a young child is associated with reversal of the container and contained function; thus the child suffers a double trauma: (1) loss of an adequately containing mother and (2) of being used as a "container" for the mother's delusional, persecutory ideas and feelings. Little wonder that the psychic digestion of the child is put out of action completely. One of the results of such a state of affairs is mindlessness (an inhibition of learning capacity), which is only a short step from antidevelopmental activities such as alcohol and drug abuse, glue sniffing, shoplifting, auto theft, breaking and entering, even mugging and murder.
4. The finding of a peer group. There is something savage about resorting to a delinquent gang, as well as something pathetically sad. The gang members have:
   (a) an apparent solidarity
   (b) a retaliation against the larger group—for example society—power that is sought and welcomed by the new recruit
   (c) the sanctioning of action rather than superego caesura and also an expectation of tolerance and not frustration
   (d) an envious outlet, clawing down the enviable "haves" using the distorted method of becoming a "have" oneself
   (e) enmeshment with material gain in the form of booty, as in war or looting
   (f) the always paramount reversal of the passive, suffering role into the active, conquering one.

Social structures such as the delinquent group, the gang, have an intrapsychic organization in the individual similar to the external one in the gang, as described by Meltzer, Rosenfeld, and me, and further developed by Steiner and a number of other workers. The gang was immortalized by the brutalization of the choirboys in *Lord of the Flies* and, on a national scale, in Orwell's *1984*.

Shakespeare ascribed the operative words to Macbeth in "Fair is foul and foul is fair," that is, a reversal of values. Faustus put it as "Badness be thou my good." The matter can be put succinctly by terming it the development of an addiction to bad parts of the self and to an idealization of them. The process is based on avoidance of psychic pain and the reversal of passive suffering by projecting it into others and inflicting the suffering on them and then attacking all good causes. The penultimate horror was reached by Stalin in dealing with his opponents, and the ultimate one by Hitler, not only to his known political opponents but also to Jewish people, gypsies, and others for what they *were* rather than for what they had *done*.

The individual finds and gets him- or herself incorporated into a gang by a combination of projective and introjective identification. The philosophy becomes a "might is right" policy as it projects all good, admiration, and confidence into the leader and ascribes all weakness and inadequacy downward in the pecking order in the form of grades of contempt. The pecking order is strict. Hatred, cruelty, and revenge are directed toward those outside the gang and, more particularly, toward any dissidents deemed treacherous and disloyal. A positive evolution can occur from gang to group, or a malign regression and brutalization from group to gang. The essential manifestation is what they "do" intrapsychically. This depends on how far toward the depressive position they have reached and sustained. If depression-position anxieties can be sustained, the gang evolves into a group and loyalty develops into a set of shared principles by the ex-gang now operating as a group. Interpersonal bonds are close but not suffocating. Dissidents are treated with sadness rather than anger and cruelty. There is less brutalization and vengeance, and more capacity to negotiate and to allow for differences of view.

A book written soon after the spectacular rise of the Beatles stated that the success in musical groups in Liverpool raised morale, and there was a shift from gang to group. The difficulty persisted, however, in those with no musical talent at all, who drifted and formed other, more delinquent groups or gangs. How seriously we should treat these facts is open to doubt, but group phenomenology is important.

In adolescence, intrapsychic balance has not yet properly developed. It can be shaken or even demolished and dismantled by the peer group, so that the individual may consciously, or unconsciously, or a mixture of both, take in the attitudes of the peer group in a chameleonlike way. This is redolent of Winnicott's "false self." The developing adolescent is both an individual and also a group person, and getting these two into balance is no easy task. Some adolescents try different styles for themselves. Life and construction are countered by greed, envy, and sibling rivalries of a cutthroat kind. The external manifestations of what is an intrapsychic as well as an interpersonal struggle can show themselves in the adolescent as he or she becomes a profound narcissist, criminal, baby, scholar, philosopher, poet, or priest in quick succession. Sometimes the roles and identifications are evanescent, but quite often one particular role stabilizes and becomes a life style.

In general, the task of becoming what one has not so far achieved is painful. A long, drawn-out course of study, an apprenticeship, a series of boring jobs can pose insurmountable problems to adolescents, who are intolerant of frustration and simply cannot work and wait for solid achievements to accrue. Also, in the course of development, the individual is thrown back on his or her own good internal objects. If, instead of helpful and encouraging figures, the adolescent has mainly critical and unappreciative objects, it is hard to sustain the effort of work and to retain interest. Here we have intrapsychic and interpersonal factors at their point of intersection. What happens if the capacity to sustain the struggle that Keats called "the fierce dispute betwixt damnation and impassioned clay" is not kept up? The abdication from struggle can be a developmental hiccup or it can initiate a regressive retreat from all endeavor. One sees this in frequent fluctuations from prodevelopmental strivings to antidevelopmental processes. The parallel of a child's game of Snakes and Ladders is apposite. Largely unconsciously determined, but with social and environmental factors providing some of the snakes and ladders, this state of affairs confronts all of us throughout life. But in periods of special frustration and fluctuation in adolescence, when the tide of impulse life runs most strongly, the outcome depends on constitutional factors such as the quantum of primal envy (Klein), the initial balance of life and death instincts (Bion), the capacity to learn from experience, to mourn and regret the harm one does and has done to others, and to recover from wrongs done to the self. Religion can exert a varying but powerful influence. Adolescence is a time when, though structurally an individual may be seaworthy, he or she cannot yet navigate the turbulent waters of development. So much for the fairly healthy. Many are not healthy, and bring to the developmental task disabilities from preadolescent life. Little wonder that they fall by the wayside. Many experiment with one or more antidevelopmental options. Relatively few become addicted to antidevelopmental living, but they are the ones who confront us. Most often, those trying out various options but who are not yet addicted to them can be helped by the sort of drop-in service provided in some places. The Young People's Counselling Service at the Tavistock Clinic offers up to four exploratory sessions to young people at their own request. These in themselves are often sufficient, though a significant percentage need to be referred for longer and more comprehensive dynamic psychotherapy.

In adolescents who have become addicted to the antidevelopmental resorts, including the habitual use of drugs, the situation can become complicated by the effect of the drug or the resort itself. If a drug, things can be made worse by the pharmacotoxic effect as well as the emotional one. If an action such as house breaking or mugging is selected, almost everyone is fearful; being wanted by the police creates a kind of paranoid supercharge. As one treats one's objects externally or internally, so one expects to be treated by them externally or internally. Hence trust is the first casualty in a person who knows him- or herself to be untrustworthy. The cruel and violent subject feels that others will treat him or her cruelly and violently.

Some antidevelopmental resorts heighten an already existing imbalance between life and death instincts, tilting them toward death. If this becomes a threat, a resurgence of life instincts but with the situation still psychically undigested can, and often does, provoke a projection of the risk into somebody else. The full sequence is that the constellation to do with death is projectively identified, that is, put into a victim and, at worst, killed in that person. The victim may or may not be known to his or her murderer. Far more commonly, it is simply abandoned in the other person. Sometimes, if masochism is a problem, action is taken to provoke a murder of the self by projective identification of the death-dominated parts of the self into someone who turns and kills the projective identifier.

Let me repeat that what cannot be psychically digested cannot be detoxicated. If the transformation from the paranoid-schizoid to the depressive position is blocked at the paranoid-schizoid position, a state of part-object relationships prevails. This is a prelude to action to unburden the self of accretions of stimuli, as Freud wrote (1911b).

In 1976 Derek Miller stated that in adolescent murderers he had found in almost every case that there had been some tacit sanction for the murderousness from at least one parent or parental surrogate. I think that the less obvious part of this statement could be that the superego of the murderous adolescent contained experiences (distorted or not) based on an internalization of murderousness or supposed murderousness experienced during development from a parent. An almost melodramatic example of this is given elsewhere of the battered baby who, when he grew to manhood, murdered a man who clearly represented his battering father. In a parody of one of A. E. Housman's poems that shook and impressed this murderer by its rather cruel accuracy, one finds the qualities of what I am endeavoring to describe:

> What, still alive at twenty-two,
> A clean upstanding chap like you?
> Sure, if your throat is hard to slit,
> Slit your girl's and swing for it.
>
> Like enough, you won't be glad,
> When they come to hang you, lad:

But bacon's not the only thing
That's cured by hanging from a string.

So when the spilt ink of the night
Spreads o'er the blotting pad of light,
Lads whose job is still to do
Shall whet their knives, and think of you.

—Parody by Hugh Kingsmill, from *Unauthorized Versions*, 1990; used with permission.

Turning from murderousness to suicidal attacks, we find that suicide may be the savage killing of the self, especially in adolescents who renounce life because of the severe psychic pain associated with the developmental processes. Suicide may be in some instances an act of heroism and constitute the ultimate in defense against uncontrollable murderousness. I have seen suicidal heroism in war as an expression of uncontrollable survivor guilt.

Achilles' heels characterize those who, by the time they reach adolescence, have made satisfactory progress in emotional development in many or most areas of functioning. Psychic digestion is not generally impaired, as a result of which psychic metabolism appears to proceed relatively healthily. Nevertheless, there are constellations of disturbance, instability, and special vulnerability. Any severe stress may overwhelm the previously apparently healthy functioning, and throw them into imbalance. When the poet Keats found himself in a state like this, he said he was "unmeridianed." Specific issues may detonate the breakdown, the breaking loose of one or more psychic constellations or enclaves. Sometimes an explosion of considerable force can occur, leading to a kind of takeover bid for the whole self by a hitherto hardly suspected part of the self. The individual in whom the phenomenon is encountered has had a sensitizing traumatic event or sequence. The whole or a large part of this event has been split off or repressed, and has seemingly given no trouble until a shocking event occurs that produced catastrophic change, comparable to the phenomenon of anaphylaxis. This may result in violent attacks on the self, other people or property, or principles hitherto held firmly and loyally. Examples given elsewhere in this book include the young man who killed the girl who suddenly turned on him and reviled his parents. Also, there was Marwood, who intended to help the policeman under attack by a gang of teenagers. He went into the fray and to his horror stabbed the policeman and killed him. Murderousness broke loose from its intrapsychic moorings and took over against his conscious wish to help the policeman.

Sanction for murderousness may have been given unconsciously years before a murderous deed against another human being takes place. An original permission arising from events—say, shooting wildlife for pleasure or for food, or defending oneself against an attack by a seemingly savage animal or bird—that have been forgotten, or split off or repressed, may be reactivated many years later in circumstances that detonate a much more violent response. One terrified child was attacked by a gander and a goose every day when he had to cross a small paddock in which they were kept. His father said geese were cowardly and that his son should chase them away. Instead, the boy attacked the gander and killed it by breaking its neck with a stick. The child was horrified. The father, evidently proud of his son, praised him. I do not know what happened when the child grew up, but this is an example of how sanction for murder can be given many years before it may result in some action upon a human being.

Hardly anyone is free from potentially dangerous encapsulations. What is important is to find out what occurs in the intrapsychic apparatus to deal with situations in which there is a lethal or potentially lethal matching of the intrapsychic situation by an external one, and to provide the appropriate therapeutic help if possible. In Bion's terms, a preconception is matched by a realization, and then the problem is how to deal intrapsychically with a murderous conception. If the apparatus present in most people is not overwhelmed by a catastrophic matching of the internal preconception by the external situation, fantasy and its working through in the mind can be a substitute for murderous action, not a prelude to such action. This should be the vital area for therapeutic intervention. In most criminals, if not all, one finds that because frustration causes psychic pain, accretions of stimuli are rapidly unburdened in pursuit of the so-called pleasure principle.

This could be expressed better by calling it the *avoidance of pain principle*. The first task is to enable discomfort (pain) to be borne without immediate evacuation of it. The second is to help to develop an apparatus to deal with unpleasant impulses from within and attacks from without. The lack of a sort of do-it-yourself apparatus to help a person tolerate and eventually detoxicate an unpleasant external or intrapsychic situation makes the transformation from persecutory to depressive anxiety almost impossible for some people to accomplish. What is possible, however, is that with a deep enough and durable enough period of dynamic psychotherapy, there can be a late development of an internal do-it-yourself apparatus. Not all people, especially in adolescence, who behave as though they have no do-it-yourself apparatus are found to be without one; this rudimentary apparatus may simply have fallen into disrepair. Once therapy is under way, the apparatus can often be largely restored.

So far, we have considered the problem of the container and what it is required to contain. Having touched on the ability of the individual to tolerate frustration, or to evacuate it, disavow it, or disregard the person or organization in which it is supposed to originate, let us look again at the fluctuation between the paranoid-schizoid position, P/S, and the depressive position, D, and the reversibility of the movement between the two positions expressed by Bion (1962), following Klein (1946), thus: P/S ↔ D. Intolerance of frustration results in a movement D → P/S, that is, from whole-object relatedness, possible at the depressive position only, to the regressed state P/S, in which part objects exist only in a state of unintegration or disintegration. What Bion called *alpha* function is lost, and the primitive *beta* elements (or bizarre objects) pervade. These cannot be used for symbolic representations or dreaming, and cannot be stored by means of memory. They can be used only for projective identification or for acting out.

A relapse from D to P/S is the first sign that a stress situation is not being tolerated, and further trouble is likely to arise. A fairly sustained holding of the depressive position is a sign that psychic digestion (and probably the subsequent psychic metabolization of the stress situation) is proceeding satisfactorily. The tide may turn at any point however—particularly in adolescents in whom the containment has been unsatisfactory and the absence of a do-it-yourself container is particularly noticeable.

At P/S there is no experienced guilt as there is at D, but rather a feeling of fear of attack, experience of being picked on by hated, hostile people or agencies (for example, the police). Fight or flight are the two possible courses to take. It is obvious that the regression from D to P/S is an escape from depressive anxiety and has made the situation harder to cope with, not better, as was intended. Let me state firmly, however, that the process takes place unconsciously. In disturbed adolescents we are often confronted by massive swings from a flimsily held outpost at the depressive position back to the supposedly safer place of the paranoid-schizoid position which, as stated, provides no safe harbor of the mind. Less violent fluctuations take place in all of us every day, of course. There is, in many destructively violent adolescents, a pseudo-reparation or a half-hearted reparation that may take the form of reparation without real regret or remorse for the harm done to other people. It may also consist of a milder substitution for the original deprivation, so that action is not to do with the forbidden thing but only a shadow of it. This is often expressed in the form of pictures, videos, and cartoon strips of forbidden violence or sexuality. This resort can itself become the nucleus of an addiction, as suggested at the beginning of this chapter.

When the sustaining of the depressive anxiety, that is, depressive pain, reaches a certain degree of effectiveness, a wish to restore the damaged object or objects emerges. The worse the actual damage and the damage perpetrated in fantasy, the harder the task of restoration becomes. Klein referred to the process of restoration as "reparation." It is a making good, a making amends for harm done in fact or fantasy, or by accident, much of which may be due to the slipping of a fantasy into action, thereby overturning the possible conscious intentions of the perpetrator.

Finally, the difference between adolescents who waver in their tolerance of frustration, challenge, threat, and temptation at some stage of the adolescent process and those who are seriously addicted to antidevelopmental resorts is so great as to be virtually unbridgeable. Fairly simple therapeutic measures may well be effective in helping to get the adolescent of the former type back on the developmental road. The more addictively enmeshed adolescent has a relatively high rate of mortality and remedial services will be taxed to their limit if any of the salvage operations undertaken by them are to prove successful.

24

Antidevelopmental Sexuality in Adolescents

During the last forty-five years or so, a different kind of problem has arisen in adolescent boys and girls vis-à-vis sexuality. Before that, the main task was to overcome the antisex and antisexual pleasure attitude that emanated from external parents and other authority figures and dominated the internalized parental authority figures in the minds of young people. Over sixty years ago I got into ongoing trouble as a boy with the senior English master at school for merely talking to an adolescent girl when our paths crossed on the way home from school. Even now, whenever I think of St. Paul, the image that comes to mind is the face of this master (whom otherwise I liked), so powerful was the superego aspect of his impact on me.

Now that a much freer social climate prevails, particularly in relation to the sexuality of young people, what would one expect? I think that the kind of young person who would strive to conform would be freer and healthier, while the rule-breaker might be frustrated by the lack of restrictions against which to rebel. Moreover, he or she might find other issues over which to express defiance, and this indeed does take place. One has only to think of drugtaking and the way it has swept through several generations of adolescents.

What I would like to consider, however, is something different. We are confronted increasingly with young people who, when adolescent, have license for sexual relationships involving intercourse before they have developed the capacity to make and sustain the relationship necessary to carry such an emotionally turbulent situation. It seems that sexual intercourse is often used as a premature escape from turbulence. The problem is based partly on the strength and pervasiveness of residues of earlier phases of emotional development that have not been worked through.

The situation is linked to the external world, of course, but less so than is generally imagined. Among the multiplicity of intrapsychic factors, one group stems from the fixation at previous levels of pregenital emotional development, that is, oral, anal, phallic, or oedipal phases. This way of looking at the problem—from the viewpoint of instincts and their aims—is the classical Freudian psychoanalytical stance. From the viewpoint of object relationships, how an individual treats his objects (other people of importance in his life) is how he feels he is, was, or will be treated by those people. His relationships to others or to parts of others are associated with two different kinds of anxiety. They can consist of a primitive anxiety rooted in the savage self (Melanie Klein's *persecutory anxiety*) or a more developed kind of anxiety associated with the more evolved self (Klein's *depressive anxiety*). Depressive anxiety is not the same as the clinical state labeled depression. The capacity to bear depressive anxiety is an indication of psychic health and well-being. It is a state of mind in which the subject is aware of his or her own capacity to harm and even destroy what he or she hates, and in doing so inevitably harms or destroys those who are loved and felt to be good or who have good and bad aspects. These attacks carried out in the mind are regretted and their consequences mourned. Persecutory anxiety on the other hand involves fear of what attacks will be leveled at the subject by the object at bay. A prophylactic silencing of the potential persecutor, or damaging of the part of the person deemed likely to attack, is felt to be necessary. Persecutory anxiety is ubiquitous throughout the animal kingdom. Depressive anxiety is specifically human. How we all move to and fro along Bion's (1962, 1967b) scale, described diagrammatically as P/S ↔ D (between a state of mind in which persecutory anxiety predominates and one of greater concern over harm done to others by the self, which is the characteristic of depressive anxiety) varies from individual to individual and from time to time in the same person. Some people are more tied to the P/S end of the scale; some are completely so. Most move back and forth along the scale, reaching what Klein described as the depressive position at times of intrapsychic integration.

One patient who was mainly grounded at the P/S level sometimes got a long way toward D but then switched back to P/S. She said to me, "You seem to make two false suppositions about me: the first is that I choose when I am depressed [meaning depressive position depression, not clinical depression]. It is not like that. I do not choose—the other thing you are mistaken about is in supposing that persecution is any less painful." These statements show clearly how the transformations from one state to another are unconsciously determined and also how P/S is no less painful than D, though it is more primitive and the outlook regarding breakdown much worse.

When the individual is stuck at the P/S position he feels threatened, picked on, aggrieved, wronged, underprivileged, often helpless, complains that life is meaningless, and states that it would be better if he or she were dead. The essential difficulty follows on what has been avoided in the negotiation of the infantile depressive position by a further such avoidance in adolescence, often soon after puberty. This involves the use of sexual intercourse as an escape from painful desires and needs into their supposed fulfillment in which the physical aspects of sexuality are gratified, but a good deal else remains unrequited. Physical sexuality without the appropriate feeling tone is not necessarily antidevelopmental, at least initially. If it continues without the growth of a mutual relationship to support it, however, it becomes a short circuit that avoids important developmental processes. I am not suggesting that the adolescent pairing couple need to be in love in an ongoing sense, but I am stating that there has to be a capacity for each to regard the other as a whole person so that, as Freud said a century ago, the two currents of sexuality can be brought together. He was referring to both sensuous and the tender currents: lust and love. Eventually young people who get together in an ongoing sexual way may well find mutual regard and tenderness to mitigate the rather nonspecific, impersonal tide of sexual desire. They may find decreasing satisfaction with each other and look for different partners, having learned much from their experience together.

If sexual intercourse in a fairly regular but purely physical relationship between two young people becomes a need, and other aspects of the relationship show no signs of development, intercourse takes on characteristics of masturbation in one respect and of various addictions in another. As with addiction, a regression tends to occur in which need and greed increase and pleasure and gratification decrease, so that a poor state of contentment results. The state then reached is one of depression, with associated elements of futility and hopelessness (ennui). At this juncture there may be clinical depression, an acting out (usually self-destructively). In the adolescent boy especially the destructiveness is often deflected from the self and enacted upon someone else—his sexual partner, for example, or someone standing in for her, or another male standing for himself and used as a scapegoat.

On the other hand, the depressive course may be countered by a manic current that sweeps young people into an anxiety-driven orgy of excitement and frenzied action in pursuit of an elusive, ideal gratification. This may work briefly for a time, as only by changing from partner to partner can depression be warded off. The usual pattern of such relationships is initial excitement and rejoicing in the finding of a new partner to whom all positive virtues are ascribed. This wonderful new partner loses the idealization virtually as soon as sexual intercourse has taken place. As Shakespeare wrote in *The Merchant of Venice*: "For women are as roses whose fair flower/When once displayed doth fall that very hour."

What we are talking about is not new, but in our complex and rapidly moving society it is more prevalent and the traditional self-righting adaptive resorts often are not available. Also, escape routes into sources of excitement are all too readily obtained. They prove to be transient in their effect, particularly in warding off depression.

The depression to which I refer in this setting is not depressive-position feeling, but is experienced in a state of aggrievement at the paranoid-schizoid end of the anxiety spectrum. In this position there is no capacity to tolerate loss, frustration, ordinary sadness, waiting, rejection. All those feelings, if borne, could lead to recovery and give evidence of the growth and integration that can derive from containing distress for a while, without a primitive rush into escape routes. The disturbed adolescent does not *suffer* from these difficult states of mind. He or she complains about them and tries to get rid of them. It is at this point that antidevelopmental options other than sexuality may be sought: drink, drugs, and pornography, to mention but a few.

As far as an unpleasant depressive state of mind is concerned, it may be engendered by something real and concrete derived from an addictive, nonloving sexuality between an adolescent boy and an adolescent girl. Take, for example, an unwanted pregnancy followed by an abortion approved by all the parents and socially sanctioned. The girl often tries to deny the implications of the killing of the first fruits of her biological creativity. The boy usually disowns the matter. It is not happening to him! Or so he supposes.

If the central problem of the sexual relationships is based on sexual need without the caring for and nurture of the partner, what kind of addictive relationship exists and from whence did it derive? Of course, the relationship may be addictive as far as one partner is concerned and the more developed and integrated partner eventually finds the situation untenable and ends the partnership. Even more disturbing to the severely addictive partner is a situation that begins with collusion; the other partner then grows and develops emotionally, finally seeking a new relationship that carries the hope of further growth and progress. The rejected, dependent partner feels aggrieved: one described it as being "as if we were on a rock climb and to save herself she cut the rope and let me fall."

The addictive-dependency relationship dates from feelings and attributes that are of the essence of predepressive position experience. It consists of a regard for the other person only in terms of what is best for and suited to the self, that is, to the subject. It consists not only of a parasitic taking from the partner, but also an extremely primitive evacuation into the partner. The partner is burdened by what in developmental terms could be regarded as waste products symbolizing urine, feces, and so forth. Fears and anxieties amounting sometimes to terror situations, also evacuated into the partner, may take hold of the partner and draw him or her into a collusive parasite-and-host dyadic relationship. There may be, or may develop, a back and forth evacuation similar to the relationship that exists between some twins. I know of one such situation that began with the boy being cared for by the girl, evacuating and projecting into her, thus leaving himself free to develop to some extent. At this point, however, beginning to resent what amounted to a reverse lend-lease situation, he deserted this girl, who had by then become his wife.

Having outlined the parasitic dependency relationship, let us look at the more developed, integrated, caring situation that characterizes the relationships of people who have made relatively satisfactory negotiations of the depressive position.

There is no growth or development when an individual is bogged down at the P/S position. Growth and integration take place only with some negotiation of the depressive position. And nobody completely, once and for all, negotiates the depressive position. It is a matter of continued struggle. Most of this struggle takes place unconsciously, that is, it seems to be automatic, the actual psychic work taking place while the subject is more or less unaware of the complicated processes going on. Misfortunes and disasters can be worked through, and the process is akin to mourning. Progress is made along the scale from P/S to D. In this way, in favorable circumstances, the individual learns from experience so that the process of working through adversities eventually results in a strengthening and deepening of the psyche (the personality of the individual). It is akin to the process of healing in a fractured bone where the site of the fracture when healed is often the strongest part of the bone thereafter. On the other hand, at the P/S end of the scale the processes are different. (Remember that the P/S end is no less painful than the D end, and the outcome is much less favorable.) Painful constellations may be repressed but more usually are split off, remaining inside the psyche of the subject or projected onto or into someone else, all too commonly the sexual partner. In the former version what one sees externally is usually what Winnicott used to refer to as a "false self."

One of the benefits of a satisfactory working through of traumatic adverse experiences is that the individual starts afresh with a clean slate. Without this working through, the mechanisms of splitting and projection put out of useful availability much of the energy of the individual, who thus becomes more and more impoverished instead of being enriched from the experiences. Thus there is greater and greater restriction and a reduction of flexibility, which is synonymous with less and less adaptability. The person who has worked through experiences of an adverse kind and recovered has demonstrated his or her adaptability, which will probably go on improving and will be associated with greater flexibility and freedom of choice.

It is not my intention to suggest that all adolescent heterosexual sexuality amounting to sexual intercourse is antidevelopmental. It is only when sexual intercourse bypasses a normal and essential period of apprenticeship and is used to avoid unresolved fixations from earlier life that the process becomes pathological. Bypassing these situations and avoiding the apprenticeship results in a precocious pseudo-adult sexuality brought with undigested infantile and childhood factors and situations that inevitably cause trouble and make the growth and development of more mature adult sexuality more difficult. The latter is needed to form and sustain ongoing relationships that act as a strong subculture to support the more flamboyant and exciting sexual interactions between man and woman.

When precocious, precariously based sexuality is the central feature of contact between an adolescent boy and girl, defects in their capacity to make and sustain a relationship are thrown into prominence, with demands on the caring agencies the likely result. In dealing with the disturbance and distress, we should not allow ourselves to be beguiled by a seeming capacity for physical sexual relationships without that substructure of a relationship required to support them.

25

Othello

The first time *Othello* was played in front of an audience was probably in 1602 when Shakespeare was 38 years old. I have always thought of the Moor as being about the same age as Shakespeare. He had reached a high position in the state he had adopted, Venice, despite his color and the prejudice and xenophobia that was rife at the time and that emerged under any kind of stress, such as the stress that overcame Roderigo when the woman he loved became betrothed to Othello and quickly married him. The attitude of Brabantio, Desdemona's father, was even stronger, and color difference reinforced her father's hostility. The manifest father–daughter oedipal theme had persisted right into her adult life. It would appear that Brabantio deeply resented her emancipation from it.

The seeds of the tragedy were incubated in Iago, resentful at being passed over by his admired and envied chief. Iago felt contempt and scorn toward the allegedly undeservedly successful Cassio. I can recall here echoes of World War II when promotion sometimes was given to someone who had not heard a single shot fired in anger! The powerful positive feelings Iago had toward the overly trusting Othello turned into implacably negative ones, and this shrewd and cunning man who had been promoted from the ranks set about demolishing the successful, enviable, and yet peculiarly uninsightful Othello.

The tragedy is built on an almost military exploitation of the weaknesses and frailties of Othello and Desdemona. It would seem that they were so locked together in their exciting love/sex relationship that those around them were excluded and neglected, like children clustered around but excluded from the sexual relationship of their parents. The two looked inward at each other and we are shown no positive dividend for their other human relationships arising from this closely bound dyad. One might have expected some benefit to accrue from such an apparently good interpersonal relationship. Perhaps there was no positive feedback because Desdemona was enthralled not only by her new-found sexual relationship, but by everything that was exotic about it. Also, positive results did not have *time* to emerge.

Unlike Chaucer more than 200 years earlier, Shakespeare sometimes appears to confuse jealousy and envy, for example: "O! beware, my lord of jealousy; It is the green-ey'd monster which doth mock/the meat it feeds on. . ." Iago said this to Othello; he calls it jealousy but he is describing envy, the envy that bites the hand that feeds it. I think Shakespeare probably did know the difference, but he made Iago call it jealousy, a lesser deadly sin. Chaucer describes envy as the deadliest of the seven deadly sins, as it attacks all the virtues and all goodness. Iago apotheosizes envy and personifies it. The other deadly sins, said Chaucer, attack only one virtue, whereas envy attacks all. On this basis Iago sets out to undermine Othello's trust in Desdemona. In pursuit of his destructive aim, motivated by envy and powered by the use of the lie, he sows the seeds of doubt and suspicion.

The love of the militarily successful Othello for Desdemona, who idealized him because of all that he had been through, was skillfully undermined, and not very slowly at that. What appealed to Othello about Desdemona, in addition to her beauty and youth, was her love for and idealization of him, her loving and generous sexual availability, her social standing, and his own ability to win and keep her despite her father's hostility. Brabantio's outraged hostility, leading to a rather vulgar efflorescence of xenophobia and racial arrogance, takes the audience by surprise. Finally, Brabantio's threat was that a girl who could turn against her father would repeat her action against her husband at a later date. Shakespeare showed complete insight into the human compulsion to repeat what has been done before. This is what Freud labeled the *repetition compulsion*, and it is important in all of us.

One is struck by the comparative simplicity of Othello, who is powerful and brave but in some ways dangerously naive. Only once in the course of Iago's depredations before the final scenes did Othello turn the searchlight of suspicion upon Iago, and that did indeed frighten the latter. Nevertheless, Othello bore what Paul Scott (1985) described as the "mark of the warrior"—a preparedness to resort to extreme measures in pursuit of his aims. These can involve death of others or, of course, to himself or to both. In the final debacle, Othello did not think of any measures to take other than lethal ones. As Othello's trust in his beloved Desdemona is undermined, one witnesses a rapid deterioration of character, suggesting the great degree to which Othello had become dependent on his wife. Instead of dismissing her, which the infidel (presumably Muslim) could have done within his religious boundaries and without offending any of his own religious or cultural laws or norms, he had to kill her. This is part punishment, part savage outburst, which he had fought against to some extent. It was detonated by disappointment, humiliation, and loss. A deep, narcissistic wound in Othello caused him to short-circuit across some sort of split in his personality, from love and marriage to his old field of endeavor: war. The event was potentiated by his being called back to action in Cyprus in response to a threat from Turkey and the consequent alarm in Venice among members of the government.

Married love, in its full sense, and war are not compatible, as Field Marshal Montgomery often stated during the time of risk of a German invasion of Southeast England during World War II. He remarked that girlfriends and mistresses were allowed in the divisional area, but not wives. The reason he gave for this was that if there were a German invasion, girlfriends and mistresses would be left by their lovers, but not so wives by their husbands. This statement, perhaps basically true, was not typical of this otherwise pillar of moral righteousness.

Othello was in a situation that demanded that he make military decisions, but he was also a newlywed. Not a lot was made of this divarication of interests, but it may have facilitated the switch from idealizing husband/lover to tortured and persecuted agent of what he felt to be retributive justice. At this turning point there is the flavor of melodrama about the play, but it is an example of Shakespeare's genius that high tragedy is restored in full when the truth finally emerges, and the complicated fabric of lies woven by Iago like a spider's web to entangle and ruin them both was revealed in all its ruthless deviousness. At this point Othello is under enormous stress and distress, but he sees the truth and appreciates it in his military way. Only tangential hatred and loathing of the guilty Iago was expressed, but Othello quickly realized that justice must be done. He must execute himself for the same reason he had killed Desdemona, and for reasons that were more reality based. The believed infidelity in love for which Othello executed Desdemona was due to what amounted to false information which, in a military sense, was intended to mislead, having been planted by the enemy, Iago. At the denouement, the truth appears, and for his own grievous and fatal mistake, based in part on lack of trust in love, Othello almost gladly executes himself.

Shakespeare shows how much insight he can bring to a situation in a concise way. At one level, a mistake in war has been brought about as a result of false information, by the general, the leader. In battle this is often fatal to many, and is therefore punishable. At a deeper level, in a love/marital relationship, being misled by information in this case completely false, brought a response that was fatal to Desdemona. Lack of trust was the cause and that constitutes infidelity in love. It may have been caused by defects in the character of Othello. One thinks of his simplicity, and his rush to action rather than wait and take a more evolved view of the situation. Above all, there is the narcissistic, brittle pride of Othello. His character was not unsuited for military leadership. There is little time for reverie and review in battle, although there may be time for review in war. Also, one is dependent on trustworthy subordinates, as Iago formerly had proved himself to be. Again, consistently, Othello soon sums up the new situation when the truth emerges. This is the military way. The mark of the warrior is displayed vividly in his rush to action and ends with an almost joyful, certainly relieved self-execution. In the audience the tears shed may even be ones of joy that the supposed villain, Desdemona, was innocent and that her soul is in bliss and that she loved him totally. Othello can then rejoin her in death, joy, and thankfulness; the hero and the heroine are together again, this time forever. One is reminded of the chorus in the Oresteia, "Cry sorrow but let Truth prevail."

Whereas Othello had the mark of the warrior in his preparedness to inflict or face death in pursuit of a perceived or assigned task, and an ability to sustain an indefatigable prosecuting of the task, his viewpoint or stance was that of a commander. He could see the overall picture and work within that conceptual framework. He became "deskilled" and thrown off balance by the articulated tapestry of suspicion Iago shrewdly wove and planted in him. This took root and grew in the compost of his character and origins. At the end of the fifth act the character balance is restored, as stated above. I am reminded of such instances in war, not over love, but over failure and defeat turned into fatal victory. For example, one of my patients won a posthumous Victoria Cross after having captured a Japanese-held village almost single-handedly.

Iago, in contrast to Othello, had the mark of the warrior but not of the officer: his was of the successful noncommissioned officer. He was a superb tactician but a poor strategist. He saw parts of the picture clearly, those that affected what he perceived to be in his own interests. He pursued his self-allocated task with ruthlessness, even unscrupulousness. Now and again there were appreciative outcrops of the truth regarding his assessment of the characters of Desdemona and Othello. Regarding the other characters, including his so-called allies (his wife and Roderigo) and his enemy (Cassio), he was scornful and contemptuous. Iago's character is made more convincingly real by these bits of evidence that he recognizes the integrity of Desdemona and the qualities of Othello.

Iago fits the requirements for a good infantry soldier as posited by the late Lord Wavell: "He must be a mixture of back-woodsman, poacher and Chicago gangster" said Wavell. In considering Iago, it must be remembered that we first see the situation after it had deteriorated, as far as Iago was concerned. He had been passed over for promotion. I suppose the rank of "Ancient" or "Ensign" or "Standard Bearer" was one held by a successful NCO, although he might well have been promoted to officer status for the job. What we see of Iago's performance makes him a perfect fit for the position, always well informed and a tower of strength when leadership was good and morale high, and a source of grave disaffection and trouble with wavering leadership and low morale. As his hatred of Othello developed (and there does seem to be an undercurrent of physical homosexuality somewhere in it), Iago deteriorates in that he becomes more ruthless and unscrupulous, promulgating lies with ever more destructive intent. The motivation was vengeance, but fueled by envy. Envy, I would conjecture, was always there, but his admiration for the militarily successful Othello and the regard and trust that Othello had showed to him hitherto had kept it within reasonable bounds. When Cassio was appointed lieutenant, however, the situation began to crumble. Finally, the *coup de grâce* with reference to his loyalty to Othello was an unconscious homosexual rejection, and the breakup of a military partnership as Othello became infatuated, fell in love, and finally married Desdemona, a beautiful woman. I would conjecture that the notion that Othello had cuckolded Iago may have had its origin in Iago's phantasies about the practice of wife swapping and may have been based on a fantasy that ran as follows: "I would even have shared my wife with him rather than lose him to that woman." We are shown only the established hate situation as it existed in Iago. What we are not shown is the scene before the debacle, when

Iago had been passed over and had lost his commander to a woman. There may well have been a kind of muted sexual affection between the two men followed by an explosive mixture of jealousy and envy in Iago.

Iago became rather like "King Rat" in his self-interest, manipulativeness, and overall incapacity to love. Implicit though not explicit is the deterioration brought about in a person when truth is deserted and all subsequent activities become based on lies. No wonder that spying is such a dangerous business as far as the mental stability of the spy is concerned. In an endeavor to keep up the impetus of his undermining of Othello, Iago needs to become increasingly unscrupulous. To sustain the network of lies, he kills Roderigo and, later, even his own wife. I am reminded of the modern process of destabilization as it is applied to governments by other governments who disapprove of them. The trouble is that the persons or establishments attacked by the destabilization process *and* those who do the attacking suffer in the end. Truth is indispensable except at the peril of everyone. The end does not justify the means if in the process the lie is dispensed and promulgated. It is pure poison. Iago does not abandon his position once the truth is revealed, but it would seem that he awaits retribution. If I know anything about old soldiers, however, he will cling to the hope that something will turn up to let him off at least some of the blame. He is a strong villain, consistent and apparently without remorse, akin to the Zeno who, when about to be executed, bit off his tongue and spat it into the face of his persecutors.

In tragedy we see how personality flaws in the people involved constitute the seeds of their own demolition. If we turn to the character of Desdemona, it would appear that her virtues bring about her destruction. She was genial and loyal, and idealized Othello. People admired and became very fond of her. Her defiance of her father over the betrothal and marriage to Othello was carried out in a mature way, and her father was by no means left unloved. Brabantio's bitter warning to Othello resonated with spite, and was the expostulation characteristic of an unfair "lock up your daughters" type of father. It may have been that her father was formerly idealized by Desdemona as a child and as an adolescent, but when it came to Desdemona the woman, her affections were firmly transferred to the man who had been "through so many dangers," Othello.

In the ambience of this supposedly strong central relationship, it was possible for Desdemona to be a friend to all the world and to espouse a cause such as that of Cassio, wounded over his demotion and loss of the confidence of the Othello whom he too idealized. It all seems so wholesome, and probably would have remained so had not the mephistophelian tongue of Iago been hard at work. In any event, her kindness to Cassio, and patronage of his quest for reinstatement, springs the trap set by Iago and she is caught, or so it is viewed by Othello. An open and florid delinquency was the next step in Iago's getting his wife Emilia to steal the handkerchief dropped by Desdemona and his insistence that he was given possession of it. Emilia became suspicious, but she was afraid to offend her chauvinistic and capricious husband, so she gives it to him and keeps quiet. The planting of the handkerchief on Cassio by Iago follows. It is the most clearly criminal act of all in the inexorable attack on Desdemona and Othello and on them as a couple. It is probable that Iago felt himself to be in rivalry with Othello for the beautiful, spirited Desdemona and in rivalry with Desdemona for Othello, the commander and victor of battles. Desdemona's lack of guile (though she knew that Othello was in the killing business and would probably kill her) may also have been related to the surprise, outrage, and depressive sadness at finding how profound Othello's lack of trust in her proved to be. Her sad song at this juncture indicates how much in search of a rehabilitation of her inner world she was after the unkindest of accusations and rejection of her by her idealized husband.

Emilia is the person who, had she acted earlier, could have prevented the double tragedy. Her reluctance or inability to speak up before it was too late is not only the pivot of the tragedy, but Shakespeare shows how evil deeds are allowed to develop until they reach an irreversible point, when good ordinary people are afraid to speak out, either because of fear of damage to themselves, or because of some desire for favor or love from the perpetrator or perpetrators of the wrongdoing. Not speaking up need not be consciously due to fear. Sometimes it is due to a failure to think through the logical sequence, and so grasp the whole picture of probabilities.

The murderous savagery of Iago is demonstrated all too vividly: once Emilia did speak up, she did so firmly, thereby drawing upon herself a murderous attack. Her husband killed her to suppress the truth. Also, there seems to have been an element of revenge and spite in Iago's attack upon her.

I have made no mention of how the characters worked together. There had been catastrophic change—the passing over of Iago for promotion and Othello's marriage to Desdemona which resulted in another, angry catastrophe in Desdemona's family. Because of Iago's activities, any resettlement was not allowed to run a benign course, but rather to freewheel into complicated tragedy.

I will not venture to create a hornet's nest by attempting to offer psychoanalytical conjectures about the state of mind of Shakespeare and to delineate what might have been going on at the time he wrote the play. As we know, Shakespeare had, to a remarkable degree, what Keats called *negative capability*. Bion referred regularly to negative capability, quoting Keats's definition of it and recommending it as a most desirable capacity for a practicing psychoanalyst to develop and to cultivate in him- or herself. Negative capability is the capacity to take in every circumstance and not to strive frantically after fact or reason. If I understand it correctly, negative capability is the capacity to take into the self experiences and to tolerate *not knowing* until after sufficient unconscious psychic work has been done on what has been taken in so as to permit a crystallization of a meaning. Primitive reaching after fact and reason leads, as a rule, to a pseudo-solution to a problem. Shakespeare was the person above all others whom Keats regarded as having the capacity of negative capability. Keats's so-called last sonnet, written on a blank page in his copy of the *Works of Shakespeare*, addresses him as "Bright star, would I were steadfast as thou art."

As I see it, Shakespeare could take into his mind all that went on and hold it there for sufficient time for some meaning to arise. This involved both fact and feeling in the context of apprehension of truth. One can make attempts to analyze Shakespeare's characters and his plays, but not the person himself, except to appreciate that the quality of taking in experience, devotion to truth, and not reaching for premature false solutions meant that he was a genuine "man for all seasons."

Despite all I have said, I am curious about the kind of man Shakespeare was. I sometimes wonder whether, in writing his plays, he may have been able to experience being everyone else, in varied complicated situations. In other words, was he able to develop or to let his psychically internalized characters work out the issues and conflicts with which they were confronted, and then unburden himself of the matured product in his plays? Clearly, Shakespeare's life was so productive because of his ability to take inside himself situations that matured in cask so to speak, and then portray them in such a compelling way that "not marble nor the gilded monuments of princes shall outlive this powerful rhyme" (Sonnet 55). Shakespeare was not boasting when he wrote this line, but evaluating the product of his creativity, the unconscious attributes and gifts that had made him able to do what he did. The evidence is that Shakespeare the man was a strong enough vessel—an adequate container for his genius. A sad contrast to this was Dylan Thomas, whose ability to write, among many others, a poem as precise and insightful as "The Conversation of Prayer" indicates literary genius. His life, however, showed that the man was not a strong or durable enough container for the intensity of his talent. It is our good fortune that so much has been given to us by Shakespeare regarding every aspect of life, so much that is invariable, so that his powerful rhyme truly does outlast the gilded monuments of princes.

To return to Othello and the play, and in particular the interplay of characters, we may ask ourselves what can we learn from this tragedy, which by "burning through the bitter-sweet of this Shakespearean fruit" (Keats 1978) we can avoid, in the concrete reality of our own lives? For example:

1. What is the difference between infatuation and the kind of love that eventuated between Gabriel Oak and Bathsheba in Hardy's *Far from the Madding Crowd*? Trust that develops through knowledge of each other, and mutual tolerance in the past and present, are the best insurances for the future.
2. How does one stop (and perhaps reverse) a bad situation? By adhering to the truth and having the courage to speak out. And to announce rather than denounce by excessive moralization.
3. Avoid rushing into action (except possibly in actual war when circumstances are urgent and threatening). Othello rushes to action instead of waiting for the situation to evolve and become clearer. The handkerchief was the concrete evidence, but circumstantial evidence can be very misleading. Othello rushed to action because he could not contain the threat to his stability that his humiliation, anger, and grief constituted. The accused was executed without trial. In less dramatic ways, we can think of many situations in everyday life when we are impelled to rush to an action, even knowing that it is wrong, because we cannot bear the internal tension of waiting until clarity dawns.
4. Beware the mephistophelian individual and the mephistophelian aspects of the self. At best, these have the characteristics of Shakespeare's Puck (Robin Goodfellow):

    Those things do best please me
    That befall preposterously.

At worst there is Iago and Iago-like persons who aim at devaluation and undermining as a prelude to the contrived destruction of a person and an enviable relationship. These people and parts of ourselves may be highly plausible and seductive. One needs time to discern the hook that is concealed by the bait, and to give a studied clearance if it is true that no hook is there anyway.

26

Life-Threatening Illness

An individual's life cycle can be, and sometimes is, threatened by an illness that could prove to be fatal. In the past, such fatalities were by no means uncommon. Since the proliferation of more and more effective chemotherapeutic agents and antibiotics, the scene has altered dramatically, so that diseases hitherto known to be killers have been brought within the realm of effective life-preserving treatment. I am thinking especially of pneumonias, tuberculosis, and severe streptococcal infections. We have also, however, been confronted by other diseases, of the heart and lungs, for example, which by and large are due to cigarette smoking, alcohol, diet, and so on. In recent years there has been the HIV illness that segues into AIDS. Many who are afflicted by life-threatening illnesses appear to have developed a special kind of splitting in which the destructive parts of themselves are expressed by means of the illness, while the creative part is left fairly free to be expressed in work, art, poetry, or other often impressive ways.

There is another way of looking at this. Some especially gifted people make strenuous efforts to harmonize two polarizations within themselves. This polarity is derived from the life and death instincts. The latter manifests itself by way of life-threatening illness, while the life instinct is shown in creative work. This is not quite accurate, because the quality of the work of art lies in the powerful interplay between the two (Segal 1962). The oscillation of allegiance is shown in Keats's "Ode to a Nightingale," in which his acceptance of the sad sights he himself had witnessed and in which he played no small part alternated with his identification with what he felt to be the freedom of the bird, the nightingale, to produce its art unhampered by the earthbound view of the human. This contrasted with his own dilemma, namely, facing in himself the threat of death, which he wished to face in his own way and at a time of his own choosing, instead of being passively held in the grip of an inexorable process. This attitude has more to it than a megalomanic defense against passivity. Keats, who had seen terminal illness, wanted none of it. The "nightingale Keats" looked back with compassion, but forward with dread to

> Fade far away, dissolve and quite forget
> What thou among the boughs hath never known,
> The weariness, the fever, and the fret
> Here, where men sit and hear each other groan;
> Where palsy shakes a few, sad, last gray hairs,
> Where youth grows pale and spectre-thin, and dies;
> Where but to think is to be full of sorrow
> And leaden-eyed despairs;
> Where Beauty cannot keep her lustrous eyes,
> Or new Love pine at them beyond tomorrow.

He would rather embrace the sentiments of the next stanza but one:

> Darkling I listen; and, for many a time
> I have been half in love with easeful Death,
> Call'd him soft names in many a musèd rhyme,
> To take into the air my quiet breath;
> Now more than ever seems it rich to die,
> To cease upon the midnight with no pain,
> While thou art pouring forth thy soul abroad
> In such an ecstasy!

Still wouldst thou sing, and I have ears in vain—
To thy high requiem become a sod. ["Ode to Melancholy"]

When Keats writes, "Where Beauty cannot keep her lustrous eyes, or new Love pine at them beyond tomorrow," I thought at first that he was perhaps referring to the sad and fairly recent death of his younger brother, Tom, of tuberculosis. I now think that it picks up the need to hold on to and tolerate and work through the mourning for one's own self when threatened by possible or even certain death. There is a link here between the need to mourn for oneself when afflicted with a life-threatening illness and the absolute necessity to mourn the killing or other crime of violence committed in fantasy only (see Chapter 1). Also, in thinking of the normal process of aging and eventually of losing all or most of one's beauty, not the least of which derives from lustrous eyes, there is the need to hold on to sadness, not to deny it and so foreclose upon the process of mourning.

Melanie Klein says something akin to this when she speaks about growing old. Two processes at least must occur. One path is illness, which requires the devotion of a great deal of the self. This devotion includes a renegotiation of the depressive position so that each fresh onslaught of the illness is first regarded as a persecutor/persecution, and the more life threatening it is, the more trouble there is likely to be at the paranoid-schizoid end of the anxiety spectrum. Psychic work can then facilitate a move along the spectrum toward the depressive end, and a whole-object relationship state. As Freud saw, internal threats are projected externally and dealt with as if they were coming from outside the self. Incidentally, what I have just described is in line with the evolutionary process. The attack is first of all experienced as though made by an unknown persecutor. This stimulates the fight/flight response. Later, the assailant becomes known and can be assessed more realistically. More thought-out, appropriate reactions or actions can follow this reality-testing operation.

To return to the other aspect of illness. It may be part of a reaction to unresolvable psychic conflict, part of an externalization that gets stuck in a body organ or the surface of the body, or related to a function. The psychoanalyst Garcia of Mexico looks on cancer as a possible psychosomatic development in relationship to an otherwise insoluble emotional conflict. My experience of patients whose conflicts were of this kind is restricted, but one I knew was responsible for the death of someone against whom he had a totally unjustified fleeting hostility and for whom he developed a relentless persecutory mourning. It was so powerful that I could make interventions that only fractionally eased the process of his unconsciously determined identification with the person whose death he felt he caused, but no mitigating circumstances could lessen his persecutory remorse. The illness he developed was rapid and fatal. To be certain about the precise psychosomatic processes is impossible, but it seemed that an extreme lack of self-forgiveness may have been related to the physical condition. It could be looked on in the opposite way, of course: the inexorably fatal illness was to him a just punishment for his having done something unforgivable (to his usual state of mind). A third way of looking at the problem would be to relate the crime and the illness to the unresolved intrapsychic situation that the crime did nothing to relieve. The crime was based on a lie, while the death-dealing illness put a stop to the entire process, which seemed incapable of yielding to therapy. It appeared that the patient's state of mind was incompatible with continued life. In such a case, the action that led to the death of another person representing himself merely delayed his own death. This seems to me to make more sense than the first two explanations.

Clinically, one finds that the individual who feels annihilated by events may attempt to evacuate the image of an annihilated object into someone else and then kill (or sometimes only attack) that person. This has in part the effect of freeing the subject from the death constellation, or at least from its clamoring, at least for a time. Reintrojection of the constellation plus a part of the person into whom it had been evacuated is usually what happens next, so the person from whom the constellation emanated is put in a situation that has worsened after only a short-lived period of relief. This reintrojection may not lead immediately to murderous feelings or impulses. A psychosomatic illness, a state of hypochondria, or one of somatic delusion may occur first.

How persons at risk look at those around them is important. One patient who developed pain in his eyes had extremely murderous fantasies, although he took no action. The ophthalmologist surprised him by telling him not to look into people in such a malevolent way. Here we have a doctor who was quite unfamiliar with formal psychodynamics, yet who linked a disorder of function straight to its aggressive emotional underlay in an instinctive way.

I am struck by the way in which fear and apprehension can be associated with the dramatic onset of physical illness. It is as if the illness is being contained, but the emotional disturbance tilts the process against containment and the illness becomes obvious. I referred to this (Hyatt-Williams 1959) by taking the example of the sudden culmination of an acute attack of malaria in both British and Indian soldiers in the Burma campaign of World War II when there was a variety of other trouble confronting them.

Physical illness can be an unconscious resort used to escape from a situation the patient cannot face. The situation may be an external threat to the patient, and experienced by him or her as a persecution, or the persecutors may be almost entirely internal. Physical illness can be the resort of a person who cannot face an intrapsychic situation in which he or she feels guilty and remorseful but experiences these feelings as persecutory in nature, and thus intolerable. In this case the manifest disturbance and distress, namely, the physical illness, is easier to face than any persecutor. A further way in which physical illness can be used is when there is a holding within the self of a frightened, angry, or guilt-ridden state of mind that is not evacuated onto or into somebody else, but proves to be psychically indigestible to its owner. I am reminded of a prisoner-patient who had been convicted for murder. This man was "doing well" in psychotherapy, and was able to face some guilt and remorse. On the anniversary of the murder he lost his voice and developed the bruise marks of strangulation on his neck. These were examined and thought not to be deliberately self-inflicted. It was concluded that this may have been an extremely concrete identification with the victim. This kind of phenomenon was found repeatedly in lifers who were beginning to work through a painful mourning process for their respective victims, who were no longer available for external reparation.

If we regard death as the ultimate illness in many people's minds, it becomes easier to see how certain people who kill project all or part of their death constellation into another person and save themselves at the expense of the victim. During mourning, whether for the killed person or for the person who has been killed in the mind of the potential murderer, re-owning of the death constellation is a crucial step. Therefore it is to be anticipated that psychosomatic illness could flare up in one form or another, though its severity depends on a number of factors. If psychosomatic illness fails to occur, accident-proneness is found frequently, and psychically amounts to the same thing. In a few cases it was found that a disturbed parent, or less often another relative, projectively identified with a child so that the child or young person received what amounted to an invasion of a death constellation. In several such instances the young person was unable to deal with what had been taken or forced into the psyche, and the constellation was projected into someone else and then killed in that person. I stress the way in which there is often a close psychic relationship between victim and killer, and this is mobilized in the mourning process. If it can be mobilized before harm has been done to the victim, the situation is immensely easier as far as resolution or mental healing is concerned.

The relationship between psychological—that is, emotional—stress and physical stress, as well as the hysterical representation or expression of emotional stress by physical symptoms and signs, has received a good deal of attention. As far as my own experience is concerned, I saw a great deal of such illnesses in the campaign in Burma from 1943 to 1945 and wrote about it (Hyatt-Williams 1959). Sometimes the identification with the damaged or annihilated person is quite clear, as in the case of a person serving life imprisonment who bled from the rectum whenever he was going through a period of regret, remorse, and mourning for the man representing his child-battering father. A man he had shot in the lower abdomen had died of an internal hemorrhage. Whenever the patient was examined by a surgeon at these times, no pathology was found, but he certainly did bleed. Jesus Christ was asked why he sometimes told crippled supplicants, "Your sins are forgiven you" and sometimes said, "Take up your bed and walk." He replied that the two statements amounted to much the same thing. This is the essential aspect of what I am trying to express in relation to a mourning process for harm done in fantasy or in action to someone or to a number of people, which gets stuck, leading to its evasion in one form or another.

Freud (1917) stated that in failed mourning there was an identification with the lost object, that is, the person who had died. It is worse when the person has been killed intentionally or in an accident. It is also worse when an ambivalently regarded person dies, so that the feeling of omniscience and omnipotence of murderous thoughts increases the magnitude of the task of mourning. If the person who has been the object of death wishes and fantasies in the subject actually dies, then the subject blames him- or herself for the death of the other person whether he or she has had anything to do with it or not. How much worse it is when the person who dies has been killed by the individual who subsequently has to mourn for him or her.

The fundamental talion law is that as one treats one's objects in external or internal reality, so one feels that one is or will be treated by one's objects and by other people. This includes external people and one's internal representations or mental images of them. In the attack upon oneself by an internal image of the person against whom the subject is harboring or has harbored ill-will, perhaps concretized in the mind as a destructive fantasy and taken no further, the counterattack by the internal image of that person can, and does, take place. It usually reflects the intensity of the malevolence of the fantasy against the person whose internal image is experienced as the source of the retaliation. If this condition can be tolerated, there are at least three ways in which a next step may be taken. The entire constellation may be resolved if the psychic pain of the guilt and remorse at the damage done to the internal object image can be sustained, so that there is a renegotiation of the depressive position. If there is intolerance of psychic pain, the intrapsychic situation may become chronic; growth and further development will be stultified. The third possibility is that there is a rejection of the mourning process altogether and any psychic pain that arrives is experienced as persecution, the obvious persecutor being the object against whom the original intrapsychic fantasy attack was directed. That person, or the internal image of that person, may thus be singled out for further attacks. These attacks are to be expected when depressive pain cannot be borne. They may well occur just as the situation begins to look more hopeful. They are due to the inability to tolerate depressive pain in the regressed mourning and remorse sequence. The person who had been injured is designated as the cause of the pain, therefore the enemy, therefore again a suitable target for attack. The state of mind into which the subject has split, that is, the paranoid-schizoid position, dominated by persecutory anxiety, is part of a regressive process in which the subject once again becomes dominated by powerful impulses in relationship to part objects, and he cannot contain ambivalent feelings. Relieving the fixity of this cycle is one of the tasks of development. Containment is required by the therapist of the person who hitherto has found it impossible to bear the depressive pain that has to be borne for some time if mourning processes are to proceed satisfactorily, and not be evaded again and again.

27

Restoring the Balance

In one form or another, the death constellation occurs in each one of us. Freud (1920), in "Beyond the Pleasure Principle," described the two polarized instincts of life and death. He stated that all of us live in a state in which we are pulled toward life on the one hand and death on the other. He wrote about the fusion and defusion of these instincts. Death inevitably won in the end, but only after the life instinct and its function of continuing the species had ensured the survival of the next generation. Although Freud remained in some doubt about the universality and applicability of his new theory of the death instinct, Klein accepted it and stated that life and death instincts operate from the beginning of life. Her consideration of their importance pervades her work. The poets write about life and death forces. Keats himself, probably burdened by the onset of tuberculosis, in his sonnet "Why Did I Laugh Tonight?" wrote: "Love, life and poetry are intense indeed, but death intenser, death is life's high mead," and, in "Ode to a Nightingale" (*Oxford Dictionary of Quotations* 1979)

> Now more than ever seems it rich to die,
> To cease upon the midnight with no pain.... [p. 291]

Segal referred to primal envy as the first major externalization of the death instinct. The idea of death is a challenge. It is universally present in all of us and tends to produce psychic indigestion. By this I mean that it fits uneasily in the psychic stomach of many people and can be neither digested nor metabolized. Therefore it poses problems to the individual and to the group to which he or she adheres. The earliest detoxication of the idea of death depends on the mother or her surrogate accepting the baby's projective identifications: "No breast, I am dying," to quote Bion in *Second Thoughts* (1967b, p. 112). This signal of projective identification is in the form of beta particles communicated to the mother by the projective identification of her baby. Mother in her reverie subjects these elements to her alpha function, converts them into alpha elements, and relays them to the baby in much improved form. She has taken the indigestible part of what was communicated to her and with her alpha function rendered it more digestible.

What can happen if mother or her substitute will not or cannot do this? If the inability to cope with the projective identification of the baby is the dominant feature, the baby does not internalize a projective-identification-accepting mother. The detoxication of the idea of death takes place in the healthy mother–baby relationship and subsequently in the healthy baby when the baby has been able to use the help of the mother. The paranoid-schizoid to depressive position transformation must of necessity be relatively satisfactory for sound development. Here we are concerned with the articulation of two transformations, container and contained, and paranoid-schizoid to depressive position, both acting synergically (Bion 1952).

Some people seek a magical denial of death, perhaps through a religious belief that can be proved neither correct nor incorrect. The moral position is retained by stating that if you lead an honest, righteous, and sober life, you go to a good place; if you misbehave in most respects, you are likely to go to a bad place.

In a number of people with murderous impulses and concretized fantasies, that is, people in whom a psychic murder has taken place many times, the murder was mainly of the internal image of a person, and had often followed some sort of nonmurderous relationship with that person. Well-known examples are Cain and Abel (the apotheosis of sibling rivalry). The Oedipus myth, son killing father but not knowing it at the time of the clash, father killing son as in the Matthew Arnold poem "Sohrab and Rustum," man killing wife, as in Dylan Thomas's "Under Milk Wood" (1959), when the husband took the tea to his nagging wife while she was still in bed. On the way he muttered to himself: "Nice cup of arsenic, my dear." When he got there it became: "Nice cup of tea, my dear." This quote shows how the poet realized how a murderer's fantasy could be tamed by expressing it and then the action could become harmless, even genial. All these situations can be matched by more modern, concrete examples. One is led to the view that in order to continue group life in the family, in the work situation, or elsewhere where there is family-close occupation in limited life-space, the healthy function of the murderous fantasy is part of essential reality testing. Only when it fails do we encounter further and dangerously escalating trouble.

In the healthy cycle there is the response to interpersonal difficulty, an indigestible experience or a series of experiences, a retaliatory fantasy, dream or token action, often of a mild kind, guilt, then persecutory anxiety to depressive anxiety transformation. The complete cycle normally wipes the slate clean, so to speak. Breakdown in the cycle may lead to further trouble, for example, a buildup of murderous hostility lodged at the paranoid-schizoid end of the spectrum and constituting what at first is a paranoid state. This may resolve itself with some unconscious switch. More discernibly, I have noticed how the resurgence of a sense of humor often sets the psychic digestive apparatus into motion again. This hypothesis is tentative, but it does cover the curious ubiquity of murderous fantasy and yet the comparative rarity of the act. Success in working through situations intrapsychically, and bringing into action container and contained and the paranoid-schizoid to depressive position transformation, usually, and quite unconsciously, clears the situation and leaves no ominous residue. Breakdown of the sequence can lead to ongoing internal risk. When it gets beyond a certain point there is real danger, particularly of a dynamic, explosive intrapsychic situation, and where that meets or is matched by a severe external threat, this threat can be actually or supposedly a threat to the life of the individual at risk. We are veering toward the viewpoint that much, if not most, murder is self-defensive ultimately. What of sadistic and sadistic-sexual murders? Most derive from long-held, often complicated masturbation fantasy sequences. When this fails to give relief, the internal situation again becomes dangerous and assertion of the long-held masturbation fantasy constellation tends to be acted out externally—psychosocially—with disastrous consequences. I am reminded of a patient who, while leading an external life of a blameless kind, masturbated with a murderous fantasy sequence. The victim was a somewhat younger boy or young man who was compounded of an enviable, admired, smug, younger male figure and himself. The younger brother who failed to match the idealized envy-provoking figure of the fantasy pattern was spared any direct hostility or attack. But the internalized figure contained a strong element of an idealized self that he wanted both to be and to reject. He had, throughout his life, an extremely difficult relationship with a demanding, coercive, nongiving, noncontaining mother, and the rejecting of her pattern for him became essential to his survival psychically. This enabled him to be his "own person," and although this situation sounds very different from the basic pattern described earlier in this chapter, it is not so different in essence, but is altered in appearance by its narcissistic elements. Would a heterosexual, murderous fantasy sequence be similar and different only in details? The answer is probably no, because the main factor is the internal object relationship. Also, the erratic switching from one state of mind to another indicates that the basic problem has been dealt with by defenses such as reaction formation or projective identification; the apparent state of being belies the unsatisfactory balance within the self so that nothing is ever satisfactorily psychically digested. "To be, or not to be, that is [always] the question."

Wolfgang and Ferracuti (1967) drew attention to the way in which, in Colombia, the murder rate had been high, but in 1926, following political assassinations, it went up abruptly from 25 to 34.4 per 100,000 of the population per annum and remained there. The basic hypothesis put forward in their book is that the idea of death, which includes the fear of death and the threat of death, would account for the escalation of murderousness in Colombia as a response to a heightened fear of death. In this switch from passive fear to actual infliction of death upon someone else, we see murder as due at least in part to a violent projection, often a projective identification, in pursuit of self-preservation. By applying this formula to murderousness in general, could it be that when the psychic digestion of the idea or threat of death becomes unbearable, that the whole or a part of the intrapsychic constellation tends to be put into someone else, at least for a period of time? In extreme cases a murderous sequence of events is triggered, though even at a late stage the sequence can be put in reverse. One woman knew about her husband's murderousness and had discovered that his violence would melt away if she became completely passive—almost feigning death. This induced in the husband a remorseful feeling, as if he had killed her already, which in his mind he had done, and he stopped the escalation from impulse to action. I think he was able to resume reality testing and did so after he had been shocked by her deathly appearance. If the view I have put forward is valid, then attitudes toward therapy could be less pessimistic than are generally believed. As has been argued, there is a scale or spectrum, based on the ability to *mourn*, the ability to make reparation internally, and the capacity to develop within the self an ability to contain one's projective identifications. Clearly important is what one has done or suffered to vitiate or complicate one's own development. To have killed someone in reality through paranoid attitudes, malevolence, jealousy, envy, spite, or perversion poses problems much more difficult than those confronting a person who has wished or fantasized somebody dead but taken no action to fulfill the wish. In the latter, therapy is aimed at restoring psychic balance rather than eradicating murderousness. However, in all therapy the method needs to facilitate intrapsychically a process of transformation from the paranoid-schizoid position to the depressive position. The development of an adequate internal container in which adverse as well as good experiences can be digested psychically and thus become more manageable is essential. This, it is hoped, may be effective in weakening the drive to murderous action and other acting out, and enable or re-enable fantasy to be used as a substitute for action rather than as a prelude to it. What about events like the sudden, catastrophic rise in the incidence of homicide in Colombia in 1926? As far as I know, there has been no report of the effects of world wars on the subsequent incidence of murder. I have witnessed the brutalization associated with the "license to kill" in war. Logically, this must put the internal control system of people who were having trouble with their own containing of impulses into disarray. I know of six cases of murder that seemed to be due to an inability of the individual to relinquish his license to kill when World War II was over. Perhaps this phenomenon may have some relevance to Colombia. One soldier I knew was cuckolded and gave his personal enemy an ultimatum—a bit like that between nations. This was ignored and he quietly executed (assassinated) his cuckolder. His war record, incidentally, was a distinguished one and his life, after he had served nine years of his life sentence, blameless. I would regard this type of instance as due to brutalization tied to the preservation of the authority-blessed, temporary license to kill. The less widely this is spread the better, and as an example one has to approve and admire the reluctance with which the police in the United Kingdom are not armed, except for short, sharp clashes with armed, ruthless criminals and criminal gangs. Could it be that the view of Bismarck that war is an extension of diplomacy expresses a characteristic of man dating from primitive times in human history, which can easily be reactivated when an alleged need arises? This, whether the reasons are in the pursuit of power or the survival of safety or of justice, alters the balance in the direction of more primitive ways of behaving. The therapeutic task is to restore the balance in the direction of more civilized behavior, and by means of the transformation from the paranoid-schizoid to depressive position and the container and contained relationship, to help people to own the various parts of themselves. This greatly diminishes people's danger to themselves and to others. In summary, it is essential to take the action paragraph out of a death wish.

References

Alvarez, A. (1971). *The Savage God: A Study of Suicide.* London: Weidenfeld and Nicholson.

Baker, K., ed. *Unauthorized Versions.* London: Faber.

Bion, W. (1962). *Learning from Experience.* London: Heinemann.

———(1963). *Elements of Psycho-Analysis.* London: Maresfield Reprints.

———(1967a). On arrogance. In *Second Thoughts: Selected Papers on Psycho-Analysis,* pp. 86–92. New York: Jason Aronson.

———(1967b). *Second Thoughts: Selected Papers on Psycho-Analysis.* New York: Jason Aronson.

———(1970). *Attention and Interpretation.* London: Maresfield Reprints.

Dicks, H. V. (1972). *Licensed Mass Murder: A Socio-Psychological Study of Some SS Killers.* London: Sussex University Press and Heinemann Educational.

Freud, S. (1911a). Psycho-analytic notes on an autobiographical account of a case of paranoia (dementia paranoides). *Standard Edition* 12:9–82.

———(1911b). Formulations on the two principles of mental functioning. *Standard Edition* 12:213–227.

———(1916). Some character types met with in psycho-analysis: criminals from a sense of guilt. *Standard Edition* 14:332–334.

———(1917). Mourning and melancholia. *Standard Edition* 14:239–258.

———(1920). Beyond the pleasure principle. *Standard Edition* 18:7–64.

———(1923). The ego and the id. *Standard Edition* 19:3–63.

Glover, E. (1960). *The Roots of Crime: Selected Papers on Psychoanalysis*, vol. 2. New York: International Universities Press.

Hyatt-Williams, A. (1959). A psychoanalytic approach to the treatment of the murderer. *International Journal of Psycho-Analysis* 41(2), 1960.

———(1971). *Risks to the worker in dealing with disturbed adolescents.* Paper presented at the International Conference on the Study of Adolescence, Guildford University, England.

Jaques, E. (1965). Death and the mid-life crisis. *International Journal of Psycho-Analysis* 46(44):502–514.

Keats, J. (1978). On reading *King Lear* once again. In *The Poems of John Keats*, ed. J. Stillinger, p. 225. London: Heinemann.

Klein, M. (1927). Criminal tendencies in normal children. In *Love, Guilt, and Reparation*, pp. 170–185. London: Hogarth and the Institute for Psycho-Analysis, 1975.

———(1928). Early stages of the Oedipus conflict. In *Love, Guilt, and Reparation*, pp. 186–198. London: Hogarth and the Institute for Psycho-Analysis, 1975.

———(1946). Notes on some schizoid mechanisms. In *Envy and Gratitude*. London: Hogarth and the Institute for Psycho-Analysis, 1984.

Meltzer, D. (1992). *The Claustrum: An Investigation of Claustrophobic Phenomena*. Strathclyde, Perthshire: Clunie.

Miller, D. (1976). Proceedings of the International Congress on Adolescents, Edinburgh.

Oxford Dictionary of Quotations. (1979). Third Edition. London: Oxford University Press.

Rosenfeld, H. (1960). Drug addiction. In *Psychotic States*. London: Hogarth, 1965.

———(1987). *Impasse and Interpretation*. London: New Library of Psycho-Analysis.

Scott, P. (1985). *The Mark of the Warrior*. Emeryville, CA: Carroll & Graf.

Segal, H. (1981). Notes on symbol formation. In *The Work of Hanna Segal*. London: Free Association Press.

Shaffer, P. (1966). *Equus*. New York: Penguin, 1984.

Steiner, J. (1993). *Psychic Retreats*. London: Routledge.

Thomas, D. (1959). *Under Milk Wood: A Play for Voices*. New York: New Directions.

Werthem, F. (1927). *The Show of Violence*. New York: New York University Press, 1949.

Williams, E. (1935). *Night Must Fall.* New York: S. French.
Wolfgang, M. E., and Ferracuti, F. (1967). *The Subculture of Violence: Towards an Integrated Theory in Criminology.* London: Tavistock.

Index